Settle for More

Settle for More

Megyn Kelly

HARPER LUXE

An Imprint of HarperCollins*Publishers*

FIRST HARPERLUXE EDITION

ISBN: 978-0-06-256531-0

HarperLuxe™ is a trademark of HarperCollins Publishers.

Library of Congress Cataloging-in-Publication Data is available upon request.

16 17 18 19 20   ID/RRD   10 9 8 7 6 5 4 3 2 1

For My Family

Contents

Settle for More

Prologue
Tough Questions

Debate day: August 6, 2015. I woke up in Cleveland, excited for what was to come. We had been preparing for this for more than two months—powering through countless meetings, calls, and arguments among members of the debate team as to which questions lived and which died—and tonight would be the culmination of all that hard work. I would be comoderating the first Republican primary debate of the 2016 election season.

The election had been a mess so far. Still in the running were nearly twenty candidates, most with impressive résumés and a long list of accomplishments. That meant we had a real job to do: give the American people some actual information on these contenders so they could begin deciding who they might want to replace Barack Obama. The lower-polling candidates, those ranking below tenth, would appear in a separate "undercard" debate. We only had to worry about those polling in the top ten: Donald Trump, Jeb Bush, Marco Rubio, Scott Walker, Ted Cruz, Ben Carson, Mike Huckabee, Rand Paul, John Kasich, and Chris Christie.

I'm an overpreparer, so I had researched and rewritten my questions over and over again until I believed they were as tight and pointed as possible. Before getting out of bed, I looked at my iPhone, which was where I kept the questions. I scrolled through them yet again, toggling back and forth between that file and incoming texts and e-mails from friends and colleagues: **Knock 'em dead! Good luck! You'll do great!**

I ordered breakfast in my room, threw on some jeans and a T-shirt, and out the door I went. I felt great. It was a beautiful day in Ohio, and I was as ready as I'd ever be for that night's event.

The car picked me up at my hotel at 10:00 a.m. to take me to the convention center. The debate team was going to meet one last time to go over the questions and logistics, and to take into account any news of the day.

"Oh, Ms. Kelly!" the driver said when I got into the car. "I'm a huge fan of yours! I want to help you. I will answer phones for you. I will do anything you want me to do today. I will iron your suit. I will run errands. May I go get you a coffee?"

"No, thank you," I said. "I'm good."

"Let me get you a coffee!" he said.

"No, thanks," I said. "I'm really okay. They have coffee there."

"I insist!" he said. "I'm going to Starbucks to get you a coffee!"

Now, I don't really like Starbucks coffee. I prefer plain old convention center coffee, and a lot of it. But I didn't want to be rude, so I said, "Okay."

I walked into the hall feeling fine, excited that this day had finally arrived.

Once there, I ran into Howie Kurtz, our Fox News media critic. I remember telling him that if the public had any idea what had been happening between me and Donald Trump the past few days, it would be the biggest story in the country. Among other things, he had threatened me in an angry phone call, called Fox News executives to complain that my coverage of him was not to his liking, and made multiple attempts to interfere in the debate process. Trump had announced his candidacy only two months earlier, and he was already the front-runner for the nomination.

Howie, good reporter that he is, wanted to know more.

"Someday," I told him.

Little did I know how that story—a few phone calls and some menacing words from a candidate few thought had any real chance—would pale in comparison to the one that would emerge that night on the debate stage and that would come to dominate the next year of my life.

The night before the debate, I'd called my friend and colleague Dana Perino, former White House press secretary under George W. Bush and now a host on Fox News. She'd already been attacked by Trump. I read her my lead question for him, the question no one was asking, even though it was key to his future as a candidate. Essentially, it was: Given your reputation for saying controversial things about and to women, how will you fare against a female candidate? Dana said she thought it was fair. So did I, but we both knew that Trump wouldn't like it, and there could be blowback. He had tried to embarrass Dana on Twitter after she criticized his announcement speech. And that was just for a passing comment she made on the air. This was a presidential debate stage. I didn't want to be attacked, but I had a job to do, and that was that.

I joined the fellow members of my debate team inside the Cleveland Cavaliers stadium. My co-moderators, Bret Baier and Chris Wallace, our digital politics editor, Chris Stirewalt, and Bill Sammon, the head of our debate team and Washington bureau chief, were all there, along with our producers and limited support staff. We tend to keep these meetings small—the questions are inviolate. Leaks would be unthinkable. This is a race for the Oval Office. There can be no improprieties. No cell phone calls inside this room, no outsiders unless they are sworn to secrecy. The five of us knew one another very well—our strengths, weaknesses, idiosyncrasies—and were full of respect for the team.

There was no time to waste, and we got right to work. Bret, Chris, and I were bunched together at the end of the long conference table. Bill Sammon was next to us, pacing. Everyone else was scattered about. We spent a fair amount of the morning reviewing Bret's opening question one last time: Would they all pledge to support the eventual Republican nominee?

We wondered if anyone would raise their hand, other than possibly Trump or Rand Paul. Were we still comfortable with that opening? It would be a dramatic and potentially important moment, we knew, and we kept it.

We had a number of other questions to discuss. What if everyone wanted a chance to respond to a likely opening attack by Trump? Would any candidates be looking for "a Newt Gingrich moment," where they went after the moderators, as Newt had in 2012? What would we do if Trump attacked me? I told Bret and Chris, "Don't jump in."

We were on LeBron James's turf, and we were pumped for the start of the game.

About ninety minutes into our meeting, Abigail Finan, my assistant, came in with a large Starbucks coffee.

"Did you order coffee from your driver?" she asked, confused.

"It's a long story," I said.

Abby put the coffee down in front of me, and the meeting continued.

Oh, what the hell, I thought, and I started drinking the Starbucks.

Within fifteen minutes, about halfway through the coffee, I got a splitting headache.

Could you get me some Tylenol? I e-mailed Abby. She sent someone in with it, but only one pill. At 12:38 p.m. I e-mailed, **There's only one here—I need two.**

Within fifteen minutes of that, I was white as a ghost. It was very clear I was going to throw up. I had a little private office in the convention hall. I sprinted out of the meeting and past Abby and my research assistant Emily Walker, ran into the bathroom, and threw up. I came out and told Abby what had happened.

Her eyes were enormous. It was just a few hours before the debate. We were expecting millions of viewers. All the candidates would be there. We had been preparing for months. The stakes were enormous. The timing could not have been worse.

"It's nerves!" Abby said, hopefully.

It was not nerves, and she and I both knew it. I'd done presidential debates before, and been on TV in front of millions of people more times than I could count. Nerves are rare for me at this point. And when I do get them, what happens is that my heart starts pounding so hard that I worry the microphones will pick it up. What does not happen is nausea.

I tried to go back into the debate room, but when I got there, I was shaky and very ill. The conversation around me was whizzing at warp speed. I wasn't able to concentrate. I felt terrible. Soon I realized I had to throw up again.

Was the milk in that coffee spoiled? I wondered. *Did I get food poisoning at breakfast?* My illness came on so suddenly, and was unlike anything I'd ever experienced. But I was in no position to open a CSI investigation. I could barely stand. (I later learned there was a stomach virus going around—Rand Paul was also sick that night.)

"I have some very bad news," I told the team. "I

don't feel well, and I need to go back to the hotel right now to lie down."

You should have seen those guys' faces. They were scared shitless. We were a team. We were going to do this together. What's more, it was very clear that Bret and Chris did not want to ask my questions. And I didn't want them to—especially my question about Trump's history of controversial comments about women. It was my question, it was on point, and I wanted to be the one asking it.

The guys were supportive. They could see that I looked like I was about to pass out.

"Go," they said. "Don't worry. You'll be fine."

"We'll see you later," they said as I walked out. It was as much a question as a statement.

It was all I could do to make it back to the hotel before I was hanging over the toilet, violently ill.

En route, Abby called my doctor in New York. He prescribed medication over the phone. Once I was back in my room, she went and picked it up.

"Take this pill," she said when she returned, after a rather horrific hour. "The doctor says if you can keep it down for thirty minutes, you'll feel better."

Who knew that, thanks to modern medicine, you don't have to throw up anymore in this country? To this day, I still don't know what Abby gave me. I didn't care; I would have taken anything if it meant I might be able to make the debate.

As I lay there in bed, curled up in a fetal position, my hair matted on my face, profusely sweating, barely able to speak, I saw the look in Abby's eyes: *She's never going to make this debate! DEFCON 1! DEFCON 1!*

It was 3:28 p.m. I did everything I could to keep my stomach calm for thirty minutes to hold down that pill. I looked out the window and stared at spiders on a spiderweb. I tried Pandora. I meditated. I started chanting, "One, one, one, one . . ." I said a prayer.

Abby was counting me down: "Eleven more minutes! Seven more minutes! Almost there!"

My husband, Doug, called, and I couldn't even speak.

Finally, I made it to thirty. Lo and behold, by forty I felt a flicker of promise. By fifty minutes later, I was definitely starting to feel a bit better. By sixty there was no question that I was going to get out of that bed.

My boss, Roger Ailes, called and offered words of encouragement: "I know you can do this." He also knew *me*: I would have walked over hot coals to do that debate.

By ninety minutes, the clock read 5:00, and I was back at the convention center. My hair and makeup geniuses Chris and Vincenza transformed that gross, sweaty, shaky mess into what people the world over saw on TV that night. I will be forever grateful.

Still, I had chills, so we traded my sleeveless white dress for a black one that covered me up more. My producers couldn't find a heater, so they gave me a blanket to put on my legs, along with an empty trash can to go at my feet. If worse came to worst, we would kill the mics and take the camera off me, and I would throw up right there on the debate stage.

The one advantage of all this was that I felt no nerves onstage. I was too wiped out physically, and focused like a laser on not vomiting in front of millions of people. I did, however, have a premonition that night. I remember feeling like the earth's tectonic plates were shifting—as if I could feel it beneath me, in real time. Somehow, I knew things were about to change. I said exactly that to Abby and Emily Walker, moments before I went out there. They locked eyes with me, and with a deep breath I looked back at them.

"Onward," I said, and walked out toward the stage.

Early in the debate, I exchanged pleasantries with Donald Trump, the front-runner. Then I asked him the question that would change my life.

"Mr. Trump," I said, "one of the things people love about you is you speak your mind and you don't use a politician's filter. However, that is not without its downsides. In particular, when it comes to women. You've called women you don't like 'fat pigs,' 'dogs,' 'slobs,' and 'disgusting animals.'"

"Only Rosie O'Donnell," he quipped.

The crowd chuckled at his Rosie O'Donnell comment. I passed no judgment on the audience, but I was not going to join them in laughing.

"For the record," I said, "it was well beyond Rosie O'Donnell."

Trump knew it too. "I'm sure it was," he said.

We had fact-checked every word of that question. Rosie had, no question, been vicious toward Trump too, and if it had only been her, I would not have asked that question. But what I'd seen in my research binder was that he'd made a habit of attacking women regularly with these sorts of terms—mocking their looks and sexualizing them. The women he'd belittled in the terms I used in my question included, but were not limited to, Arianna Huffington, Bette Midler, *New York Times* columnist Gail Collins, and a lawyer requesting a prearranged break to pump breast milk for her baby ("disgusting"). There were many, many others.

"Your Twitter account," I continued, "has several disparaging comments about women's looks. You once told a contestant on *Celebrity Apprentice* it would be a pretty picture to see her on her knees. Does that sound to you like the temperament of a man we should elect as president, and how will you answer the charge from Hillary Clinton, who is likely to be the Democratic nominee, that you are part of the 'war on women'?"

First Trump said that we'd gotten too politically correct in this country. And then this: "What I say is what I say. And honestly, Megyn, if you don't like it, I'm sorry. I've been very nice to you, although I could probably maybe not be, based on the way you have treated *me*. But I wouldn't do that."

He looked angry, I thought. After all my planning for that moment, I was relieved that he hadn't attacked me personally in his response. Still, I felt his anger, and understood him perfectly. He was making a veiled but very clear threat.

I'd known Trump for several years by this point. We'd had a mostly good—but also complicated—relationship. Seared into my mind was a threat he'd made to me by phone just four days earlier to "unleash" what he called his "beautiful Twitter account" on me. I expected I would find out what he meant by that soon, and indeed I would.

Trump's answer—"What I say is what I say"—would become a mantra for his campaign, and it would be very successful for him. *I'm not like the other politi-*

cians, he told America. *I don't care if you don't like it.*
His willingness to drop a swear and cut through the
bull and tell it like it is—it was refreshing in a way.
And it made for great TV.

But of course, as with anything along those lines,
there are limits to that refreshment. Someone can tell
it like it is and then drop the N-word on you, and suddenly you're not feeling refreshed any longer; you're
just feeling offended. I'm no lover of being overly PC,
but there is a limit to how far the overcorrection to that
can go. You can't justify everything that way. We still
want to live within the bounds of decency with one another, or so I hope—especially when choosing leaders,
whose behavior should inspire us and may be modeled
by our children. They should be held to a higher standard.

For what it's worth, I thought Trump did fine with
the question. But I do believe that in that moment he
felt betrayed. He said it: "I've been very nice to you."
As if we were friends in the sandbox and I'd stolen his
toy, when in fact he was a presidential candidate trying
to get elected, and I was a journalist trying to do my
job.

". . . although I could probably maybe not be . . ."

I knew what he meant: *I told you if you gave me a
hard time, I would come after you, and now I will.*

Then, as the world knows, he did.

And then, as the world also knows, I survived.

I was raised with strong values, and had spent much of my life to that point seeing my character tested. I was viciously bullied in middle school. My father died when I was a teenager. As a lawyer, I worked eighteen-hour days immersed in acrimony. As a cub reporter, I was targeted by a violent stalker. Once I became a well-known news anchor, I accepted without complaint the scrutiny that comes with that role. I'd also navigated my way through plenty of sexism from powerful men. So I suppose I was as prepared as anyone could be to spend the 2016 election being targeted by the likely Republican nominee.

Yet still, the chaos Trump unleashed was of a completely different order than anything I'd encountered before—than anything any journalist has encountered at the hands of a presidential candidate in the history of modern American politics.

This is the story of how I found myself on that debate stage, and how asking that question led to one of the toughest years of my life.

1

No False Praise

To know who I am, you have to know where I'm from.

My family raised me in upstate New York with the core message: Be whoever you are. That person may (or may not) be extraordinary. We're not going to lie to make you feel better, but we'll love you no matter what. In our house, it wasn't "You are special." It was more like "You don't seem that special so far, but we don't care."

That foundation of you-are-nothing-remarkable-and-that's-okay worked very well for me. When I was growing up, I felt zero pressure to achieve. I mean zero. As a result, I was able to figure out for myself what I wanted to do and find my own motivation. I grew up happy and, thanks to my parents' honesty, had no delusions of grandeur. Early on, I knew what I was and wasn't good at, because no one ever oversold my talents.

My parents would never have even considered the trophies-for-everyone parenting philosophy now so in vogue. In our family, trophies were for winners, and there was no pressure to win. If you did win, you were praised. If you didn't, everyone would have a laugh and a big meal and call it a day. My family simply did not believe in false praise. As a result, I grew up the opposite of spoiled. Everything about my outlook—my values, my sense of right and wrong, my independence— began there.

The same went for my sister, Suzanne, and brother, Pete, who are six and five years older than me respectively. We spent our childhood in the suburbs of Syracuse and Albany, attending public school and going to Catholic mass most Sundays. In the summers we went swimming at the town park or ran under the sprinkler in our backyard. We played kick the can on our street and rode our bikes everywhere. In the winter, we went sledding on a trail nicknamed "Greased Lightning," thanks to my obsession with the movie Grease. We ice-skated on a nearby pond. My brother mowed the lawn and took out the garbage for his allowance; my sister and I unloaded the dishwasher and cleaned up after dinner. It doesn't get much more Norman Rockwell than us.

My attitude started with my parents. I lived simply and honestly because they did. I adored my father, Edward Kelly, a college professor and meat-and-potatoes Irishman with a huge, bellowing laugh. He had beautiful blue eyes and salt-and-pepper hair that he kept on the longer side. He is still the man against whom I measure other men.

My mother used to say I was the female Ed, minus the beard and mustache; from the eyebrows down—eyes, nose, cheekbones—I look exactly like him. Tall and slim, he always wore his college ring, a houndstooth newsboy cap, and glasses with thin gold rims. He had a space between his two front teeth, which I had too when I was young.

My father never had a harsh word for me, and he made me feel loved and valued. He would come home from work in the evenings and scoop me up in his arms, saying, "Hiya, tiger!" before taking off his heavy navy trench coat.

We would sit around our upstate New York dinner table each night, and Dad would ask each of us, "What's the report?"

We'd have to tell him what we'd learned or done that day. When it was my turn, I would prattle on.

"Make her shut up!" my brother and sister would plead.

"You had your chance," Dad would say. "And now you will listen to her."

Worldly and erudite, Dad traveled as an education consultant to exotic locations such as Bali, Tehran, and Africa, and he used sophisticated words all the time.

"Dad!" I'd complain when I lost track of what he was saying. "Speak English."

"Megyn, I will not lower my vocabulary to meet yours," he said. "You must raise yours to meet mine."

Still, he was fascinated by us—these little, increasingly intellectual beings. He wanted to exchange ideas, to talk about language and the power of words, sentence structure, what was proper and improper. He made me feel interesting, and I worked hard to keep up with him.

He once wrote a hundred-page grant proposal and gave it to me to proofread. I was nine.

I sat down with a dictionary and I read the entire proposal.

"This is really good, Dad," I said.

He dedicated the work to me: "This is for my daughter Megyn, who read this and said, 'This is good, Dad.'" (He got the grant.) I felt respected.

He always had his nose in a book, and these were not

beach reads. When he read *Shogun*, I remember marveling at how long it was, and after he finished that, he picked up an even longer book. He could quote *War and Peace* and *Moby Dick*. He loved to write: education papers, a book about teaching that he never got to publish, and poems, some of which I have framed and hanging on my wall to this day.

Dad worked a lot, but still found ways to be present—he read and sang to us, took me to clarinet lessons, sat down on the floor to play jacks after work. He was such a natural father that it's hard to believe he almost forewent having a family. As a young man, he'd considered becoming a Christian Brother and taking vows of chastity, poverty, and obedience. While he chose (good news for me) family life instead, he still lived a life of faith and scholarship, talking to us often about what kind of a man Jesus was. He said we needed to picture the son of God as a man, doing all the things men do, to truly understand him. He taught me to value education and faith, and he made me believe that what I had to say mattered, regardless of whether my siblings agreed.

That's not to say he didn't worry about us. Dad observed his children's habits almost anthropologically. Circa 1983, I went through a phase of painting my nails in elaborate patterns: with stripes and dots and zigzags, all different colors. And then I'd put decals on them.

"Linda," Dad said, watching this ritual. "I am concerned about Megyn's values."

"Ed, get over it," my mom said. "She's twelve."

This was their dynamic in a nutshell. If my father taught me to take myself seriously, my mother, Linda, taught me not to take myself *too* seriously. For her, laughter is the secret of life.

A second-generation Italian American, Mom was—and still is—a force of nature. From my earliest memories, she was always beautiful, with a larger-than-life personality. For me, her best attribute—and there are many to choose from—is her self-deprecating sense of humor. She is the kind of person who lights up a room. When she's there, everyone feels a bit brighter. When she walks out, the room is unhappier.

She has brown hair, or blond, or red, or some other color, depending on the season and her mood. (She died it pink once, "for breast cancer awareness.") She has never struggled to attract attention. For as long as I can remember, everyone has wanted to be around my mother.

Mom's sense of humor is among the greatest influences in my life. She is one of the funniest people I have ever known, though not always intentionally. One time, there was an ax murder in Delmar, our Albany suburb. I grant you, it doesn't start off funny—bear with me.

The suspect in the case had been identified but not yet arrested and was still free and working—at our local vet, as it turned out. My mother brought her enormous mastiff mix in one day for care, and the suspect helped pick up the dog. He looked a bit wary of the animal.

My mother reassured him: "Oh, you have nothing to worry about! An *ax murderer* could come through our house in the middle of the night, and she wouldn't do a thing!" Thankfully he chose not to test this theory.

Mom has a condition we've dubbed chronic lyricosis. She's always singing—poorly, and with the wrong words. She loved Prince's "Raspberry Beret"—or, as she prefers to sing it, "Strawberry Beret." And then there's Creedence Clearwater's hit "There's a bathroom on the right." Some prefer to sing it with its actual lyrics: "There's a bad moon on the rise." In fact, she often mishears or mispronounces things. She refuses to properly say the names Rachel or Paige, preferring Racial and Peige, to rhyme with *beige*. One summer our family was served Stoli O vodka and sodas at the Saratoga racetrack. My mother was determined to recreate this later but had a tough time finding the ingredients. No liquor store in the Albany region, strangely enough, carried the brand "Smolio."

Nine times out of ten, the family stories we devour revolve around something hilarious my mother has done or some fantastic embarrassment she has brought upon herself unwittingly. Like the time she bought a FUBU sweatshirt at a garage sale and wore it around town without knowing what it stood for. (Google it.)

Or the time she told everyone her cough sounded just like the theme from *Ghostbusters*. Or when she got a tattoo at age seventy (a rosary, on her foot). Or when she told us she was the voice twin of Tina Turner and sang "What's Love Got to Do with It" nonstop for weeks. Or told us she had the perfect country twang and sang "Peace in the Valley" with the worst country twang ever. (She says that when she dies, she's going to leave a recording of her terrible singing, and if we don't play it at her funeral she'll haunt us from the grave.) Or when she decided at age seventy-three that she wanted to be a security guard and signed up to take classes, but then backed out when she realized they weren't going to give her a gun and she'd have to work weekends. She later told us: "All I really wanted was a job where I could put my thumbs in my belt loops."

I could go on.

To this day, my mom keeps me laughing . . . and humble. She is proud of me, but the moments in my career that might lead to a Linda phone call are less about any kind of high achievement on my part and more typically along the lines of that time I tried to say

"Huckabee" and instead said "Fuckabee" on the air. She speed-dialed me on that one!

My mom has always wanted to keep my head from growing too big ("You don't look good in gray." "How long are you going to keep your hair like that?"), but she loves the fact that as I have become better known, so has she. She said her physical therapist told her, "Whenever I see Megyn on TV, I think, Wow, her mom is my patient!" And my mom responded, "And you must always think exactly that—whenever you see Megyn, you think of her amazing mother!"

One time we went out to dinner in Albany. "Stand up so people can see who you are!" she told me. I laughed, firmly attached to my seat. But Mom gets her way with just about everyone else. For example, when one of her doctors seemed cold to her, she told him, "Look, I know you have no bedside manner, but if you are going to operate on me, you have to start talking to me."

That's how she is—she lays it on the line, but charmingly. On command, her doctor struck up a conversation, and it turned out he was a Fox fan. Now he talks nonstop, and she loves regaling him with behind-the-scenes stories about Bill O'Reilly.

In February 2016 I was on the cover of *Vanity Fair*. A full month went by before she mentioned it to me. Maybe she didn't see it, I thought—after all, she doesn't really peruse those kinds of publications. She'd much prefer a *Reader's Digest, Parade,* or *People*—all of which I love too. More likely than not, I assumed she just didn't see it as a reason for a chat.

Weeks later she casually mentioned, "All of my doctors saw the *Vanity Fair* cover. They loved it."

"How did they see it?" I asked.

"I showed them all."

This is vintage Linda. She's tough at times, but she's always in my corner—the way she has been my whole life. And while she is happy for my success, she's perhaps a bit surprised by it, too. I think it's fair to say my mother never anticipated great achievement on my part, nor did my slightly-above-average grades give her reason to expect great things. She made me take typing—twice—so I'd "always have something to fall back on." (I am a fast typist.) She was never hoping to raise a doctor. I think she thought my best hope was to marry one.

"They don't give cheerleading scholarships, Megyn!" my mother said if I blew off homework. The truth is, they do, but certainly not at my level. All I had going for me was school spirit and the ability to rhyme. To this day, I can't even do a cartwheel.

In truth, though, I think she just never much cared

about academic details. Like my father, she wanted me to love learning, and I did, but neither of them rode me about grades or extracurricular activities. Nor did they really have to. She could not tell you how I did on the SAT (not that well) or where I graduated in my law school class (with honors)—not because she didn't want good things for me, but because she could always see I had decent grades and seemed to be happy enough.

Still, she had fun letting us know where things stood. When Mom went back to school to earn her master's degree, she posted her grades on the refrigerator next to ours.

"Mine are better than yours," she'd say.

It wasn't mean; it was true.

In my family, we are proud of and kind to each other, but we often show our love not by being falsely polite, but by letting our guard down and saying what we really think. We're on the radical honesty program, which has led to greater intimacy.

This no-bullshit approach goes all the way to the top. My now-hundred-year-old Nana (my mother's mother, naturally) once stroked my long blond hair and said lovingly, in her New York/New Jersey accent, "Ya hay-er is so lowng . . ." Then her tone changed to displeasure: "Too lowng!" Once I came downstairs after getting dressed for a friend's wedding. "Is thatcha dress o' ya petticoat?" Nan asked me. Apparently it was a bit short.

Whenever you talk to Nana on one of her birthdays—her real name, by the way, is Antoinette Frances Holzworth DeMaio, though she's better known as Tebby—she'll tell you how old she is, quickly followed by "Ain't that revoltin'? Da woy-ums should have me by now. I should be playnt-ed. Why ain't I playnt-ed yet?"

"Because the Lord doesn't like complainers," my mom will say.

So my mother comes by her bluntness honestly.

Speaking of which, when I played Jack's wife in our elementary school production of *Jack and the Beanstalk*, my mother's first reaction was to criticize my onstage sweeping. Of course, since Linda is not much of a cleaner, this one didn't have much of an impact.

"Mom, am I really smart?" I asked her once.

"You're about average," she said.

Now that we're older, the rules have changed a bit. I'll get a haircut, and I can feel the windup: "Honey, I have to tell you something," she'll say.

"Mom," I'll reply, "you can criticize me, but just know, that for every one you lob my way, I get to give you one back."

It's amazing how much less criticism she levels at me now.

My parents met in New York City in the early 1960s. My dad was studying at Manhattan College, and my mother was in nursing school. He would visit her in her school's "beau parlor," where they would share scotch he'd smuggled in via shampoo bottle. From there, they would go out to the White Horse Tavern in the West Village, where inspired patrons like my dad would get up on the tables and recite Shakespeare. He was clever. She was a riot. They adored each other.

My father had a great combination of intellectualism and romanticism, and I think that's why he and my mom got along so well together. My mom was not the philosopher type, but she was savvy, whip-smart, and she loved his erudition. They had a yin-and-yang thing going in that regard.

Both devout Catholics, they married not long into their courtship. She was twenty-two. He was twenty-three. One year later, they had my sister. A year after that, they had my brother. They'd tried to follow Catholic guidelines against birth control. "Then I had two babies in two years," my mom said, "and *forget that!*"

I was born in November 1970, when they were living briefly in Champaign, Illinois, which lets me brag that I was born in champagne. Far from it, in fact. The apartment we lived in was so small, my nursery was my parents' closet.

When I was seven months old, we moved to the Syracuse suburb of DeWitt, and our house was decked out in the latest style. The split-level ranch I spent the first nine years of my life in was classic 1970s: thick orange shag carpet, orange drapes, a black, orange, white, and red couch, all lit up with orange lamps. My favorite of these was a lamp whose shade was a spinning forest-fire scene. This being the seventies, naturally there were beanbag chairs, but only in the basement—we kept it classy, of course.

My parents had parties all the time at our house. There was always a guy named Malcolm playing the guitar, barefoot, and a few others just like him. They weren't hippies—they were academics, and creative types. My father spoke passionately about religion, philosophy, life's purpose. He loved music. At these parties, people would come with instruments or sing or read a poem. You could perform a verse if you wanted to act a little. One way or another, you had to be willing to put yourself out there.

During the parties, I got to serve the drinks. I loved using the tongs to put in the ice. They would play Don McLean's "American Pie" and I would dance and dance. At the end of the night, I would escape to my room, where I had a small white-and-green record player on which I played Alfred Hitchcock stories read by Hitchcock himself. (In retrospect: How creepy! Why didn't my parents just buy me the 45 of Leif Garrett's "Runaround Sue"?)

My mother managed a lot back then, and even today I'm not quite sure how. She was working as a nurse and studying for her PhD and raising three kids and yet still throwing these parties, doing all the cooking, serving, and clean-up on her own. Maybe that's why she's still nine credits short on that doctorate, and why my parents didn't have much time for recreation—they rarely took a couples vacation, and never exercised a day in their lives. My mom worked very hard, and she was my role model.

Like all couples, my parents fought sometimes, but they never lost their sense of humor. One time my mother and father were sitting in the living room, and she was giving him a hard time for something. He said very little, which was typical when they argued. After a while, he stood up, walked over to her, and silently dumped his Manhattan over her head. Then he massaged it into her hair. I still remember how the maraschino cherry looked as it rolled down her face. She had to laugh. They made up.

They rarely stayed angry long, because they prioritized their relationship and always made time to check in with each other. After he greeted the kids, every night Dad would go in the living room with Mom and talk. They'd sit and catch up. We were not allowed to interrupt. This was their time. Then my mom would make dinner. Dad came from a quiet family, so our big loud family dinners every night and the big loud parties and Mom's big voice were all very attractive to him. For my mom, the half Italian, food was important, and she was always quick to feed our emotions.

"You hungry?" she'd ask.

"No, Mom, I'm good."

"Okay, I'll just make you a sandwich then."

When I was growing up, Mom liked to say we were "upper middle class," but that was a bit of a stretch. In the summer, typically my family would drive to Lake Ontario and rent a small log cabin in the Selkirk Shores State Park along with our cousins. We hiked, painted sticks, sang songs around the campfire, and ate hot dogs. I loved it, especially when there weren't enough beds and I got to sleep in a lawn chair in the living room. My dad would play guitar and sing us Neil Diamond and John Denver songs, along with personalized versions of the era's greatest hits. When he sang our names, we had to get up and dance, which we did with glee.

Extravagant trips were rare in our house. We took a big family vacation exactly once when I was growing up (Disney World). The one time in my mother's life that she's been to Europe was for her fifteenth wedding anniversary. At their anniversary party, my father got dressed up in a tuxedo. One of the party guests told me, "Hey, your dad's wearing a tux!"

"What's a tux?" I asked. I was seven.

"Something that makes you look like a penguin!"

"Why would anyone want to do that?" I said.

Then I saw him, and wondered why anyone would ever wear anything else.

At that moment he presented my mother with a card that turned out to be a clue. He had created a scavenger hunt through the house. At each location there was a balloon, and inside each balloon was a twenty-dollar bill. We didn't have a lot of money, so this was a huge thrill.

We kids had helped him set it up, and it was exciting to be in on the ground floor of the big surprise. The five of us plus the guests ran from location to location as my mother solved each clue. At the end, it became clear that this was not just about giving her cash. The very last spot had two tickets to Paris. The money was for them to spend there, on their very first—and what would be their only—trip to Europe.

My parents encouraged gratuitous acts of kindness—whenever someone in town was hurting, my mom and dad would bring over a pot roast or lasagna, or go sit with them for a while. In this spirit, when Nana reached her eighties, I sent a letter to her Park Ridge, New Jersey, high school. I told the principal and superintendent how she had been forced to drop out of school during the Great Depression to help her family by taking purchase orders at the Comfort Coal Company, where her father worked shoveling coal. She'd dreamed of being a nurse, but because of her lack of education she ended up at the phone company. She always regretted not graduating. I asked them to consider granting her an honorary diploma. Almost a year later, I received a letter saying it had taken them six months to track down the records. Not only did they want to give her a degree, but they also wanted to have her walk through the graduation ceremony with the class of 1997.

Every member of our family went to the ceremony. Nana declined to wear the gown; she preferred a flowered dress and her favorite sneakers, along with a corsage we got her. But she was ecstatic. "I was da belle o' da bawl," she said. Her local paper ran a story about it, noting: "Frances DeMaio's priest this morning asked if she's going to Harvard or Yale. But a high school diploma is good enough for her."

I was happy to pay back a little of the joy she's given me over the years. As kids, Nana always let us do whatever we wanted. Sleep on the dining room table? Go for it. Play with balloons filled with food coloring? Have fun. Want to sleep in the jeep outside overnight? Sweet dreams. I particularly remember the monster stories she used to tell me on her porch in a rocking chair while I sat, riveted, in her lap. I ate them up.

Her husband, my Pop-Pop, was a volunteer firefighter and paper mill worker, and he ran a boatyard on the Hudson River. He's passed, but as of this writing, Nana is still with us and continues to be a huge influence in my life. When we go to diners, she steals the bread and the napkins and reminds the waitress that she should get a senior citizen's discount: "Would ya like ta see my license o' my wrinkles?" She walks into the pharmacy and asks, "Whey-ah's Steve? I like ta aggravate him!"

While my mother insists we play her terrible singing at her funeral *or else*, my Nana has a different deal-breaker: she hates carnations, and says if there is a single carnation at her funeral, she'll come back to haunt us. My brother and sister and I worry about how many mourners we'll offend, running around the church with clippers. Apparently, we're in store for either some very awkward funeral proceedings or a lifetime of apparitions and noises in the night—the choices are not ideal.

As good as she is to me, Nana drives my mother crazy. When Nana started getting a bit older, if a light-bulb went out at her place, she'd guilt my mom for not driving two hours to change it. When Nana turned ninety-nine, Mom brought her to the doctor.

"How's she doing, Doc?" she asked.

"Great, Mrs. Kelly. I just had a patient leave here at a hundred and four. She's going to outlive him."

"Oh, Jesus," said Mom. "Please tell me you're not that good a doctor."

Nana loves that story.

Nana and I are still close. Every night at 9:00 p.m. she turns on Fox News. "I can't undah-stand a day-mn word ya saying," she says, "but I like ta make shu-ah yer okay." If she thinks I'm looking too skinny or tired, I'll hear about it. As she got closer to a hundred, we all volunteered to take her in or pay for an aide or get her some assistance. But Nana always refused—"I got my aches an' pains, but I get around okay," she'd say. "'Specially fer an old buzz-ahd."

Given this cast of adult characters in my young life, it should come as little surprise that my siblings and I were raised to take care of ourselves. Back in those pre-helicopter-parenting days, we were often our own primary caregivers.

Once when I was five, I woke up and asked for food. Mom said, "You're old enough to make your own breakfast."

I went into the kitchen thinking, *I'm sure I can figure this out.* I spotted a box of cereal. Bingo.

My brother said, "All you need to know is this: Put the milk in first."

I wound up with a bowl of milk and about nine Lucky Charms floating in it. (I'm a *slightly* better cook now.)

Another day I overslept and got to the breakfast table late. Pete had eaten all of the marshmallow charms out of the Lucky Charms box. I was left with only the cereal.

"Mom! MOM!" I yelled to her. "All the charms are *gone!*"

In response to which she opened the kitchen cupboard and pointed to her favorite sign: "Lack of Planning on Your Part Does Not Justify an Emergency on My Part."

We ate all sorts of junk: soda, Twinkies, Ho-Hos, McDonald's, Wild Berry Hi-C. We watched a lot of bad TV, like *The Brady Bunch, Gilligan's Island, The Love Boat*, and *Fantasy Island*, and some good stuff too, like *Little House on the Prairie, The Waltons*, and *Willy Wonka & the Chocolate Factory—Wonka*, about five hundred times. (My mom's favorite movie was actually *Animal House*. My brother begged her to take him to see it, and she laughed so hard that he eventually changed his seat out of embarrassment.)

In any case, things were up to us. There was no regulation. We rode around in my dad's black VW Bug with both parents smoking, the windows rolled up, and the three kids bouncing around like monkeys in the back with no seat belts. No one thought it was a problem. They didn't even put sunscreen on me. For the love of God, have you seen how pale I am?

But just because my parents gave us the space to be kids didn't mean we ran wild. We grew up knowing right from wrong and good from bad. No moral relativism at our house. And we knew there were consequences if we misbehaved. If Dad was disappointed in us, we felt shame deep in our souls, and if Mom was mad, we felt it somewhere else.

We did a feature at Fox News about how spanking makes children more aggressive. I cued up a bunch of clips of me challenging people on the air, and then I had my mom call in.

"See?" I said to Mom. "You spanking me is why I'm like this."

"No," she said, without missing a beat. "It was that sort of behavior that made me have to spank you."

I don't spank my own children today, but I don't think my mom did any damage to me and my siblings with corporal punishment. She never really hurt more than my feelings.

Those punishments aside, she didn't keep us on a tight leash. For the most part, I was able to roam free. I used to leave in the morning on the weekends on my bike and play around the neighborhood all day. My parents had no idea where I was. The only rule was that we had to be home by dinner. When I was about eight, I used to ride to a nearby thick patch of woods with a stream and go exploring. I'd be outside all day in the winter too, except on those mornings when the snow was over my head. One time I decided I wanted to run away. I came downstairs with a suitcase packed. My mom said, "Did you pack socks?" I cried. She hugged me. I stayed.

Perhaps then it's not shocking that my mother was not one for beautifying her children. Most days I dressed like a cowgirl, which was what I wanted to be when I grew up. My mom still has the Olan Mills shot of my family in front of the fake woodsy background on the wall in which I'm sporting my favorite outfit: a black-and-red cowgirl jumper. (My parents did make me remove the accompanying holster and two silver toy guns for the shot.)

Mom used to cut my hair to save money, and she once cast a disapproving eye on her own work, remarking that it looked like the bangs had been chewed. I remember leaving for the bus stop one morning. I was about seven. My mom was fixing her own hair and looked at me. "I know a little girl who didn't brush her hair this morning." I shrugged and walked out. She didn't stop me.

Apart from making us obey laws and common courtesy, my parents never much tried to rein me in, the way people so often do with their girls. They taught me manners, but didn't put much stock in me acting "ladylike." My parents always encouraged my self-expression, even if we were in a restaurant and I decided to dance near our table. They never told me to sit down. My parents let my whole self shine.

One time, my Pop-Pop, Nana's husband, was very ill after a series of devastating strokes. He could no longer go to church, so Nana had a priest come to their house on Sundays to give him communion. Pop-Pop sometimes couldn't take the communion without putting it in pudding or something soft. The priest objected, and Pop-Pop got teary—his dignity was being stolen from him, little by little. I watched the whole thing from the kitchen. I knew there was no better way to cheer him up than to dance, as ridiculously as possible, right in front of him. Pop-Pop loved it when I did this. The priest saw me edging in out of the corner of his eye and shot me a disapproving look: *Keep out.* But Mom and Nana smiled, and off I went, spinning and moving my arms like a madwoman, and singing my own made-up tune. Within moments Pop-Pop was laughing, his eyes again sparkling. He relaxed a bit, and got the communion down.

So much of how we think we're supposed to act comes from the signals we get from our parents. I'm grateful that my parents never tried to box me in, and that they encouraged me to break the rules here and there. I'm also thankful they helped make me self-sufficient.

I worry about the young children today who seem like perfect little ladies and gentlemen, ready for brunch at Buckingham Palace. Isn't this the time to let your spirit soar? Nor do I think it's good to do everything for your kids. Why not let them spill, make a mess, accidentally break a thing or two? Being left to figure things out for myself—to pour my own sugar cereal and to run around with unbrushed hair—was a great gift in retrospect. And so were the moments they permitted—even encouraged—me to challenge authority.

My mom raised us not only to take care of ourselves but also to stand up for one another. When she was in middle school, my mother once punched out a boy named Rennis who had been bullying Mom's kid brother Donald. She took ol' Rennis down by the railroad tracks and let him have it. He never bothered Donald again. And she encouraged us kids to look out for our siblings and our friends.

My sister, Suzanne, nearly seven years my elder, clearly got the message. She has always taken particularly good care of me. My second-grade teacher, Ms. Clancy (isn't it funny how we remember our grade-school teachers' names our whole lives?), had a stuffed bear named—wait for it—Clancy. Ms. Clancy let each student take Clancy home for the weekend—she went through the class alphabetically. I was thrilled to have my turn one Friday, but that afternoon I felt sick.

"Ms. Clancy," I said. "I think I'm going to throw up."

"You're fine," she said. "Sit down."

I obediently went back to my desk. A few minutes later, I was proven right.

Ms. Clancy scolded me in front of the whole class for the mess, and angrily sent me to the nurse. Worse: she refused to let me take home Clancy the bear. I was so disappointed.

Upon hearing this story, Suzanne went directly to the mall and bought me my own Clancy, an exact replica.

God, how I loved that bear. And I loved Suzanne for giving it to me.

Pete, on the other hand, teased me, sprayed me with water from the sink, and gave me noogies. In retaliation, I constantly got into his things, threw my sneakers at him, and did whatever I could to annoy him. We argued a fair amount, and my mom would sit us down and encourage us to talk it out. She was big on conflict resolution. I used to storm out of the room, go up to my bedroom, and slam the door. My mom would give me some time to calm down ("Let her have her upset," she'd say) and then would always come up with a soft knock on the door.

"Can we talk?" she'd ask.

"I'm still mad."

"Forgiveness is something you do for yourself, honey."

And my brother and I would always talk it out. My mom, too, if she and I were arguing, would be the first to come to my door. She never let pride prevent a healing moment.

When Pete turned ten, we were camping, and my dad said we should all make his gifts that year. My dad wrote him a song. He also helped me use sticks to make a stand on which I presented Pete with a perfectly oval stone I had found. On it I painted, "Pete Kelly is grate!" (I was only five—spelling would come later.) Pete kept it through his high school graduation on the shelves in his room. It always meant so much to me to see it there.

Today, Pete and I are great friends, but, growing up, we tested each other. I like to think he helped toughen me up, and that I learned to give as good as I got.

Case in point: one year on my birthday, my mom presented me with a key lime pie.

"Key lime pie?" I said. "I hate key lime pie."

"No, you don't," my mother said. "You love it."

"No, Mom," I said. "Peter is the one who loves key lime pie."

"Oh," she said, as the truth dawned on her.

At this point, my brother had a great idea. He was very enthusiastic. What if we all put our names in a hat, and whoever had their name picked by me would get the key lime pie in the face?

We all agreed. There were about ten of us there.

I picked a name out of the hat and then walked around the dining room table as my would-be targets blinked their eyes in fear. I had decided from the start that no matter which name I picked, my brother would be getting the pie in the face, since he had been so excited about his idea.

Sure enough, when I got to him, I planted that pie square in his kisser, making sure to massage his hair with the whipped cream on top. It was spectacular, among the best birthday presents I've ever received.

Growing up in such a family will keep you full of humor and humility. It's hard to feel like the king of the world when on special occasions you stand a very real chance of getting a pie in the face. But it also raised my standards for human kindness. My parents always valued honesty, but they softened the sometimes harsh realities of life with warmth, jokes, and cheerfulness.

I knew there would be no shortcuts for me in life—we didn't have money or access to people of power. I knew, if I was going to have any success, it would be a result of getting educated and working hard—as hard or harder than my parents did. If I was going to enjoy life to its fullest, it would be because I inherited my mom's sense of fun and my dad's intellectual curiosity. Most of all, as a Kelly, for the rest of my life I would have no choice but to tell the truth, and to get up and dance when someone called my name.

2

Mean Girls

As tight-knit and loving as my family was, nothing could have prepared me for the gauntlet that was seventh grade. It was a horrible year for me. It was also a year that helped make me who I am.

For much of my school life until then, I'd been subject to the usual whims of social groups, with things going up and down year to year. At a birthday party in third grade, I overheard the adults talking.

"Well," a parent said, motioning to me, "it's very clear who the leader in *that* group is."

Wow! Me? I felt flattered. I had never thought of myself as a leader before. And the adult attention felt good. Of course, at that age it's the most and least popular kids who are the most vulnerable to changes in fortune. That's why so many kids try to keep their heads down and blend into the wide middle. But I was Linda's daughter, incapable of not putting myself out there.

Usually I was rewarded for my courage. But not always. In fourth grade, I was the subject of very different attention. For some unknown reason—in retrospect, I think the most powerful girl in the group was trying to neutralize a perceived threat—I was targeted at a birthday party. The girls at the party turned on me and started flicking me, hard, with their fingers. They were yelling "Flick!" as they did it. I clearly didn't like it and was trying to get away from them. I started crying, but still they wouldn't stop. There was of course no adult present, because this was 1979. Somehow I got away, went inside, and called home. My dad came and picked me up early from the party. When we walked through the door back home, my mom looked at us.

"How was it?" she asked.

My dad made a thumbs-down gesture.

I was hurt and confused by what had happened and completely without the skills to handle it. I guess I did the right thing. What would I tell my child to do in such a situation? Call me. Go get a grown-up. The upside of all the hovering we do today with our own children is that a responsible adult is usually only about three feet away when we need one. Maybe that's why we stick so close to our own kids now—because we remember from our own free-for-all childhoods what can happen when you don't.

When I was in fifth grade, things were on the upswing again. My father took a teaching job at SUNY Albany, so we said good-bye to Syracuse, and I transferred to a new elementary school in a suburb of the capital city. As the new girl in Delmar, I was fairly popular. I even ran for class president. Each candidate had to come up with a nickname appropriate to her platform. Mine was Penny Preserves, because I stood for thriftiness and saving the environment. Alas, I was defeated by "George Brett." His platform was that the Kansas City Royals were awesome.

In sixth grade I met Kelly McGuiness, one of the best friends I would ever have. We had both been marked as students who might belong in advanced math, so they had us take a test. We met in that test room, sitting next to each other at the desks. We laughed and bonded. Neither one of us made it into advanced math, so we were math-whiz also-rans together. She and I were inseparable for the next decade.

Decent grades came fairly easily, and so I focused more on my all-consuming social life than my schoolwork. While I was outgoing enough to have friends, I was not cute enough for most of the boys. I was a bit overweight, with my dad's gap between my two front teeth and acne-prone skin (something I struggle with to this day).

"She's going to be with us for a long, *long* time," my parents liked to joke. That idea didn't bother me. I loved my parents and was happy they might be stuck with me.

"Don't worry," a friend of mine said. "Farrah Fawcett was an ugly duckling, too."

This did not offend me either. I knew I was not attractive. It was encouraging, however, to think I could be one day.

Kelly, on the other hand, was always very pretty, and she helped me discover the joys of Sun-In highlights, curling irons, Clearasil, and Forenza V-neck sweaters. Kelly and I would wear matching leg warmers and rugby shirts. We became quite popular, and were asked to most parties, which was about all we ever really wanted.

Then, a year later, in seventh grade, it started. Over the years I've looked back, trying to understand what began it all, but I've come up empty. One day, almost literally overnight, I was on the outside—not just of my friend group, but of what felt like the whole world. It was as if I'd gone to sleep myself and woken up as a ghost. No one would sit with me at lunch. No one would stand next to me at gym. No one would choose me for their team. No one would take my calls. Kids flicked spitballs into my hair and made nasty comments about my looks. Girls tried to trip me in the hallway.

It wasn't so much the targeting in class, it was the total elimination of me as a person. I used to be so social, walking through the hallways, talking with friends. Now I would try to walk up to a circle of girls and they would disperse immediately, with eye rolls and pained expressions, as if it was ridiculous that I would even try to talk to them. I went from spending all of my time with these girls to being treated like I had killed one of them.

The cruel expressions, their obvious disdain for me—it was as if I had a putrid smell, as if just being seen near me could result in a hideous illness. They looked at me with such disgust, it made me feel disgusted with myself. I would walk by a circle of the girls at the entrance to a class, and they would laugh—loudly—to make sure I knew it was about me. They would pick something on me—my sneakers, my jeans, my large backside—and mutter an insult as I walked by, like "Try the salad, for God's sake!" Or "What is she, four? What's with the decorated sneakers? Grow up."

We used to get together every day after school somewhere—hanging out around the outside of our school, or going over to someone's house. Now I'd see them going off, and I'd be by myself on the bus or in the schoolyard, trying not to make eye contact with anyone. My home phone, which had constantly rung when I was getting along with The Group, now never did. I had not a soul to talk to.

Not even Kelly. She never actively targeted me (and in fact she lobbied unsuccessfully for the bullying to stop), but her entire social existence depended on not angering The Group. I didn't hold it against her. I had done it at one point to her, too. The cost of breaking stride with The Group was just too great. I was ashamed to sit at home in front of my parents without my phone or doorbell ever ringing. I wanted my mom and dad to think everything was fine.

The Group had power. Not just with girls, but with boys, too. One of the cute guys in the grade ahead was with the female ringleader and a few of her friends in the hallway. I, like most twelve-year-old girls at the time, had acne. "Try some Windex on that face!" he yelled as I walked by. I held it together in the classroom, but I'd go home and cry, and cry some more. My mom took me to a dermatologist. That helped, but only a little.

As hopeless as I felt, I knew I could never hurt myself. A young man close to our family killed himself when he was sixteen. His parents heard the shot ring out from the living room. They ran into his bedroom to find him. He had failed his driving test, and a girlfriend had broken up with him. He was a little slow. Perhaps sixteen years of feeling different had finally caught up with him. His poor parents—who had been loving and generally happy—were never the same again. A week later his mother was found wandering aimlessly in a park, crying. A man sat her down and comforted her. The kindness of strangers. The powerful shoulder of a real man. He brought her back home.

The bullying shattered my confidence. I went from being a social butterfly to keeping my head down and practically running from class to class. I felt relieved when I got to my desk, as at least my teachers would stop the worst of it. It was like what happened at that birthday party, only instead of being one day, this went on for almost the entire school year. Alone and terribly sad, I felt too ashamed to discuss it with my parents, and was powerless to change my reality at school. I went to see a guidance counselor, but he was of no help. Things were different then. I had no solace—I had developed no sport, or hobby, or other potential friends outside The Group that I could cultivate to take my mind off what felt like emotional torture. I went to school and came right home, where I would watch TV by myself, usually eating too much to make myself feel better.

One Saturday night I was home with my parents. It was dark and cold outside, the dead of winter. The phone rang, and I answered it. I stood in the kitchen, with my parents steps away in the family room. It was the ringleader of the popular kids, who was having a party.

"Hi, Megyn," she said. I couldn't believe it. She was calling me! It felt like a glimmer of hope. "Do you have any idea where all the kids from my party are?"

"No," I said.

"We're *HERE*!" they all yelled, right into the phone. Then they hung up.

My parents were looking at me. I held back my tears and said, "Wrong number."

It was nighttime and freezing, but I went out into the backyard. I knew the tears were coming, and I didn't want my parents to have to see it. We'd had a lot of snow recently, followed by freezing rain, so the snow had iced over on the top, and it was possible to glide across the surface on my sneakers. I skated back and forth, hands in my pockets, tears running down my face in the darkness. It was raw, terrible pain, and I can feel it to this day when I think back on that night.

I talked to my mom about the bullying somewhat, but never told her of the full extent. I felt ashamed of it, as if it were a reflection on me. Not opening up to her more was a mistake, of course, but the truth is, those were different times. It was 1982. Parents weren't as involved as they are now. Bullying hadn't been recognized as the abuse we now clearly know it is. Having said that, I think if I had shared with my mom the full extent of my pain, she would have intervened, as she had once years before.

When I was in first grade, a fifth-grade girl had assaulted me on the bus. She was in the seat in front of me, and she leaned over the back, reached down, and slapped my face, over and over and over again. To this day I don't know why. Maybe I said or did something to anger her. I cannot remember. She slapped me hard, five times in a row. This was the first and only time I had ever been slapped across the face—my mother spanked us, but the most we ever got was a whack on our clothed bottoms. I was crying and confused. The bus driver paid no attention at all. I got off the bus hysterical, and my mother was angry at what she saw and heard. After she comforted me, the first thing she did was call the girl's mother and lay into her. I remember feeling vindicated, happy that this girl was in trouble. And I got back on the bus the next day. (I wonder if I would let my kids back on that bus again; I doubt I would.)

With no one intervening on my behalf this time around, seventh grade continued to be miserable. Then, toward the end of the year, a miracle: Heather Sheppard. Heather lived not too far from me, and we had always liked each other but hadn't really hung out in the same group. At great personal risk to her reputation, she sat down next to me in the cafeteria.

"Hi," she said.

I had never been so grateful for a simple hello.

Heather and I ate lunch together that day, and many other days. We became friends. *All you need is one*, my mother had told me, and I learned she was right. All it takes is one brave, decent person to change your life by thinking that you're worth something. And then there were two. Heather brought around another friend, Jennifer. I remember sitting with the two of them in Heather's bedroom, listening to Quiet Riot and talking, and feeling for the first time in a long time that *I belonged*. There is nothing else like it for a pubescent girl—or boy, for that matter. And I was grateful. So very grateful.

Months later, an amazing thing happened. As quickly as The Group had abandoned me, they came back. I wish I could say that I told them all to go to hell, but I didn't. I was profoundly relieved not to be ostracized anymore, so I welcomed the détente.

I saw Heather at my induction into my high school Hall of Fame last September. There she was again, showing up to send her love. I hugged her, and we spoke for a while. She still means so much to me. I wonder if she knows just how much.

Seeing Heather and other former classmates brought back some painful memories of that time. I thought about how I'd been a different person before the bullying. I was more trusting, more open, more cheerful. Going through severe social ostracism at such a precarious point in your life—it changes you. In an effort not to be hurt again, I had put up a rock-solid wall. Even once I'd recovered socially and felt more comfortable in my own skin, a part of me still felt uneasy about letting others in. I decided, consciously or not, that I could avoid being hurt again by projecting strength. That meant not owning up to any vulnerability, and spinning a narrative about myself that would convince others I was too strong to attack.

Ultimately, I emerged from the experience both

stronger and weaker. Stronger because I vowed never to tolerate that kind of relentless targeting again, and weaker because I still didn't fully understand the true toll the abuse had taken. It would be many years before I really came to understand what a problem the protective veneer I was creating could be.

In eighth grade, just to show how insanely fickle middle-schoolers can be, I was voted Most Popular Girl. There was no pleasure in that for me, only a tentative sense of security. It meant nothing more to me than insurance against another round of targeting. Perhaps now I had some power. I resolved that I would do whatever it took not to go through that misery again. I also vowed to protect my friends from bullies whenever possible.

A short time later, Kelly told me the class ringleader had begun to torment her again—The Group was starting to turn. Kelly had already had her turn of torture as their target.

"Not again," Kelly told the ringleader.

"She's already been through it," I said to the mean girl. "Stop." Amazingly, she stopped.

To this day, I can handle people who are dumb, lazy, or generally annoying. The one thing I cannot and will not tolerate is a bully.

Still, I was never able to reclaim my innocence about

humanity. The most enduring legacy of being bullied was that I understand on a cellular level that other people being cruel to you is part of life, but that this too shall pass. And that every time you drag yourself to school or your job even when you don't want to go, you make yourself a little more resilient. It's like working out. Every time you do it, your muscles break down. The tiny fibers tear a bit. Then they grow back stronger and more defined. And the next time it happens, you can take more weight.

That doesn't mean bullying is a good thing. It can create very deep wounds. But enduring it does develop some life skills, as long as you can get past the scar tissue. And until about two decades later, I thought I had.

That summer after middle school, Mom took me to get my teeth fixed. I took up running and lost fifteen pounds, and entered high school looking like a new person. I wondered if this was the beginning of my Farrah Fawcett moment.

Looking somewhat prettier and having been through the grind once already, I felt my own power much more in high school. I was done being an outcast, and I refused to put up with any bullshit. I became head cheerleader and president of our high school sorority.

One day in the locker room, an older girl growled at me and then called me a bitch. Twice.

"If you call me that one more time," I said, "you're gonna regret it."

She said it again.

I let her have it. We ended up rolling on the ground in our cheerleading uniforms, pulling at each other's hair. (This sounds sexier than it actually was.) The gym teacher had to pull us apart. I'm no advocate of violence, but I do believe in self-defense.

And the growler? She never bothered me again.

3

Silent Night, Holy Night

At the start, high school was a breeze. I was happy and popular, getting mostly A's while also finding time to work—first as a babysitter, then as a salesclerk. My planned pursuits, according to my yearbook, were "college, government, and wealth." For the record, I have no recollection of wanting to be in government.

By my sophomore year, I was fifteen years old, and the last child living at home. My parents and I loved one another, and still had dinner together almost every night, but I tested the limits like all kids do, including shoplifting once. One Halloween, Kelly's mother denied us some costume jewelry we wanted from Kmart. So we stole it.

Later we put the jewelry on at Kelly's house, right in front of her mother.

"Where did you get those star earrings and plastic necklaces?" Kelly's mom asked us.

"Megyn's mother gave them to us," Kelly said.

Mrs. McGuiness knew better. "Megyn's mother had two pairs of enormous plastic star earrings and necklaces?"

"Yes," we lied.

"I'm calling Mrs. Kelly," she said. "And you two girls better go down in the basement and pray to God that she tells me she had two pairs of that hideous jewelry and gave it to you in between the time you asked me to buy it for you and right now."

So we did. We went down in the basement and prayed that my mother would lie.

Yeah, right.

"I just got off the phone with her," Kelly's mom said.

"What'd she say?" I asked, as if I didn't know.

"She said your father will be over to take you both back to Kmart as soon as he finishes his meat loaf."

We had to return the items and apologize to the store manager. He was gracious, but told us we could have been arrested, that he's seen it many times. I never stole another thing.

Another time, Kelly and I threw a boozy party when my parents were out of town. Stupidly, we took pictures and neglected to hide them, landing us in huge trouble.

My sister was the first to talk to my mom after she saw the photos on the kitchen counter.

"Well?" I asked Suzanne.

"She said you have no life left."

Yet another time, Kelly and I told our parents we were going to the Saratoga racetrack, but actually went to see some boys on Long Island.

"How was the track today?" Mom asked.

"It was great," I responded. "We won big."

"The track's closed on Tuesdays," she said.

Busted.

Suffice it to say, Kelly and I weren't exactly criminal masterminds, but thankfully our rebellious streak was a minor thing. While Kelly was a devilish influence on me, all my memories with her are good ones. We were more like sisters than friends (she spent so much time at my house, my mother used to call us "the boarders"), and we had a lot of fun. It was in no small part because of her friendship that school and life were both going smoothly for me. But that's often how these things are right before everything changes.

Ten days before Christmas 1985, my family was beginning to gather together for the holiday, with Suzanne home from college. Pete was attending college nearby and was frequently underfoot, though on this particular day he'd opted to watch a football game with his friends rather than at home. I wanted to get the same class ring Kelly was ordering. Dad said it was too expensive. I kept complaining, and he kept saying we couldn't afford it.

I wouldn't let it go.

He'd had it. He turned and walked out of the kitchen. That was the last exchange I would ever have with my father.

I watched him walk toward the living room, and then I stormed up to my bedroom without saying good night or even acknowledging him. I turned out the light and went to sleep angry. The last image I have of my father alive is of him alone on the couch, staring at the Christmas tree. That sight would haunt me for the rest of my life—the picture of a good man, exasperated and alone.

Just before midnight, Suzanne ran into my bedroom.

"Wake up!" she shouted. "Daddy had a heart attack."

I ran downstairs just as the paramedics arrived. They began performing CPR on Dad. Red lights were flashing into our living room. Mom, Suzanne, and I struggled to push our large German shepherd, who was trying to be by my father, into the basement to keep her from getting in the way. The EMTs hastily loaded my father onto a stretcher and then into the ambulance.

One of them was a friend of my brother's. I remember his face vividly—it was grave, and he had tears in his eyes.

The ambulance raced to the hospital. Mom, Suzanne, and I followed behind, driven by our neighbors, who had heard the commotion and come over. When we arrived, we were told to wait in a private room. It seemed like we were there for many hours, but it was probably less than one.

At last the doctor came in and looked at us, shaking his head.

"There was nothing we could do."

I remember standing in the corner of the room and feeling my knees bend. A small green metal trash can sat beneath me, and I felt it hit the back of my legs as they buckled.

They invited us to see him. To take a look at my dad, who had been alive two hours earlier and looking at the Christmas tree. To say good-bye to my dad, with whom I had argued over a class ring, and whom I had disappointed with my selfishness.

He was lying on a hospital bed with a cut on his upper nose, where his glasses hit him when he went down. He looked peaceful. And it was clear he was gone.

One by one, we held his hands. It was too much to bear.

We were all in shock. At about three o'clock in the morning, as we were leaving the hospital, I stood next to my mother in the parking lot under a pitch-black sky.

"Will you ever be happy again?"

"Of course I will, honey," she said. "And you will be, too."

Mom couldn't afford to take time off from her job. Just a few months before my dad died, he had canceled an extra life insurance policy, thinking that he was forty-five and healthy, and we needed to save money. When she got home from work at the hospital, she would sit in the garage and sob, alone, before she came inside. She tried to put on a brave face for me. But I knew.

Money was certainly a stressor. My dad had bought a new car a couple of weeks before he died. The car company gave my mom a terrible time about the payments, even though they knew the situation in full. She just wanted to give back the car. It was two weeks old. It hadn't seen a lot of wear and tear. And yet they wouldn't take it and were threatening to sue her. It was more than she could handle at that moment.

Our family lawyer, Peter Walsh, had been one of my father's closest friends. A well-respected attorney in

Albany, he shared my dad's passion for religion, philosophy, and music. He told my mother not to worry.

"I'm going to handle this, Linda," he said. And he did. He sent the car company a one-line letter: "Go fucketh thyselves."

As someone who later became a lawyer and a communicator for a living, I think about that letter often. Sometimes less is more when it comes to showing someone what a moron they are.

The company took back the car.

But money was such a small piece of what my mother had to deal with in her grief. A person can encounter such inadvertent cruelty after losing a spouse. Most of my parents' friends were married. Once she lost her other half, so many people seemed to write her off. It was as if she had ceased to exist outside of her marriage to my dad. This was driven home when some friends of the family were in town right after the funeral. The husband and his wife took my mom to the store, trying to get her mind off of things. They meant well. When she came home, it was clear she was upset. Later she told me how affectionate the man had been with his wife. He held her hand. He helped her in and out of the car. He kissed her. My mom saw it all, and felt so alone. He didn't do it on purpose, but sometimes people don't recognize life's little cruelties.

The number-one thing I remember from that time was overwhelming sadness, which we each dealt with in our own way. My mom was strong but in deep mourning for a very long time; for the next year, she went to church almost every day. I preferred biking to my father's grave, to sit there and be with him. His tombstone has a fishing pole on it—Dad loved to fish. Every time I'd see an impossibly long book, or hear a word I didn't know, I'd think of him. I still do.

One of the only releases we had was TV. Mom loved *The Golden Girls* and *The Jeffersons*. It's actually one of the reasons I love TV as much as I do today: during that awful time, it was an escape for both of us, something we could do together on the weekends. Mom would say, "Let's have a TV marathon!" We'd light a fire in the fireplace. Kelly would come over. We'd all get under blankets, order dinner in, and watch a marathon of *Little House on the Prairie*. And for a while we would forget how sad we were.

My other strategy for coping was to throw myself into school life. I had been voted homecoming princess and started dating a popular boy in the junior class. Socially, I felt accepted. Kelly and my other friends were there to cheer me up and to make me feel cared for during that awful time.

We asked God for signs a lot in those days—signs

that my dad was still around. Every time we asked, we received. Not long after he died, Mom had a bad asthma attack and wound up in the hospital. She was upset and overwhelmed, and asked for a sign. Sure enough, later that day, she was looking for something in her purse while still in her hospital bed, and out popped a small card my father had sent her with some roses *years earlier.*

I realize this kind of thing can be explained in any number of ways, but my own belief is: Who are we, as mere mortals, to say there is no power beyond? To presume all of this energy, this beautiful, strong, complex energy, just dies when our hearts stop beating? I believe my father's spirit lives on, and I believe somehow he got that card to my mother that day.

Whether it was through sitting at his grave, or in church, or in front of the TV, we had to endure. It was like giving blood at the doctor's office. Sometimes you have no choice. The needle is going to pierce your vein. Your blood's going to pump out. It is going to hurt. So too it is with grief. There will be a bloodletting, whether you want it or not. You grit your teeth and bear it until the acute tenderness has passed. And then one day you realize it has.

It took years to feel anything but deep regret about the terms my father and I were on that last night. I wished I'd made up with him before I went to bed, or that I'd been less shallow. Me being bratty and him being fed up—that had never been what our relationship was about. I hated that it ended on that note, rather than after any of the days we'd spent talking about books or playing music and dancing. It's taken years to get to a place where I can believe that my father has forgiven me for my pettiness and vanity in those hours before he died.

I try not to let that memory make me paranoid about my relationships with others. At first, when I would fight with my husband, Doug, I would wonder if we should try to make up before bed, because what if . . . When they say you should never go to bed angry, I know why firsthand. But the truth is that even after my dad's death, I found this adage unrealistic. Sometimes you're angry. Sometimes you're tired. Sometimes you can't resolve things before you close your eyes. If I ever fall asleep mad at Doug, and then die before we make up, I just have to trust that he knows I love him. As for my kids, I've never gone to bed angry with them; in fact, I've really never been angry with them. Of course, they are not yet teenagers who want meaningless and expensive class jewelry. Still, like my mom, I believe strongly in conflict resolution. And never more than a day will pass before Doug and I work out our differences.

For a very long time, I was consumed by thoughts of our loss.

"Mom," I said one night, "I keep dreaming about Dad. Then when I wake up, I remember the truth. It's awful."

"Why don't you think of it as extra time with him?" she said. "Try to enjoy that time."

I looked at her, thinking of everything I was going through and how she had to be feeling just as much, and more. I felt like I would never be as tough as my mother.

"How are you so strong?" I asked her.

She came over and held me.

"Anything is doable as long as it's time-limited," she said. "This pain will never go away, but it will get easier."

My mother was so sad, but so brave at the same time. Once, when she was at work during this time, she had a contentious exchange with a table full of doctors at the hospital. Uncharacteristically, she burst into tears. While crying, she choked out: "These tears are not about you. They are about my husband. But don't let the tears dilute the content of my message."

What a great line.

She is so right. Like my mom, I am by no means a woman of steel. And as the years have gone on, I've come to realize the truth of what she modeled for me: It's okay to get emotional. It's okay to cry—and this is key—*as long as you can play hurt.* My mom always told me one of the tests of an emotionally healthy person was how quickly they could recover from a setback. The test of strength is not avoiding emotional distress; it's functioning in the face of it.

Those first few Christmases after my father's death were rough. We took comfort in each other, and in the maintenance of our family routines. Mom would always cook a big breakfast Christmas morning—she even did it the Christmas right after my dad died, a week to the day after we buried him on a bitingly cold, gray, snowy day. Every year thereafter, we always got a tree and decorated it, drank eggnog, and sang Christmas carols, with one less stocking by the fire.

We worked hard in those first years after my father's death to find opportunities to smile. One Christmas, Mom sent me and Suzanne to get the tree, insisting as she always did that it be a Fraser fir. She said Douglas firs shed their needles everywhere.

"No problem," we said.

"Go now," she said, "or they will all be gone."

But we were watching our favorite Christmas special, *The Christmas That Almost Wasn't,* and this was before the invention of DVR.

"We'll be fine," we told her.

"Go!" she cautioned.

Sure enough, by the time we got to the tree farm, there were no more Frasers.

We bought a Douglas, and before we brought it home, my sister looked at me. "This *is* a Fraser," she said. "Got it? Repeat after me: This. Is. A. Fraser!"

When we got home, Mom took one look at that tree, and with hands on her hips, said, "That is *not* a Fraser!"

"Yes, it is," Suzanne said.

"It is," I said.

We had barely gotten the tree decorated when needles started falling off. Suzanne and I doubled down.

"This year's Frasers seem off," we remarked.

My mom rolled her eyes.

To this day we have never admitted it was a Douglas. (I'm having my mom skip this chapter.) It was an extra boon that the sheer absurdity of our lie, and the intensity with which we maintained it, gave me and Suzanne a good laugh in a dark time.

In the years since my father's passing, I've found different ways to remember him at Christmas. The very first time I played a guitar was Christmas 1997, twelve years after my father's death. I wanted to surprise everyone by playing "Today" by John Denver, which has always been such a special song in our family, as it was one of my father's favorite campfire songs during our summer trips. My friend at the time said, "I don't mean to discourage you, but it is two weeks until Christmas, you don't know how to play guitar, you don't own a guitar, and you don't have the music to the song."

I was undeterred. I bought a classical guitar for $100. I found the sheet music by walking into about seven guitar stores and singing the song until someone knew it and how to get it. I taught myself how to finger-pick the tune late at night after work. And then I sneaked the guitar home for the holiday, having a cab instead of my mom pick me up at the train station so no one would see I had it.

On Christmas morning I came downstairs in my red pajamas, and told my brother, my sister, and my mom I had a special gift for them. And I started to sing.

Today, while the blossoms still cling to the vine.
I'll taste your strawberries. I'll drink your
sweet wine.

A million tomorrows shall all pass away,
'ere I forget all the joy that is mine today.

I played and sang "Today" for them. And I wrecked Christmas. I could barely make it through the song without breaking down. Okay, I did break down. And so did every member of my family. It was like I set off a sadness bomb. I went to the bathroom to clean up my tearstained face, and my sister Suzanne came in.

"Meg, that was wonderful," she said.

"No, it wasn't. I ruined Christmas."

"You didn't," she said.

"I made everyone cry."

"You made us feel him, Meg. You made us remember what it was like to have him here. You didn't ruin anything."

In truth, even now, all these years later, I'm never far from my father's life and his death. Ever since his passing, the fear of my own mortality has haunted me. For many years, I worried that I had some gene that would take my life early. There were some advantages to this. After my dad died, I started eating well. As soon as I could at sixteen, I started teaching aerobics and did that for ten years. I was determined to try to stay alive. And then when I started having children, that desire became even more acute, and I began to obsess over mortality.

For years, starting in high school, it was as if I could hear my heart beating, each *thump* a reminder of the passage of time. Every time I hit that brick wall of unhappiness, I hear my heartbeat grow louder. Because of that night, with my sister coming into my room and the paramedic's face and my dad on the gurney and my mom in the parking lot, I know I only have limited time here. I mean I *know* it, not just in my head the way everyone does, but in my heart and in my gut, the way those who suffer great loss do.

But this newfound sense of urgency didn't immediately bring a higher level of clarity or calling to my life—on the contrary, it sent me reeling. Recently, I came across my old journals, which I've been keeping since I was a kid. Here is an entry from June 12, 1989, three and a half years after my father's death:

> *I feel so helpless sometimes. I know that my destiny is in my own hands, but to what extent? There is so much to think about—family, friends, career, LIFE! Will my grandchildren read this, years from now, and see it as the only thing to remember me by? No legacy? We're here for such a short time.*
>
> *But what exactly are my ambitions? I thought ambition was viewed as bad, as wrong. It turns out*

it's the key to everything. Where will I be in ten years? I want to be successful.

What do I believe in—really believe in? Hell, Megyn, what do you even know about the world? I want to know what my teachers know. Where is it all? In books? I know where it is—it's in years and years of research and experiences. That's not something I can just have. I have to get it all for myself. I'm just sitting here wondering who I really am inside and—who am I to become?

A few years after my father's passing, Mom met a wonderful man, Peter Kirwan, in a support group for widows and widowers. He'd lost his first wife to brain cancer and nursed her himself to her dying day. Peter was great for my mom, and for me, too. He could never take the place of my father, but he was a good-hearted, good-humored, strong male presence in my life at a time when I really needed that.

Peter came to the relationship with three children of his own—Paul, Patrick, and Liza. Paul was strong, good-looking, and easygoing—he's now a police sergeant in Albany. Patrick was about the gentlest soul I'd ever met, quirky and loving and all kindness. If any of us needed anything, Patrick would be there, first in line with a screwdriver or a moving truck or whatever else, and probably a corny joke too. And Liza, now a critical care nurse, was full of fire—she loves music, sings like an angel, and floors us all with her acerbic wit.

Like my dad, Peter is a devout Catholic, and as a young man he too had considered the priesthood. (When my mom's friend heard this, she asked Mom, "Does your mother know you're boinking all these priests?") When Peter and my mom got married, they had five priests standing at the altar. Two were friends, two were from their respective parishes, and I don't know where they found that other guy. It was a beautiful service—very pious, as you might guess—and full of family. All six of us looked on, relieved to see our mom or dad finding love again, but also deeply saddened at the reality that life really does move on.

I don't call Peter my father, because my father didn't abandon us, and I want to honor his memory. But Peter is as much a father figure to me as any man could have been. He's provided a shoulder to cry on more times than I can count. He's given counsel in the dark times, and shared my joy in the highest moments, always with a thoughtful word. We tease him because he tends to see things in extremes—everything with him is either "magnificent" or "devastating." There's very little middle ground. Conversation with him is exciting.

My dad was an intellectual. Peter never finished high school, but has a college degree in Life. He's a true partner to my mother. Peter is the first to go with my mom to the garage sales or grocery stores. He would happily drive down to Nana's apartment to fix her TV or take her to the craft fair. He brushes Nana's hair and dyes my mother's. He and my mom laugh and fight and make fun of each other and knock things over out in public. They're like a comedy act. They kill at the Grand Union. He is an excellent dancer and roller skater—like Deney Terrio of *Dance Fever* on skates. I know this because we used to go roller skating as a family, even though it was long past that sport's heyday. Peter also happens to be a neat freak, which is good, since my mother hasn't ironed a piece of clothing since 1980. One time they were having an argument in their upstairs bedroom. Suddenly we heard some sort of glass break. Moments later, we heard Peter's footsteps, *step-step-step-step*, then the sound of the vacuum cleaner. Then the argument resumed.

Peter has always honored my father, often going to plant flowers at his grave.

"You're just going there to complain about me," Mom teases him.

"Yes," says Peter without missing a beat. "And there's usually a line when I get there."

4

Who's Getting Hit First?

When my mom told me she was marrying Peter, I was a sophomore in college. I loved Peter, and I was happy for her. But I also felt a renewed surge of mourning for my father. It had been four years since Dad had died, and it still felt like yesterday to me. After I'd congratulated them, I went back to my college apartment in Syracuse and wept. My boyfriend at the time, Jim, came over and held me for a very long time. I leaned a lot on Jim in those days.

College until I met Jim had been pretty predictable. I'd always known I would go to Syracuse University, though I'd never thought much about why. It just felt comfortable. My mother had gone there. My father had taught there. It had this air of home. I remembered my years in that city so fondly, and I wanted to be where my dad had been. I walked through the Syracuse Department of Education, where I taught aerobics for a time, and saw a poster for the Edward F. Kelly Evaluation Conference, an educational competition that was started the year after he died and which exists to this day. Someone there told me about how much my father had meant to him, and dug up a photo of me from a work picnic, a tomboy swinging on a tire swing, smiling, a picture that captured exactly how I felt as a kid—free, full of life, loved.

But mostly I just ambled through my days, obsessed with college boys and my weight. I skipped classes to hang out with friends. My journals are replete with messages amounting to "I don't know why he's not calling!" or "I have to lose these last five pounds!" How I would love to go back and talk to that girl.

Some of my apathy came from not having gotten into the journalism program. When I was accepted to Syracuse University, I applied to the famous Newhouse School of Communications, but was turned down. And so I entered the Maxwell School of Political Science instead.

I had set my sights on the news business after my sophomore year in high school, when they gave us a written aptitude test. Mine said I should be a journalist. I did a two-day internship with the *Albany Times-*

Union. I got to follow a reporter around all day as he talked to politicians and worked his sources. I thought it was thrilling. I also took a journalism class in high school. We watched *All the President's Men,* and I found it deeply inspiring. Less inspiring was the day when our teacher wrote the following on the chalkboard and told us someone had actually written it on an exam: "Pullet Surprise" (for Pulitzer Prize). (No, it wasn't me.)

Other than that, my news experience consisted of the time my high school cheerleading squad won the Northeast Regional competition, and we stormed the studios of the local CBS station, did a cheer, and insisted that they mention our victory in the nightly newscast, which they did. It was the first, but not the last, time I would cajole a newsman into putting me on TV.

Anyway, when I started at Syracuse in political science, I figured I'd eventually transfer to journalism. But then I got sidetracked.

At a recent event, I sat next to Steven O. Newhouse of Condé Nast. I teased him about how the school named after his grandfather had turned me down.

"I read that someplace," Steve said, "and I called up an administrator at Syracuse and asked, 'How did that happen?'"

"That's all I ever wanted to hear!" I told him. Vindication is sweet.

When I started college, it had been less than three years since my father's death. I was still mired in sadness, and it influenced the way I socialized. After I left home, I noticed that it was harder for me to enjoy things on a superficial level. In college, I pledged a sorority, Tri-Delt. I fell into a group of six women—people called us the Six Pack. They were fun, kind young women, but they were also normal eighteen-year-olds. Secretly, I felt like I had nothing in common with them. I recently heard from one of them—she remembered me as "quiet" and "serious."

It was in this mess of emotions that I met Jim. Jim had the greatest impact on me of anyone in my life at the time, outside my family. He changed me as a person in profound ways and was easily the most important thing that happened to me in college. I met him sophomore year. He was a senior. I was working as a waitress in an on-campus cocktail bar called Harry's, where he was a bouncer. He used to walk me to my car at the end of the night after our shifts were over.

One night we kissed. He came back to my apartment, and we fooled around a bit. I fell asleep, and when I woke up the next morning, I was fully clothed, Jim was gone, and his T-shirt was in my bed. Immediately, I drove to where he lived.

"I have to talk to you!" I said.

"I'd imagine so!" he said.

"Did anything happen?"

"No, but only because I'm a nice guy!" he joked.

We hit it off instantly. I was very attracted to him. He was so strong in so many ways, but as I would later come to see, so damaged in others.

Jim was the youngest of nine. He grew up in Yorktown Heights, outside New York City. His dad was a cop, and his mom worked in a factory. Jim had eight older siblings, some of whom had severe substance abuse problems, as did his dad. His father and some of Jim's older brothers used to get very rough with each other. They never hit Jim—they called him "the Christ child"—but as a little boy he'd have to jump out the window and go sleep on the neighbors' couch to feel safe.

He was the first person in his family to go to college, and it came through, of all things, lacrosse, which he'd become quite good at as a kid. I came to know the lacrosse world very well. Lacrosse communities have a lot of blue-blooded kids, but they also have a fair amount of tough kids like Jim from more blue-collar areas. Jim got into Cornell and was told he could have a full athletic scholarship.

After his first year there, his brother called and said, "You have to leave."

"Why?" Jim asked.

It turned out there was no lacrosse scholarship. Jim's parents had been working double shifts for months to try to keep him there. Jim left Cornell the next day.

He started shopping himself around to any place that would give him a full ride. The legendary coach at Syracuse, Roy Simmons Jr., brought him on, all expenses paid. Simmons later told me that in all his years of coaching, he'd never seen all seventy guys write down the same name for captain until Jim. He was a natural leader. He was courageous. They won three Division I national championships. Jim knew a thing about grit.

Jim always said the key to winning a confrontation is for the other side to believe you'll fight. Then you won't have to. One time we were taking a vacation, and two punk kids were crossing in front of us in the crosswalk. One of them punched the front of Jim's car.

Jim was out of that car in a flash. "All right," he said matter-of-factly, "who's getting hit first?"

They ran.

He defended my friend Marla in a bar. Some guy wanted her to dance, but it was clear she didn't want to. The guy wouldn't take no for an answer, and was grabbing Marla. Jim pushed the groper against the wall. "She said she doesn't want to, pal!"

I never saw him actually throw a punch.

He was quick to downplay his own accomplishments, which were plentiful, certainly on the athletic side. And he wasn't afraid to show who he was and where he came from.

One year we went to a Final Four championship dinner; the teams included Yale, Loyola, UNC North Carolina, and Syracuse. Each captain gave a speech to a packed hall. The guy from Yale said, "There have been a lot of eyes on Yale this year, a lot of questions about us. People wonder why we do drills the way we do, why we warm up the way we do. . . . The way we wear our socks is very innocuous. It's all about teamwork and brotherhood."

Jim gets up there for the Syracuse team and says, "I can't speak for all the teams, but we at Syracuse did not have our eyes on Yale, and we didn't wonder about their drills or their socks. But we *were* wondering what the word 'innocuous' means."

To this day, I admire the way Jim owned his roots. I learned from him that being self-deprecating doesn't show weakness. It shows strength—just as those who tell you how amazing they are all the time are probably masking something absolutely not amazing. The six-foot-seven center doesn't tell you how tall he is.

Jim made me laugh. When we met, he had a lot of

acid-wash pants. It was 1989. I didn't like them, and I made sure they went away. (This would repeat itself later with Doug.)

Then one day I came downstairs to meet Jim, wearing a black velvet bodysuit.

"What is *that*?" he said.

"I have to express my individuality," I said.

"I tried to express my individuality," he said, remembering his jeans, "and all my clothes got sold in one of your mother's all-you-can-grab-for-a-dollar garage sales."

(I felt his pain years later when Doug and I were going to a prom-themed party and I went looking through the basement for my prom dress. When I asked my mom what happened to it, she said apologetically, "All you can grab for a dollar.")

Once I met Jim, all bets were off. He filled a void left by my father's death. We were inseparable. And he gave me the first real confidence boost I'd ever had. I knew I could perform socially. I had a high EQ. But before him, I didn't think "I can do anything!" Jim helped me focus on the importance of believing in myself. He helped me clear out the negativity and self-doubt in my mind. My journal entry from the summer after we met reflects this:

I'm young. I can do so much with my life. I can really be somebody. But not without effort. I see opportunity, but I've got to go seize it! I have to work twice as hard. I can succeed. I can do it. Take control, Megyn. Nothing is holding you back.

Jim used to call me "little girl," which was ironic; his attitude was the opposite of belittling toward me. It was tongue-in-cheek, like calling a big guy Tiny. He would say, "You got this, little girl." He was sweet, but tough—chivalrous, which is a great thing for a girl missing her father. He made me feel like no one was going to hurt me while he was around. I felt connected, believed in, and supported.

We had a lot of fun, too. I studied abroad in Florence, Italy, my junior year. I created a job for myself teaching aerobics over there. I brought my mix tapes from the States, rented a big room in an office building and a stereo system, and did it all in Italian. I figured the room could take fifty girls, and I charged each girl $100 a semester. Suddenly I had $5,000. That was a lot of money for a broke nineteen-year-old girl in 1990, and I used some of it to fly Jim over. We had a romantic week together, culminating in a trip to Elba on our last day. It was a wonderful time. If you told that girl that her future wasn't marrying Jim and living happily ever after by his side in upstate New York, she would not have believed you. But time would prove that Jim was not the man for me. As the years went by, it became quite clear we were very different people, with divergent goals. It eventually ended with great sadness and affection.

I will always be grateful to Jim for the support he gave me. He was there for me during many dark moments of missing my father. No one else was as much of a comfort to me. I think it's because his childhood had been rough, and so he had the wisdom and gravitas to handle my grief. When my insecurities would creep up—about school, or friends, or my future prospects—Jim would tell me, "Don't let them get to you, little girl. You know who you are." He believed I was strong, and helped me believe it too. Sometimes I wonder if he has seen me on TV, and whether he knows that what I've accomplished is in part an accomplishment of his. He gave me the confidence to do everything I've done. I doubt I would be here without him.

By my second year of college, I found myself thinking more and more about law school as a next step. I'd actually been considering it since my freshman year, when I had taken a class with a political science professor named Robert McClure. He was a tough, no-nonsense professor whose class I loved. I learned quite a bit from him about how to make an argument—and, more importantly, that I loved to argue.

By the time I was a junior, I had decided to become a lawyer, which was empowering as a decision. I'd been searching for what my path would be and how I'd take control of my life. Now, finally, I'd seized upon one. From my journal entry on January 26, 1991:

> *I am twenty years old now and have actively begun to make what I want happen. It's a good feeling, though certainly frightening. I know who I am becoming and who I want to be. The horrifying threat of misplaced nostalgia will never affect me as I age, for—succeed or fail—I will have accomplished the satisfaction of attempting.*

When I applied to law schools, initially I thought I wanted to go to Notre Dame. It was Irish and Catholic, it was in South Bend, Indiana, and I thought it might be fun to see a different part of the country. Plus, it was a great school. I was turned down by Notre Dame, but got a yes from Albany Law School (ALS), right in my hometown, so I could live at home and save some money. Besides, everyone says it's the Notre Dame of Albany.

I would need all the confidence I got from my family and from Jim, because law school was not for the faint of heart. The work was intense and the competition fierce. However, to my mother's delight, not only did I thrive in law school, but I paid for it myself.

My favorite class was taught by Professor Bob Tyman, a crusty old guy, good-humored but sarcastic as hell. He taught torts and contracts—or, as he put it to folks at cocktail parties: "I use a little blue book, and a little green book, and I teach people how to think like lawyers." Tyman paced around the well of a grand amphitheater-style classroom, with about a hundred students wrapped around him, going up several levels, like a waffle cone. He, like most professors at ALS, used the Socratic method to teach—walking you through your logic until you at last realized the folly of your position, or the soundness of it. Imagine skipping the homework and then being subjected to that.

At ALS, often we were forced to make our arguments on our feet, going at it with our professors, with an audience around us. I loved every minute of it. Tyman once pulled me aside to tell me, "You really seem to be enjoying law school." *My God*, I thought, *I made an impression.*

Not everyone was pleased with my classroom enthusiasm. I sat near a woman I will call Jane, who informed me that some had taken to referring to me as "Barbie." Jane would often tell me the negative things people had to say about me. I was offended by the nickname, but also a little inspired by it. *You think I'm a ditz? Stand by.* I've had this feeling many times in my career. Being underestimated is a gift in many ways.

One day it dawned on me: Jane enjoyed relaying this information a little too much, and she was not my friend.

"You know what, Jane," I said, "do me a favor—stop telling me the bad things people say about me. I don't need that kind of negativity in my life."

"Fine!" she said indignantly. "I was only trying to help."

I put up with her for a long time, but by our final year of law school I'd had it.

"Hey, Jane," I said, trying to figure out a class's seating chart. "Do you know where we're sitting?"

"Figure it out yourself," she said.

To which I responded, "Shove it up your ass."

That is the only time I have ever used that phrase in

my life, mostly because once you've really nailed it, you should leave well enough alone.

Though Jane probably wasn't rooting for my success, I could feel myself gaining a self-assurance that I had never felt before. I was coming alive, but it wasn't just in my classes. As much as I loved studying and arguing and learning, the thing I was absolutely dying to do was moot court. Students were not allowed to audition for the trial team until their second year, and even then the team consisted mostly of third-year students, with only one or two second-years. So my first year, I watched with envy as the upperclassmen practiced and competed.

By the time second year rolled around, I could barely contain my anticipation. I checked the door of the coach's office several times a day, awaiting the sign-up sheet for tryouts. I could think of nothing else. In all there were eight spots, four on the first-tier team and four on the second tier. I was determined to be first tier, and I knew in my bones I could do it.

This was not the result of some unbridled confidence in myself. I never thought I'd be a great scientist or dancer or contestant on *Jeopardy!* I also knew I would never be number one in our law school class (those folks seemed to have truly special brains). But

I knew almost as soon as I got into law school that I could stand up and make an argument.

It's not like I had been winning arguments my whole life. I hadn't. But in the same way my friend Bob Clyatt picked up clay from his son's middle school art class and suddenly knew he was meant to do something with it, and now is a successful sculptor, I saw the students on their feet making arguments during my first year and knew it in my bones: *Yes, I can do this.*

I am a big believer in that old Henry Ford quote: "Whether you think you can or you think you can't— you're right." Moot court is where that all started for me.

In retrospect, there were signs to support my confidence. While I hadn't been focused on academics in high school, I loved public speaking. It was my favorite course. After my father died, I'd written and read aloud a poem about loss that took every ounce of strength in me. I swallowed hard to make it through without crying, only to look up and see I was the only one who wasn't. And like my mom, I also enjoyed being "on" in a room. I had her authoritative voice. A good voice is important for any public speaker, but especially for a woman. In fact, I believe women with very high voices should consider voice training; there is no better way to be instantly dismissed—other than bad wardrobe or makeup choices—than to sound like a child when you talk.

I'd used my voice to great effect during one of my jobs in college as a telemarketer. Though I'd continued teaching aerobics throughout college, I'd also taken up selling 1-800 numbers for businesses as a way to make more money. At first, I found I couldn't sell very well if I used my own name. I did much better if I used a fake name: "Hi, this is Rachel calling . . ." (Or, as my mom would say, "Racial.")

That kind of acting was an effective tool, and a skill—one that I honed later as a young lawyer, when I was deposing powerful, high-rolling clients in cases where millions of dollars were at stake. If I failed, it wasn't really me, but an alter ego. That took some of the pressure off. With "Rachel" and my voice, I became a killer telemarketer and made excellent money for a summer job. They never made it official, but I felt sure I was chief telemarketer.

The end result of all this was that I knew I was good enough for the trial team, even though it was quite competitive. Still, there was no question I was going to have to work at it—everyone wanted one of those spots. I spent the summer of 1993 studying the sample criminal case they gave us, a notebook filled with transcripts and other "evidence" against a young fictional man who'd kidnapped and raped a fictional woman named Lynn Anne Montoya.

They left it up to us whether to argue the prosecution or the defense case. I was always more inclined to put criminals behind bars, rather than keep them out, so that's the side I chose. Not to diminish what criminal defense attorneys do—I respect them greatly. They serve an important role in our criminal justice system, which is stacked against defendants and does get abused. But I found the idea of prosecuting cases honorable, and that's what I wanted to do.

For weeks, I prepared, studying the case and crafting the best legal argument. Night after night I sat in my bedroom, working at my assemble-it-yourself particleboard desk with one bright lamp. I wrote and rewrote the most compelling closing argument I could. I spent days tightening the logic and tying the evidence together. I looked deep in the case file for clues that might bolster my circumstantial case.

In the end, after many weeks of writing, I knew I had something that would sing. I practiced in front of the mirror, my friends, basically anyone who would listen, which more often than not meant my mom, my stepfather Peter, and my sister Suzanne. I remember sitting my mom and Suzanne down in foldout chairs in my sister's backyard one day and delivering the whole closing without notes, spelling out what had happened to Ms. Montoya in great detail.

When I got to the most gruesome part, my sister said loudly, "That's disgusting!"

It appears we've won over juror number two, I thought.

The day of the tryout, I was like a racehorse in the starting gate. I walked into the classroom where tryouts were. It was cold and white, with about twenty desks and chairs and not much on the walls except a blackboard in the front, where I was.

And then I saw him. In the back of the room by the windows, the legendary Ken Melilli—Yale and NYU law grad, former federal prosecutor, head trial team coach, and beloved criminal procedure professor. He was about six feet tall, with a full head of dark hair—smart, confident, and infamously unsparing in his analysis of students, and life.

Next to him was his assistant coach, a young blond woman I had never seen before. *Glad to see there's no bias against young blond women in this room,* I remember thinking.

There were very few words between us before I got started.

"Hello," I was told. "State your name. Please proceed."

The room around me seemed to disappear. This is something that happens to me to this day. It's as if adrenaline shuts out all stimuli outside of the thing on which I have to concentrate. I took a deep breath, looked them in the eye, and before I knew it, I was off.

For twenty minutes, I waxed on about the defendant and Ms. Montoya—hitting the crescendos and decrescendos, holding back at moments, raising my voice a bit for dramatic effect, and building the drama to the end. I wasn't nervous. I was exhilarated. I could do this. This felt right. I believed in my case. I knew I could convince them. *Stay cool, stay collected*, I thought. *Don't get too emotional, don't oversell it.*

"The defendant is guilty," I said. "He kidnapped this woman in broad daylight. And then subjected her to hours of unspeakable cruelty. What will he do if you acquit him, ladies and gentlemen? Do you want this man back on the streets? Around your families? Don't make the same mistake his victim did. Don't trust him."

When I was done, all Melilli said was "Thank you."

I was a little disappointed. I thought I had nailed it, and I half expected on-the-spot feedback. Maybe a "Great job!" or, in a perfect world "You did it! Welcome to trial team!" What I got instead was a nod toward the door, which I opened and walked through.

What I didn't know then was that Melilli and his assistant coach had looked at each other after I closed the door and high-fived. Melilli later told me in his office that I was not only the highest-scoring candidate for the team that year but the highest-scoring candidate they'd ever had. He also kept my ego in check, telling me never to refer to the jury as "ladies and gentlemen" because it's alienating, and that I had violated a major ethical rule by trying to make the jury fear for its own safety. Whoops.

Overall, it had gone great, though. As a kid who never excelled particularly in anything but being popular, that moment was the first taste I can ever remember of knowing that I could do something, and then hearing someone else confirm, "You're really good at this."

That's a marker in time for anyone. More than simply boosting my confidence, it confirmed that my instincts about myself had been right. Because I grew up the way I did, I'd been honest enough with myself to know what I could and couldn't do. With moot court, I'd been able to sense that fine line between hoping I would be good at something and actually being good at it. That kind of self-awareness rarely just happens—it needs to be cultivated. Having that intuition about my own abilities validated was a crucial first step toward believing I had promise in this field. It started to dawn on me, sitting in that office in my jeans and a T-shirt, sporting a ponytail of blond hair, that I really might be more than a cheerleader who could type fast.

5

Trial Team Barbie

L aw school was challenging, in a great way. Generally, with every tough class I weathered I grew more certain of my abilities. But then, a setback: at the end of my first year, I failed to "grade on" to the *Albany Law Review*, the prestigious student-edited law journal.

"You didn't grade on? Wow," said Jane, a little too gleefully.

Being on the *Law Review* is basically a yearlong homework assignment, but it is also a huge résumé builder. If you finished the first year in the top 10 percent of your class, you automatically "graded on." I was in the top 12 percent, but anyone in the top 20 percent could attempt to "write on" to the *Law Review* instead, which required a hell of a lot of work the summer after first year. I was determined, and I just about killed myself working to write on in the summer of 1993.

Every spare hour of every day, I was working on that *Law Review* piece, finding holes in my arguments, perfecting the language. At the same time I was preparing my trial team audition, as well as working nights and weekends teaching aerobics, and working full-time during the week for a local law firm, at which I was busting my ass. The senior partner and I worked together all summer on a case involving a patron at a bar who got drunk, drove home, got hurt, then sued the bar. I had done a ton of research and witness interviews, and spent a fair amount of time briefing this partner. One day he called me into his office.

I walked in full of hope. *This is it*, I thought. *He's seen how hard I've been working. He's going to give me a really good case, or a job offer, or a recommendation . . .*

"Megyn, I've been thinking," he said. That was good. He was thinking! About me! Surely about the long hours I was putting in for the firm. Then came the kicker: "I'd really love to set you up with my son."

I stood there in shock. I didn't want to go out with his son. I wanted an assignment.

Here I was working tirelessly at this firm because

I wanted him to see me as a future associate, not as a future daughter-in-law. He went on to tell me how attractive I was, just his son's type, and would I consider a dinner out with the two of them?

I realize he meant no offense. This guy was born around 1930 and raised in a different time. That's not an excuse, but it is an explanation. These days, I think we are much more conscious of the fact that we don't only praise the girls for being pretty and the boys for being smart. Many women I knew at the time were sent similar messages—that no matter how tough they were or how hard they worked, ultimately they were more likely to be pulled in for a chat about their dating status or their looks than for a conversation about their career.

No real harm was done to me in this exchange, but it was a moment in which I remember realizing that I might have challenges getting some men to take me seriously. I didn't spend much time thinking of it as good, bad, or otherwise; I viewed it as information. This was something I would encounter, so I had to learn to deal with it. The bottom line for me was, no, I did not want to date his son. Besides, who had time to date? I had to write on.

In August the letter arrived with the *Law Review* decision inside. I picked up the envelope, praying. I understood how much was riding on it. This was my last shot. There were no do-overs here. I held it up to the light, trying to see through the envelope, as if that protective layer between me and the news might somehow cushion the blow. After about a minute of that nonsense I ripped open the envelope. I had done it.

The significance of that moment cannot be overstated. In fact, one could argue that my entire future depended on the strength of the article I submitted for the write-on competition. Without that feather in my cap, I almost certainly would not have caught the eye of my eventual law firm, which only accepted one or two students from my class in a very competitive process. I came away feeling empowered: *I am in charge of changing my life, and hard work matters.* I didn't need money, or connections to power, or the natural advantages some of my classmates had. Through sheer force of will, I could get myself where I wanted to go.

Between writing onto the *Law Review* and making the trial team, I was feeling increasingly confident in my skills as a potential lawyer, a feeling that only got stronger once I actually started competing in moot court. To this day, my moot court experiences in law school are among my best memories.

In my second year of law school, my friend David

Hillman and I partnered up for the Gabrielli Appellate Advocacy Moot Court Competition. We were given a case to study. Then we had to write an appellate brief, and for months on end we argued the case before appeals court judges—sometimes real ones, sometimes professors playing the part.

For weeks at the beginning we toiled away in the small, run-down law school cafeteria, arguing over what each of us believed were our most persuasive positions. We both had strong personalities, which led to many heated discussions. Generally, however, we worked things out. In the afternoons, we hunkered down in the school's one-room computer lab along with dozens of other competitors. As this was before the days of everyone having a personal computer, we hovered over each other to type the brief and make it look professional.

I remember looking out the window at the gorgeous upstate New York fall day and thinking, *I want to be out there.* But I knew I was working toward a goal. Beauty, nature, and fun would have to wait. As it turned out, they would wait a long damn time.

When the competition began, Hillman and I wouldn't find out until right before we got up whether we were arguing for the appellant or the respondent, so we had to know both sides of the argument cold.

This required a ton of work, but made us much better advocates. It was also a skill that would serve me well later in my law career and my TV job. I used to say at Fox News, when we still had a show called *Hannity & Colmes*, which involved a conservative versus a liberal, that I could sit in for either guy on any given day. So, by the way, could Hillman.

Hillman and I were very frank with each other. He spoke with a charming Queens accent. There is no accent I like more than the New York City one. "I like ta read tha paper in the maw-ning—that's vehry impo'nt ta me," Hillman would say. And, after the arguments, "I thawt you've done betta—I'm not gonna ly-e."

I enjoyed being with him even given the sharp elbows, which I threw right back. Come to think of it, moot court was actually excellent training for the debate prep I do with my colleagues Bret Baier and Chris Wallace to this day. And just as Hillman and I gave each other a hard time, Chris and Bret and I never mince words: "That's too wordy!" "No one will understand that!" "Aren't you missing the real issue?" In both cases, the combative preparation made our work better.

We made it to the finals on November 18, 1993, my twenty-third birthday.

The competition was held at the law school's biggest auditorium, a gleaming brand-new amphitheater that commanded all eyes to a stage down below with an elevated judge's bench in the front. There were two lecterns in front of the bench, with a desk for the advocates beside them.

The room sat several hundred people. That night, it was standing room only. People filled the stairways and balconies and doorways, and I was both thrilled and nervous as hell to get up there in front of them. Then, as now before a big event, I would look at the clock a day earlier and say to myself, *Twenty-four hours from now, it will be done. Just get through these twenty-four hours.*

The argument was before three judges from the New York State Court of Appeals—the highest court in New York State. Knowing the legal brainpower that would be testing our positions was disconcerting. But it was also good practice for being a lawyer, when your adversary is getting paid to destroy your argument.

Before we got started, the four finalists had dinner with the judges at the law school. I was starstruck by the intellect in the room. *This might never happen to me again*, I thought.

One of those judges, Judge Vito Titone of Staten Island, in appearance and demeanor reminded me of then–sitting Supreme Court Justice Antonin Scalia, and he was one of the most respected people on the court. In one quiet moment, Hillman told Judge Titone how honored we were to be there.

"Really, no matta what happens tonight," Hillman said, "we've awl-ready won."

I looked at my partner (who, by the way, is now a gifted and successful lawyer in New York). *What are you saying?* I thought.

And Judge Titone said what I was thinking: "Second place is losing, son."

When it was my turn to argue that night, I got up, looked at the judges, and had a bit of a moment. *There they are, I thought . . . and here I am. On my feet. Making an argument.* And ready, I knew, for anything they might throw at me. Well, I hoped that was the case. *Please God, let me be ready for anything they might throw at me.*

I started talking: "May it please the Court . . . Counsel . . ." And I was off to the races. By the time I sat down, I felt as if I'd swum the Atlantic. My adrenaline was pumping, but the relief at being done was enormous. The arguments went well on both sides, so much so that when it was all over, it was not clear to me who had won.

Much as they do with the Miss America pageant, they read the results of other, lesser awards first. Of the three hundred people who participated in the competition, so-and-so wins Most Improved, such-and-such wins Best Brief (we won Third Best Brief), and so on. By the time they got to the winner of the finals, my heart was in my throat.

Hillman and I held hands and waited, eyes on the table in front of us. It had been our friends—two guys we really liked—opposite us that night. It was a little tough to root against them, but we wanted to win, and badly. *If we have to lose*, I remember thinking, *it wouldn't be terrible to lose to these guys.*

What I was doing was something Dr. Phil McGraw advises: Answer the what-if question. When something is bothering you, answer the what-if question and get yourself okay with that imagined result. It's a technique for handling stress, and it works like a charm.

Finally, they announced the competition's Winners of Second Place—a preposterous term—and we heard our names.

All the blood seemed to drain from our faces. Dejection immediately set in. Those warm feelings I had been having about our friends across the aisle turned to sour, biting ones. These two guys? Seriously? Suddenly we wanted nothing more than to get out of there. I hated the feeling. And yet I knew I could do something with this misery. After all, how can you know how much you hate losing if you never experience it? I can draw on that dejection right now—it's still there at the ready. And it is, indeed, a powerful motivator.

Before the night was over, the woman who ran the competition—Patricia DeAngelis, who went on to become a tough-as-nails district attorney in New York State—presented a special award. I had known Trish, a slender brunette with a take-no-prisoners style, since my days as a Pop Warner cheerleader, and we had become friends again when I got to ALS, where she was a year ahead of me. She stood before the auditorium—packed with my classmates, professors, and some high school friends who had showed up to provide moral support, along with my mom and Peter—and said she had one more special announcement to make.

This year they were presenting a Best Individual Advocate Award—the top advocate in the competition as decided by all of the judges throughout the year. She talked about the amount of work the contestants had put into this competition: the number of mock arguments, and the scores we had accumulated over many months before dozens of judges who tested our mettle.

Hillman and I sat there, half dying to just go home, half hoping we might still turn the night around and hear one of our names. I was too afraid of the terrible losing feeling hitting me in a one-two punch again to get my hopes up.

Trish, holding the award in her hands—a wooden gavel engraved with the winner's name—said, "I remember when I first began planning this year's competition, I asked the person who has now won Best Individual Advocate what date I should have the finals on. And she said to me: 'Have it on my birthday, November eighteenth.'"

You could hear my mother's loud, joyful sob from the audience. You would have thought this was an Academy Award. My mom gives me a hard time sometimes, but she's also my biggest fan. She may not believe in false praise, but when praise is due—as in this moment, when I was rewarded for what she knew to be months of insanely hard work—she has always been quick to offer it. She's not the kind of parent for whom nothing is ever good enough; some things are good enough. And this award was one of them. Peter later told me it was magnificent.

Trish concluded: "And when Megyn Kelly thinks back on her twenty-third birthday, it will be a day she never forgets." And she was right.

It was an incredible moment, and yet, despite my growing confidence in my ability as a lawyer, I never got too drunk on my own wine. Then, and now, I was Linda's daughter. I knew who I was, and what mattered. I could fill this book with things on which I need to improve and at which I am simply no good. But I also know what my strengths are—and this self-awareness has served me well. This approach was later encapsulated by Professor Melilli in what I now call my Albany Law School Theory of Life.

One day Melilli said to our first-year class, "Look, for those of you sitting here feeling bad about yourself because you're in danger of failing out, don't beat yourself up too badly. Just remember, you're still in law school—something thousands of others wanted but were denied. And for those of you at the top of your class, feeling great about yourselves and thinking, 'I've got it made,' just remember: you're still at Albany."

That's pretty profound if you think about it. However low you are, there is always something to feel proud of, and however high you are, there is always something to humble you. I hold on to that to this day. My mother is only too happy to help.

6

Legally Blond

When I started at ALS, I didn't have a master plan for what kind of lawyer I would be. I just knew I was there to get great at preparing cases and making arguments. I also had begun to suspect that if I played my cards right I might end up making real money at this job. I was thrilled by the notion that I'd found something I was genuinely good at that could actually lead to some financial security. By my last year of law school, though, I couldn't afford to spend too much time daydreaming about what might be—I needed to find a job, any job.

In fact, I was already supposed to have one. My second summer of law school, I'd worked at a firm in Syracuse doing real estate, contract, and employment law. It was a nice firm with pretty offices right in the heart of Syracuse, and I had a great summer there. One of the unwritten rules of law school was that it was "expected" we would get offers from our second-summer law jobs—this was the basic understanding among firms and interns, barring a catastrophic development.

In spite of this pressure, I worked hard, but also managed to have some fun. My friends Joan and Isabel were there with me, and we loved going to a dive called Roman's Tavern, where the owner played his trumpet on the bar and insisted you do a shot if you were a "Roman's virgin," meaning new to the establishment. The Dinosaur was another great place, its walls covered with biker paraphernalia and its booths filled with actual bikers, with whom we'd drink and play Quarters until the wee hours before getting up for work and acting like grown-ups.

In many ways, that summer was a preview of sorts of what I expected my post–law school life would be. At that point in my life—twenty-three years old and not long out of Syracuse University—I thought making a home and a life in Syracuse was what I wanted, a peaceful suburban existence with a job that would allow me to pay my bills, have a house, and raise a family. Just as my parents had done. As a result, I desperately wanted an offer at this firm, understanding the mad dash I would be in if I returned to school in the fall without one.

I'll never forget the day one of the partners came to see me in my tiny office, in which you could barely even turn around. It was the end of the summer, and he sat down across from my desk and told me, flat-out, that I wouldn't be getting an offer. They claimed they didn't have the money in the budget, even though they loved me, yadda yadda yadda.

I was speechless. I didn't want to hear what I was hearing. I muddled through the awkward conversation, then went to my car in the parking lot and sat there, alone, for a very long time. I remember John Mellencamp was playing on the radio. I took the news as a rejection of my work that summer, of me, of my potential as a lawyer. It was particularly upsetting because this wasn't some big New York law firm where the competition was cutthroat and the practice top-notch. It was a fine law firm, don't get me wrong. But it was in Syracuse, and I was the only intern. Everyone back home would be expecting me to return with an offer. Had I spent too much time at Roman's and the Dinosaur? Could I only succeed as a lawyer if I cut out all the fun in my life?

I would do it. I didn't care. I wanted a better life. I

fell asleep that night feeling humiliated and like a failure. I resolved to do whatever it took to succeed, even if it meant sacrificing my social life on the altar of law.

Luckily, I'd built up a reservoir of confidence and a tough shell, so I was spurred instead of crushed by this failure. Back at the office, where I still had a few days to work before the summer was over, I put on a brave face. Really, I wanted to never return, to show them I didn't need them. But I realized that would have been self-defeating, so I donned a smile and tried to finish off the summer graciously. Not only did I not want them to know how upset I was, but I also didn't want to burn any bridges, just in case the no-money-in-the-budget story was true and they might be in a position to hire me down the road. This experience of showing up at work with a positive attitude despite feeling like hell inside was quite valuable. I would come to draw on it many times in my career.

When I got back to Albany to start my third year, I was too humiliated to tell people the truth. I told everyone I got an offer but didn't want to stay in Syracuse after all. It was easier than confessing that I had failed. I couldn't let the Janes of the world see me as weak.

In order to achieve, I believed I had to be perfect. My success thus far felt like a house of cards that might collapse with the tiniest wrong move. I didn't yet have the confidence to admit my failures. When I did well, it would build up some reserves. But when I failed, I convinced myself that the failures were evidence of the "real" me, and the successes were the "fake" me fooling people. What I didn't realize then was that my real friends wouldn't have celebrated my sadness—they would have helped me through it. I had plenty of friends who would have been happy to provide a sounding board. I was just too focused on seeming strong to let them in. And so I was all alone in my anxiety and disappointment.

By the time I returned to Albany that fall, I was committed to turning things around. I marched into the career-planning office and began researching the firms at which I might still have a shot. Most did their main recruiting from the second-year, not the third-year, class, so I was late to the party, and I knew it. One firm, however, did stand out: Bickel & Brewer. They were based in Dallas, with smaller satellite offices in Washington, DC, New York, and Chicago. They liked to hire third-year law students, and at New York salaries.

William Brewer bears a decent resemblance to a young Robert Redford. He walks with a strong gait and wears a tan Burberry trench coat over perfectly tailored navy or gray suits. He was also legendary in the halls of Albany Law School, where he had studied law. I researched him and his firm with vigor and soon found that Brewer's looks weren't the only thing attractive about this firm. The term "Rambo litigation" was coined there. They took no prisoners. You hired them when you wanted a fight.

At twenty-three years old, I loved that. Kill or be killed! We're not here to make friends, we're here to win! You sue my client? F— you and your request for an extension! You want a settlement conference? Pound sand! Our offer is screw you!

Looking back, this feels a little silly, but as a young gun it sounded very sexy to me. I could enter a frat or a brotherhood of sorts. The bravado naturally appealed to me, given the protective armor I'd built up since being bullied, not to mention the fact that I'd probably always had a bit more testosterone than most girls. Going on the offensive was thrilling, and the more I acted tough, the tougher I felt. Being a litigator was the perfect job; it not only let me hide my insecurities, it felt like a tool for conquering them.

I was determined to learn everything I could about the partnership. I studied up on Bill Brewer, John Bickel, the firm's reputation, everything I could about their identity and how they saw themselves. I researched who at the law school was still connected to them that might be able to put in a good word for me. As luck would have it, one of Brewer's good friends, Shelley Stevenson, was still teaching at the school and was a beloved professor of mine. She had given me two straight A's. I liked her so much I had earlier recommended her classes to many of my friends, including a guy I'll call Bob. I asked Professor Stevenson if she would put a good word in for me. To my astonishment, she refused: she had a policy of only recommending one student a year, and she had already put forward Bob.

I was a bit worried, since Bickel & Brewer notoriously only accepted one or at most two associates from ALS a year, and there were many top students in the hunt this year. They agreed to grant me an on-campus interview, which was a good start. I wore a cream pantsuit from Casual Corner. It had flare bottoms, and the jacket was cream and yellow plaid. I accessorized with a fake strand of pearls and white—yes, white—pumps. Finishing the picture were my big glasses with blue tortoiseshell rims (gone today in favor of contacts, which I couldn't afford back then) and a big polyester hair bow that I used to tie back my long hair at the base of my neck. I thought I looked great. One of my classmates who had family dough and always looked very put-together saw me after and said, "Is *that* what you wore?"

I left feeling hopeful about a callback. Sure enough, I got one, which meant a trip to Dallas along with all the other recruits. I was nervous about going up against so many other aspirants at once. These were guys from Harvard and Yale and the University of Chicago, and I was the girl from Albany who had to write onto *Law Review*.

Still, I knew it was death to worry about them. Jim had told me long ago that you can always tell which team is going to win before the game even begins.

"How?" I asked.

"Because one team is running drills and practicing plays and focusing on their game," he said, "and the other team is looking at that team."

Before I knew it, I was in a first-class seat to Dallas. While there, I stayed at the Mansion, a tony hotel with thousand-thread-count sheets and great-smelling body lotion. They put on a weekend of parties and extravagant dinners for us. I could see that this place spared no expense.

I was mesmerized by how *luxurious* this world looked up close. I'd never had a lot of money. I was used to struggling to get anything. For seven years of college and law school, I had lived on a shoestring budget. I survived on student loans and the money I made teaching aerobics and doing odd jobs, which was barely enough to cover my tuition, never mind room and board. My apartment for many of those years had a tiny freezer so iced up that I could fit only one Lean Cuisine in there. Later I learned to defrost my freezer with a hair dryer.

I had terrible credit and was constantly dodging calls from bill collectors, doing my best to either ignore or stave off the next demand. I went into collection on more than one account. I tried to borrow money, but there was no one in my life with enough to lend. From time to time my mom and Peter would slip me $25, and you would have thought they were delivering a private plane. My brother Pete, who is a successful business-man in Atlanta, helped when he could. But he drove a tough bargain. He used to joke that the motto of his "Bank of Kelly" was: "You don't pay, you go away."

By my third year in law school, my phone was shut off, I had over $100,000 in school loan debt, and my kitchen had been hijacked by a particularly diligent ant colony. A few months later, I moved in with my mom and Peter to help minimize some of my expenses. I used to have stomach acid burn when I went to the mailbox. When things got particularly tight, I'd try to pick up extra aerobics classes—so I was not only very poor but also very thin.

The most powerful people I'd dealt with up to that point were the bosses at my Holiday Inn "front desk girl" job during college. Looking at this world of Big Law, with its crisp suits and expensive wines, I realized for the first time: *I could get rich doing this.* I hated that sickening feeling when the bills came. This job felt like a golden ticket. This was my shot. It was like getting plucked from obscurity. I would do whatever it took.

On Saturday we were individually shepherded from office to office, meeting with lawyers. Rumor had it that if things went *really* well, you'd be brought in to meet John Bickel or Bill Brewer, but we were told not to expect it and not to panic if it didn't happen.

I'll never forget sitting in one senior associate's office. He was telling me this place was like being in a foxhole; everyone there would take a bullet for the others. This is not the way most law firms recruit. Typically, they want to know why you wrote your *Law Review* note on "The Dangerous Instrumentality Exception to the Negligent Supervision Doctrine." This guy wanted to know if I was a fighter.

I knew in my heart that I was. Of course I did worry that all I had to offer by way of proof was that I'd led my high school cheerleading squad to victory in the regionals. Meanwhile, my ALS pal Brian Farrell was down the hall, telling them about the Bronze Star for Valor he'd received in the first Gulf War.

But somehow I must have impressed him, because moments later the associate picked up the phone and called Bickel's assistant, saying, "John needs to meet this candidate. Today."

In I went to John Bickel's office. We hit it off instantly. I did something all job applicants should do—I asked for the job. I told him that if they extended an offer, I would accept it on the spot, that I had done the research and investigation, and this was where I wanted to be. Don't underestimate the power this message can have on a potential employer. Everyone likes to be flattered. Of course it works better if it's true. I left the office cautiously optimistic. That night, between my ridiculously soft sheets, with that feeling of a new city around me and a new beginning on the horizon, I stared at the ceiling and felt elated at the possibilities. Things were happening that could alter the course of my life. One step at a time, I was starting to run. I hadn't grown up with high hopes for my future, but in that moment I had a sense of opportunity knocking, of imagining that I might actually be able to make something out of my life.

The next morning, I had breakfast in the hotel restaurant. There was Bob. I ordered eggs, and he ordered the tallest stack of buttermilk pancakes I had ever seen. As his food arrived, he regaled me with stories of how he'd killed the interview.

"Don't worry," he told me, patronizingly. "You may not have Stevenson's rec or gotten to meet with everyone I did, but you'll probably be fine. And I hear that stuff about them bringing people in to meet with John or Bill was bullshit."

"Actually," I said, "I met with John. It went great."

He looked at me as if I'd run over his dog. He didn't eat a bite of those pancakes.

From that day forward, I thought of him simply as "Buttermilk." A few days later, I got the job, and so did Brian of the Bronze Star. Buttermilk? Take a guess.

When I was hired, Bickel & Brewer told me I could go to any office they had, but they were hoping I would join their guys in Chicago. They flew me out one weekend and put me up at the InterContinental. I looked out the window at the twinkling lights on Michigan Avenue, also known as Magnificent Mile, with all of the cosmopolitan women carrying briefcases or hailing taxis, looking like they had someplace important to go, and thought, *That could be me.*

Walking down the sidewalk that weekend, I saw a woman talking on an early cell phone. *What could she possibly have to discuss that is so urgent it cannot wait until she arrives at her destination?* I thought. *So obnoxious!*

The sum they offered me seemed ludicrous: $85,000 a year. I would be able to pay my bills, every month! Little old me. A girl from Albany, or, as we called it, "Smallbany." I wasn't yet twenty-five. It was more money than either of my parents had ever made in a year. I had no idea what it was like not to dread getting the mail, or to simply pay a bill when it arrived, stress-free—but now, for the first time in my adult life, that would be in my future.

And that firm I had interned for in Syracuse that didn't make me an offer? Well, guess what—they came through. Called me up and offered me the job, and the life I had thought I wanted in Syracuse. But it was too late. I had already found a new dream, and a new me: Megyn Kelly, Esquire. Attorney and counselor at Bickel & Brewer. Big-city high flyer.

I moved to the Windy City in August 1995. I had rented an apartment in a high-rise near Oprah's apartment building on Navy Pier. The night I moved in, I remember looking out the window in an apartment furnished with a bed, a love seat, a TV, and two milk crates, drinking white Franzia boxed wine and playing Tina Turner's "I Don't Wanna Fight" on CD. *I did it*, I thought. My "real life" was starting. I was somewhere, and on my way to being someone.

I had never lived in an urban center before. The sheer number of restaurants, bars, museums, and parks was spectacular. Lake Michigan was lovely—vast and clean, more like an ocean. It was also a hotbed of social activity. On the weekends the locals would Rollerblade, bike and walk lakeside, and the parks were filled with adults playing softball and baseball. I fell in love with it instantly.

At work I was the only female lawyer, but I was surrounded by a great group of guys. I never was one to call BS on salty language or off-color jokes (use of the former I inherited from Nana, affinity for the latter came directly from Linda), and that made things easier from the get-go. I adored my colleagues, who were very smart lawyers, and they set the bar high for me in this, my first professional job.

One early brief I turned in was less than stellar, and a senior associate sat me down.

"Look," he said, "we are American Airlines First Class. Our clients expect the cloth napkins and the glass cups and the real silverware. You can't half-ass things here."

I worked like a dog. Many nights I stayed past midnight. Saturdays were not a day off as much as a chance to catch up on work you hadn't managed to get to during the week. On Sundays we worked a laid-back noon to 6:00 p.m.

I didn't mind. I understood the enormous opportunity I had been given—the chance to prove myself, to make something of my life.

Around this time, I shared a cab with a lawyer who'd been in the game about eight years. We struck up a conversation. "Do you hate it yet?" he asked.

"No!" I said. "I love it!"

"Just wait," he said to me. "About eight years in is when you decide you're either in it for the long haul or ready to make a change." If that were true, I had seven years left on my clock.

Even though I was the only female lawyer in our Chicago office, I didn't deal with much in the way of sexism, though occasionally there was a waft of it. For example, when Brewer came up to the Chicago office from Dallas, all of the women in the office—yours truly plus the support staff—had to change from our pants into skirts. We weren't supposed to be wearing pants at all, ever, but the rule wasn't enforced unless Bickel or Brewer came through.

It seemed ridiculous to me. The guys could wear

pants, but we had to freeze our asses off in the dead of winter in Chicago because the boss thought our bare legs were more professional? It wasn't like I wanted to go casual—I just didn't want to be cold. But I researched it and learned that it was perfectly legal.

So I didn't push back on that, but later there was a dust-up about something else.

The senior partner in our Chicago office was a very well respected attorney. I'll call him Michael. I learned a great deal from Michael. He terrified most of the office back then, as he had zero tolerance for mistakes and did not like being challenged. He was the elder statesman, in his sixties as compared to our twenties and young thirties. Everyone usually deferred to him, which was clearly the path of least resistance and led to the least brain damage.

When Michael got mad, he got really mad—red in the face, clipped words, and he would yell. To a young associate like me, it was downright intimidating. I thought any mistake I made could wind up costing me my job. Having said that, Michael was a talented lawyer, and I knew how lucky I was to have him as a mentor. He used me quite a bit for legal research on the office's big cases. He also used me for photocopying. A lot. All the time, actually.

Now, the problem with this is that copying cases

is not the job of a junior associate. It's staff work. Clients shouldn't be paying for a lawyer's time doing menial tasks, and lawyers shouldn't be wasting their legal education standing at the Xerox machine hitting COPY.

But Michael wanted his cases when he wanted them, and if his assistant wasn't around, he figured I was his next best option.

I didn't complain at first, because I realized that I was low on the totem pole, and my general philosophy was to say yes to everything when trying to prove myself in a job. However, it soon became clear that I was the only attorney in the firm who Michael used for copying cases. There was another junior associate—a man—who was never asked. There were plenty of other associates—all men—who were never asked. And then there was me. It bothered me a little at first, and then it bothered me a lot. It actually also bothered the male associates in the office.

Gender, typically, is not something I spend much time thinking about. When I was a kid, I wanted to play baseball at a time, roughly 1978, when there were no baseball or softball teams for girls in my town. I wasn't trying to break a gender barrier, or make a statement—I just wanted to play. And not surprisingly, it's how I was raised.

"There are only teams for boys," my mom said when I told her I wanted to play.

"Okay, I'll do that," I said.

My mom didn't push back and say, "You sure?" She just went and signed me up.

I showed up for the first day, and I was the only girl anywhere. There were no girls on my team or on the other teams. I wasn't fazed by it. And no one gave me too hard a time.

Throughout that season, I was never focused on being the only girl. And that was how I'd been ever since—often finding myself in situations where I was the only girl or woman, but never feeling the need to give too much thought to it.

Finally, though, the situation with Michael became too much. I resolved that I was going to address it. I was twenty-five years old at this point, and not very sophisticated or experienced in dealing with powerful men. And I certainly needed the job. But your ethical code is your ethical code, and I knew there was only one path forward. I worked out in advance how I would handle it. I walked through in my head what I would say and how he was likely to respond, and then planned out my rebuttal.

To this day, I believe planning out confrontations in

detail is key. It prevents regrets in the moment (e.g., your temper getting away from you) and lets you control the exchange.

Well, the day arrived: Michael asked me to copy another case. He said it in passing as he walked by me in the hall and into his office.

"Meggie! I need you to copy a case for me." He called all of us in the office by some similar nickname (Johnny, Jeffy, Stevie . . .).

I turned and followed him into his office, where he was now sitting behind his desk. My heart was beating hard, and I was conscious of it pounding in my chest, but I tried to sound calm and authoritative.

"Michael," I said. "I'm done copying cases for you. It's not an appropriate use of an associate's time."

"*What?*"

"I said I'm done copying cases for you. If you would like to discuss a case with me, I'm happy to retrieve it and have that talk. But if you just want me to do secretarial work for you, I won't."

Michael's face was getting red. He was clipping his words.

"Do you think John Bickel copies his own cases?" he demanded. "Do you think Bill Brewer copies his own cases?"

"No," I answered. "I think they have their paralegals or secretaries do it."

The universe did me a little favor in this moment; just as he was edging toward genuine anger, his phone rang, and it was an important client. I took my cue and scurried out of there, but it was not over.

I later learned, from one of the senior associates, that Michael called up John Bickel to complain about our interaction. God love Bickel, because I was later told he responded: "Not only is she right, but if you ever ask an associate of this firm to waste her time doing your secretarial work, it'll be the last thing you do at Bickel and Brewer."

Michael never asked me to copy a case for him again. The story went viral through our office, and it gave me some street cred there. I didn't do it for any accolades—indeed, I was expecting the opposite—but I did learn that standing by your principles is always the right call, even when dealing with people in positions of power.

I realize many people are not in the position to always choose principles over a paycheck. Sometimes there really is not another job out there, especially in the job market we've had in this country for the past few years. This is why it's important to build up your value. You need to make yourself indispensable in whatever post you have, whether it's the cashier at the grocery store or a burger flipper at McDonald's. The harder you work, the better attitude you have, the more your colleagues come to feel they need you, the greater job security you earn, and the more risks you can take.

In my heart I knew this firm was not going to fire me for pushing back on a sexist request. Like the matchmaking senior partner at that Albany firm where I once interned, Michael was not a bad guy, he was just of a different generation. I actually liked him quite a bit and remain fond of him to this day. (I changed his name only because he is not a public figure, and I don't want to cause him any embarrassment here.) I had every reason to believe that, when challenged, Michael—and our bosses Bickel & Brewer—would do the right thing.

In spite of that issue over photocopying, life at Bickel & Brewer went well—until a couple of years in, when it dawned on me that I had very little in my life but work. I remember hearing that some firms had cots and showers for the associates, and feeling jealous because we needed that. I had no friends outside of work—there was zero time to cultivate any. And the kill-or-be-killed nature of the firm that at first I had found so attractive? The shine was wearing off that too. The constant acrimony was tiresome, and more than a little soul-killing.

There was no question I was staying in law, but I thought that if I switched to another firm, I could bring some balance to my life. At the time, I naively believed the hours were inherent to the firm and not to the industry, or to me. (I would later come to understand that quote: "Wherever you go, that's where you are.") And so, despite many fond memories, I ultimately decided to leave Bickel & Brewer.

I figured a change of scenery would be nice. I loved Chicago, but having done all right in a city of that size for a couple of years, I felt optimistic that I could handle something even bigger—and Manhattan would bring me much closer to my mom, my family, and most of my friends. At first I hired a headhunter to shop my résumé around.

One firm (solid, but second-tier) interviewed me several times—I went for two callback interviews and felt certain I was likely to get an offer. Instead they told the head hunter they were passing. I'll never forget his report: "They think you're a little too perfect."

What nonsense. He said he was being honest, that's what they said, and urged me to write a letter begging them to reconsider. I knew I couldn't do that. As badly as I wanted the job, I didn't have it in me to beg for it from a firm that had just rejected me. So I refused. And then the head hunter got angry, because he wasn't going to get paid. We parted on unfortunate terms, and I was left without any offers.

I decided to go back to square one. I had a law school professor who had worked at the prestigious international law firm Jones Day, and I called him and asked him if he would forward my résumé to the hiring partner. He did so, and within a week I was walking through Jones Day's New York office. This felt like real Big Law practice. There were Warhols in the conference rooms. The receptionists were attractive and well dressed. The lawyers looked busy and important, with tastefully appointed offices and great views. It felt like a promotion in every way.

As it turned out, they made me an offer, and so did two other Big Law firms. I couldn't believe it. I went from "Why don't you try begging?" to three great offers, none of which would have happened if I hadn't taken a risk and called my law school professor about forwarding my résumé to Jones Day. I chose Jones Day because I believed it was one of the best law firms in the world. I knew that if I could succeed there, my legal pedigree would be unassailable. Just like that, I was heading to New York City.

As I prepared to leave Chicago in August 1997, I met a young medical student named Dan Kendall while out dancing. It was the night Princess Diana died, and I'll never forget coming home and seeing the makeshift memorials to her in front of Buckingham Palace and the sea of people gathering to mourn her. Another reminder of the fragility of life. I went to sleep in my Lake Shore Drive high-rise, wondering about the road ahead and what my life in New York would look like. The future Dr. Kendall made it very clear he was determined to be a part of it.

7

Self-Pity Is Not Attractive

I arrived in New York in the afternoon, long before any of my boxes would show up. Thus I entered my new apartment on the southern tip of Manhattan to find it empty, with no phone line, no electricity, and no warmth. It felt a little scary. I waited all day for my things to arrive, and when they finally did, I felt more overwhelmed than before they got there. All I could think of was a conversation I'd had with my brother:

"I'm moving to New York City!" I said.

"Why?" said Pete.

"What do you mean?" I said. "It's the big city of dreams!"

"Yeah," said Pete. "Scary, nasty, wake-up-in-the-middle-of-the-night-screaming dreams."

Hmph.

But I was starting to come around to Pete's way of thinking. I felt overwhelmed and alone. By nightfall, I left the apartment to find a phone. I wound up walking a few blocks in the darkness to the Millenium Hilton hotel. The Financial District was deserted at night, not at all the "city that never sleeps" you see in the West Village or Midtown. There were no stores, no restaurants, nothing going on except some street cleaning.

From the hotel lobby, I called my mom. As soon as I heard her voice, I burst into tears.

"I don't know anyone," I told her. "It feels so cold here, so harsh."

"You'll meet people," she reassured me. "Put up some family pictures as soon as you unpack. First thing tomorrow, figure out where your grocery store, your dry cleaner, and your post office are. Start getting to know your neighborhood. And Peter and I will be there soon to visit."

Mostly she listened as I had a good cry. I wondered if I'd made a terrible mistake leaving a town I loved for a job so far away.

The next morning, I felt better. I tackled the boxes. The phone guy showed up. The electricity came on. Still, I came up empty in my search for the neighborhood staples my mom had recommended. Even by day, there was nothing going on downtown other than Wall

Street business. I also took note of how unfriendly everyone seemed. The clerk at the Duane Reade pharmacy didn't make eye contact when she rang me up. I smiled at people on the street. No one smiled back. How did people live like this?

I went into the office at Jones Day one morning to get my bearings. The secretaries sat in pods outside of the attorney offices. Not a single one of them said good morning when I walked by them; some were silent even in response to my hellos. What had I gotten myself into?

I called my mom again that night and again broke down in tears, feeling sorry for myself. I told her about the coldness, my loneliness, my self-doubt. She listened, was supportive, and gave me another few ideas for how to help things a little.

The third day wasn't much better. Some guy in a hurry nearly knocked me down without so much as an "Excuse me." I took the subway to and from work; it smelled like urine and vomit, and there were rats on the tracks. No one seemed to care.

Still very unsure about Manhattan, I called my mom once again and cried. She listened to me: "There are no people at night in my neighborhood! It feels desolate! It smells bad! The secretaries are unfriendly!"

Finally, she said, "Megyn, stop playing the victim. Not attractive."

Man, what a wake-up call.

I felt embarrassed. I, who had a great job, a great family, a nice, safe apartment, and everything going for me, had been wasting time wallowing. True to form, my mom's honesty snapped me out of my pity party and gave me some perspective: *Seriously? You're crying three days in a row because your apartment feels "cold" and you have to take a subway to get groceries and the secretaries didn't smile at you? Grow up.*

This is one of the many things I love about my mom. She's empathetic, but always has a good perspective on what's worth a wallow and what's not. And she's gentle but brave about sharing it.

So I toughened up and stuck it out, and soon my legal career took off. The most significant case I tried while in New York was against our client, a luxury jeweler. A woman who ran their salon was let go by the firm and sued, alleging wrongful termination. We had a December trial date, and went in that November for a conference. The judge in the case did not suffer fools gladly. I had appeared before him many times.

Like most trial judges in the New York State Supreme Court system, he was overworked and understaffed. When he heard that we had a December trial date, the judge made it clear he did not want to hear the case.

My co-counsel pressed the judge hard on how important that date was to our client. The judge said the case sounded boring. I marveled that this was apparently relevant. That's when my co-counsel started to dazzle the judge with the most salacious details of the case.

"Judge," he said, "this case is not boring! This case involves a beautiful blond plaintiff who claims that one of the most respected jewelers in the world wrongfully fired her."

"BORING!"

"Wait! Our defense is that the plaintiff was actually fired for cause—"

"BORING!"

"And that cause was: she was sexually harassing the male employees of the firm. She would show her breasts and rub up against the men. She engaged in X-rated discussions at the office place regularly. She propositioned more than one man in the salon."

The judge started looking more interested. Suddenly he spoke to my fellow lawyer, looking at me: "Is *this* the plaintiff?"

"No, Your Honor. This is my co-counsel."

Cue the look of disappointment on the judge's face.

"But she'll be trying the case with me!" he said. "She'll be in court every day!"

Thinking about it now, I see that this was a bit like being asked to go out with the boss's son. Here I was, having appeared repeatedly before this judge, but still the assumption was that I was not a lawyer. I'm sure it had something to do with my youth and blondness (and, once again, my judge's advanced age), and again, in the moment, it didn't bother me much. We wanted that December trial date. And even though I could have taken offense, I was content to be offered up to this judge like a shiny toy before a distracted baby to get what my client wanted.

We got our December trial, tried it in a week, and won a jury verdict vindicating our client entirely. The joy of that win was unlike any I had ever experienced. It was exhilarating.

Meanwhile, I had begun dating Dan long distance, and it was getting harder and harder to be apart. I initially thought this was going to be a fling. But we really hit it off, and so from the fall of 1997 through August 1999, we tolerated the plane rides between New York and Chicago.

Dan is six feet tall and has brown hair and brown eyes. He's good-looking. Athletic. Fun. He is a nice guy—happy-go-lucky. I don't know if I've ever really seen him in a bad mood. He likes to have a good time. He's smart. He loves sports and medicine—two things in which I have no interest. But this didn't strike me as a problem, because I enjoyed his company so much.

He was also a welcome distraction from the constant drumbeat of work in my life. Yes, the long hours and contentious nature of litigation had followed me to New York. Days would go by when I talked to no one except the people with whom I worked, and corporate litigators, while very dynamic, aren't as a rule the most emotionally in-touch people on the planet.

Workdays were full of fights with opposing counsel. The acrimony was never-ending—it's the nature of the beast. When we won a case, it was electrifying in the moment. The losses, however, were incredibly harsh. I would drag myself back to my apartment at the end of the day, eager to flip on the TV and steal a few hours of sleep. I'd put on *Oprah* and marvel at how others were working to improve their lives. Sometimes in the mornings, I'd put on *Little House on the Prairie* reruns instead of the news. It felt like a comfort from home, an escape. I didn't have time to think or even really feel.

I wasn't yet thinking *I'll do something else for a living,* but it struck me that if I had Dan closer, I might be happier. So my third year in New York, Dan moved to town, and in with me. His medical school allowed him to complete his last year working at New York hospitals, which we figured would be good for both of us. The long-distance courtship had been wearing thin.

Before I knew it, Dan surprised me with a proposal. I could hardly believe how everything was lining up. High-paying legal job at a Big Law firm? Check. Nice apartment? Check. And now a future doctor husband? Check. The lady at the Saks Fifth Avenue counter exclaimed, "A doc-tah and a loy-yah! Does it get any bettah?" I loved Dan, and I loved how he fit so perfectly into this new ideal-on-paper life I was making for myself. If life was a contest, was I ever winning it.

In case you haven't noticed by now, I really like to win.

In the spring, Dan learned that he had been accepted at Northwestern University Hospital in Chicago. It was clear to us both we were heading back to Illinois. I asked Jones Day if they would consider allowing me to work out of their Chicago office, and they graciously agreed. They were always so good to me.

I wasn't sorry to go. New York had never grown on me; it had never felt that warm, nor like I had mastered it. I was looking forward to a fresh start in a familiar city. We left Manhattan in the summer of 2000.

I was in Chicago on September 11, 2001, which happened to be two weeks before my wedding to Dan. I remember sitting on my couch watching the TV and calling Dan, who was already in surgery, and telling him—and thus his entire OR—that the first World Trade Center tower had just fallen. They thought they had heard me wrong.

"It's *gone*," I said again. The second tower fell, and the world changed forever.

Like so much of America that day, I couldn't tear myself away from TV news. I found myself hypnotized in particular by Ashleigh Banfield and Peter Jennings, who were on competing networks. She was on the street for NBC; he was in the anchor chair for ABC, and I felt like they were both talking right to me. I'd always had much respect for journalists, and here was as clear an instance as I'd ever seen of the nation benefiting from their calm professionalism. They had a higher calling in those terrible days, and they fulfilled it with human- ity and grace. Like a lot of people, I felt like I wished I too could do something to help the country through it. For the first moment I could remember since entering law school, I felt regret at not becoming a journalist. It wasn't that I was second-guessing my legal path yet; it was that I was envying someone else's choice, admiring a service whose value was so apparent.

Beyond that, all I could think about was the people in my former apartment building, which was steps away from the WTC. My doormen, my neighbors, the people who worked in the Millenium Hotel, in which I had made that phone call to my mom. The humorless clerk at Duane Reade. The ones who worked in the towers, whom I would see on the subway late at night when I came home from my law practice.

As it turned out, my old apartment building was badly damaged by the attack, and had to be closed for months afterward for repairs. I was told that a large piece of one of the plane's engines had been found on our rooftop. I cannot imagine the hell those in my old neighborhood went through at that time, nor what the fallen experienced as their lives were cut short that Tuesday in September—the day America lost its innocence.

Dan and I went ahead with our wedding, though naturally the nation's agony cast a pall over it. It was a lovely ceremony at a Catholic church in Chicago, followed by a reception at the InterContinental—the very one I had stayed in when Bickel & Brewer first flew me out to the city on a recruiting trip, six years earlier.

We spent our honeymoon in Bora Bora, which is a spectacular place, or so I hear—it rained the entire eleven days we were there. I kept abreast of the news back home, which was full of stories too awful to really take in; on top of that, an anthrax scare was terrifying the nation.

Although the wedding and honeymoon were off to a somewhat somber start, when Dan and I returned to Chicago, a rich life awaited us, full of challenging careers and a terrific social whirl. Finally, I thought, everything was clicking into place. Now that I was married and back in a town I loved, surely I would be more fulfilled.

We made many friends through Dan's anesthesia residency program at Northwestern. The hard work kept all of the young doctors busy, but also ready to seize upon whatever fun was available. We spent the weekends out with friends at the Chicago restaurants or attending Chicago's many street fairs or parties. We loved to go with our friends to one bar in particular, the Hangge-Uppe, where we would dance to 1980s music until the wee hours and cheer for the Elvis impersonator who would sometimes appear. If we had any concerns about marriage or our careers, we drank and danced and laughed them away.

We spent most of our time in a group setting, so Dan and I didn't get a lot of one-on-one time, especially because we both worked so much. Of course that was a problem, but we couldn't see it at the time. We were so focused on our careers. He would go on to become chief resident and was well respected at Northwestern. I was trying and preparing cases and learning a ton.

Dan and I had each other's back, and we figured that meant giving each other freedom to work crazy hours in the pursuit of our dreams.

We didn't think it was unusual to go days, weeks on end, without spending any real time together. All of our friends were busy too. They were mostly lawyers or young doctors, so in a sense, we were all in it together. There was a coming of age and coming into our own professionally, and living on the promise of what might be.

This was actually a very happy time for me. I met two of my best friends—Rebecca and Andrea, with whom I am still very close. The three of us still take a girls' trip every year, usually to one of our hometowns—Chicago, Detroit, or New York.

My girlfriends and I formed a wine club. I lived on the second floor of a three-story brownstone, and there was a tiny back patio in the rear. My friends would come over on the weekends, and we would sit with lit candles all around us, playing music (plenty of the Smiths), telling stories about our work and our relationships.

It wasn't until my third year into this stint that my work life again morphed into an exercise in survival. I never said no to work. I considered it a badge of honor to be asked to be on the best cases. And the firm rewarded me with plum assignments and tons of responsibility, not to mention big bonuses and raises. I was succeeding by any professional measure. And I was not the only one—there were plenty of lawyers going full throttle. I remember saying to one female partner whom I really liked, "Did you see that article in the *Tribune* this morning?"

"Oh, you misunderstand me," she said. "You see, whenever I'm not at the office, I'm intoxicated." She was only half joking.

I loved the praise that came with doing well. It's hard to get hired at a firm like Jones Day, at least for someone like me, let alone to be recognized as one of the best. I had made it. I was competing—successfully—against the Ivy grads. Me, a girl from Albany.

I enjoyed my colleagues and had many fun times. But it's fun swimming in the ocean, too, until suddenly you realize you might be about to drown. It's still beautiful, and the water's as blue and warm as ever, but it's up above your lips and climbing, and you quickly find yourself desperate to get back to shore.

What had started as a step up in intensity and opportunity at work had transformed yet again into nonstop hours, acrimony, and the elimination of the social life I had come to love. Those wine club get-togethers went away, and soon Dan and I barely saw each other at all.

I talked to some of my colleagues about switching careers. "You're thinking of leaving law?" my friends at work would ask. "Are you *insane*?" One brilliant appeals lawyer pulled me aside, saying, "The law is your highest and best calling; you'll never be as good at anything as you are at this." Your ego gets tied to being a lawyer. Mine was. I thought it was the only way for me to be taken seriously, especially by powerful men. The people I dealt with all day—judges, my bosses, clients—were almost all men.

My legal training gave me several skills, but knowing how to handle men in positions of authority was easily one of the most valuable. I would call on it many, many times. I endeared myself to them by working incessantly and by figuring out what made each of them tick. This one partner used me a lot on his cases because I worked hard and I knew how to get to the point. Once, a junior associate saw him in my office. She ran in, trying to regale him with her totally irrelevant knowledge on a case. Sensing his frustration, I found an excuse to send her off. He looked at me and deadpanned, "Don't ever let her speak to me again."

I became good at reading powerful people and managing their egos. The most challenging thing was dealing with opposing counsel. At that level of practice, these are killers, formidable adversaries, and they want to embarrass you. Every day is fraught with peril. When I started out in law, I felt insecure and was easily angered by these guys. I'd play right into stereotypes about "hysterical" women. I would get spitting mad at a deposition. I regret that now, looking back on it.

But I learned. A few years in, I had turned the tables. I might say something passive-aggressive just to get opposing counsel mad, and then when he got worked up about it, I would say calmly, "You seem upset. Do you need a break? We can take a moment if you'd like to step outside and get yourself together." I became an expert in making them lose their cool.

For years I did that. And then it lost its luster.

8

Calling and Calling; Nobody's Home

In 2002 the chickens came home to roost. I was driving home on Chicago's Kennedy Expressway in the darkness, tears streaming down my face. *If I could only break a bone,* I thought. *Nothing too catastrophic, but something significant. A femur? No one could argue with time off for a broken femur. They'd have to let me rest then.*

I had been working around the clock—eighteen-hour days for weeks on end. In one way, it was paying off: seven years into my career, I'd become one of my law firm's top billing associates. The cost, though, was brutal. For months, I hadn't seen anyone except co-workers. I had blown off friends' weddings. I cried a lot. I was sleepless, and sad, and lonely.

Gone were the days of law school when I'd been

devoted to my studies because I loved learning. Now I was just cranking out work like a machine. And I'd come to realize that the joy of winning did not come close to justifying the pain of losing or the long, long hours of legal paperwork and intense strife that characterized the practice of law on a day-in, day-out basis.

One case in particular, representing Bridgestone Firestone, had been consuming every waking hour of my life. It became the straw that broke the camel's back. I was flying all over the country, from Wisconsin, to Texas, to California and beyond. One particularly rough flight to Greenville, South Carolina, is seared in my memory as a metaphor for how I felt during that time: helpless, trapped, and terrified.

Another lawyer on the case and I boarded a plane at O'Hare Airport in Chicago in the middle of a significant thunderstorm. It wasn't terrible yet on the ground, but you could see the dark skies in the distance, and the rain was pounding. I remember wondering if it was safe to fly. The pilot came on the overhead shortly after takeoff and said, "We're coming up on an area of bad turbulence. Don't worry, folks, we would never fly in that. We're going to take the long way around, but it won't add too much time to our trip."

Flash forward about ten minutes, when the we-would-never-fly-in-that clouds were upon us and the plane was getting tossed around like a toy in a tornado. Suddenly the flight attendant was thrown to the floor, and began crawling up the aisle to the front of the plane.

People were screaming. I was one of them.

The plane kept dropping as if in free fall. We could see lightning out the windows. We had no idea if we were going to live or die. Some people were crying. I was holding on for dear life to the eighty-year-old woman next to me. All of a sudden, from the seat behind me, I felt a hand grabbing my arm. It belonged to the other lawyer, whom I barely knew. He was scared out of his mind and thought he was about to die. I reached one arm back in between the seats to hold him. We kept silent, and prayed. We all have these brushes with death, these moments that remind us of our tenuous connections to life. But I think for those of us who lost someone young, there is something particularly sharp about those reminders: no, *really*, you could die at any second.

After what felt like an eternity, things settled down. No one on the plane spoke. Finally, the pilot came on the PA. (Why must they maintain total silence in these situations? Just one calm word from the cockpit would help so much. I suppose it's because they are busy trying to keep us alive.) "No extra charge for the fun ride," the pilot said. "We're out of trouble, should be a relatively smooth ride from here."

The flight attendant, who was now vertical, said, "Anybody need anything?"

A loud voice boomed back: "*Where is the alcohol?*"

It may or may not have been me.

As is often the case, it's the rare near-death experience that actually forces you to reevaluate your life. Those things are traumatic, but they are so packed with adrenaline that it's more cinematic than life-changing. Rather, my awakening came from something far more, for lack of a better word, *innocuous* (hi, Jim): a trip home to see my mom.

I had been working myself into a frenzy, billing more than 3,000 hours a year. The better you are as a lawyer, the more work gets loaded on you as a "reward." As they say, working in law is like a pie-eating contest in which the prize is more pie. Which is about when I realized: just because you're good at something doesn't mean it makes you happy.

It sounds so obvious now, but for most of my adult life I'd been chasing success with such single-minded determination that I hadn't thought much about my long-term goals, only about acing each new challenge as it came. I'd come of age believing so strongly in the value of hard work, and it had paid off for me many times already. Only now was I starting to see that I had taken it too far. There was nothing wrong with working hard—but without a plan it was more like running in a hamster wheel than running toward some place I wanted to be.

"Mom, why don't you meet me at the racetrack in Saratoga?" I suggested before boarding my plane home. "I'll call you when I land and tell you where I am."

When I arrived in Saratoga, I went to a restaurant and called Mom. She didn't answer her phone, so I left a message.

"I'm here," I said. "I'll wait for you at the restaurant."

I waited and waited, and still she didn't show up. I called again and left another message. An hour passed. On the third call, Mom finally answered her phone.

"Mom, where have you been?" I said. "I've left you two messages!"

"You didn't leave me any messages," she said. "I've been right here, waiting to hear from you."

It took a minute, but then I figured out what had happened. I'd called *my own* answering machine in Chicago. On my voice mail were the messages I had meant to leave for my mother. That meant I had listened to my own voice—"You've reached Megyn and Dan. Leave a message, and we'll call you back"—then left messages for my mother. Twice.

It was a little bit like coming to consciousness covered in blood, standing over a dead body, so startled was I by how checked-out I'd become. Clearly, I was operating in a kind of fugue state. My body was out there, moving around in the world, but without much of a connection to my brain. I was dissociated from my own life. It was in that moment that I knew, with total certainty, that things had to change. I had to improve my life. Sitting in that restaurant near the racetrack, I had to admit to myself: I wanted to leave the practice of law, just as that man in the taxi had predicted. I hated the anger. Hated the hours. Hated what I'd become.

Yes, I was making money. I had friends at the office. But I had to sacrifice everything else: family time, time with Dan, reading books, seeing friends, travel, giving back. I felt like I'd lost so much time. These should have been wonderful years, but they weren't. I knew I had so much more to offer: I enjoyed talking with other people, hearing and telling stories, solving problems, traveling. I wanted to do something creative. Not just argue, dodge, provoke, and compete. The verdict was in: the money and prestige were not worth the sacrifices.

That night, back at my mother's, I sat on her couch and wrote in my journal:

I am more exciting than this! I am more interesting than this! I am more interested than this! I need more out of life!

Then I wrote down one of the most important commitments I've ever made to myself:

I will be out of the law by this time next year.

I knew this time that I didn't need to move to another firm, or to another city. I needed to move to another profession. That is a watershed moment for any professional person. I'd spent seven years pursuing an education that would let me do this job. And more than seven actually doing it. I knew I was going to make partner at Jones Day at the youngest age possible. That meant a lot to me. It was a feather in my cap. But I knew I couldn't stay just to get that feather. For one thing, it would be taking the opportunity away from someone else. For another, I knew that if I took it, I'd have to stay at least a couple of years. I simply didn't have that kind of time left in me at that job.

Everything in my life looked great on paper. I was a lawyer. My husband was a doctor. He was kind and supportive. I might not see much of him, but I knew he cared for me. We had great friends. It was more than anyone had ever hoped for me. How could I not be happy? How could I not feel whole? But I wasn't. And I didn't. I felt miserable. And I thought to myself: "Hurry up, you're dying."

Around this time, I found myself mesmerized by midnight reruns of *Oprah*. Eating microwaved Lean Cuisines after yet another endless day of brutal litigation, I would watch her talk about living our best lives. It was almost as if her words were coming to me from another planet, so little did my frantic, empty life resemble the considered one she described. She spoke about how we are all one decision away from changing our lives.

Then, one night, her guest, Dr. Phil, said something that made me drop my fork: "The only difference between you and someone you envy is, you settled for less."

It was as if he were describing my exact situation. It looked from the outside like I had everything anyone wanted, but I knew in my heart that I was settling for less—less than I had to offer, less than I deserved. I wanted love and freedom and creativity and adventure.

I wanted friendship, time to think and feel, a sense that I was making a difference in the world, food that did not come out of a frozen box.

It was so simple, but so clear to me—this was the moment when I realized I could change my life. I did not have to settle for less. I could settle for *more*.

It took many years for me to see my father's death as anything but a burden. But in that moment sitting on my couch in Chicago, I realized that his death had given me a gift: the clear awareness that I couldn't afford to waste a second. The value of hard work, that other tentpole of my existence, had stood me in good stead up until that point, but it had taken me as far as I could go without a new value: *meaning*.

None of us knows how long we have on this earth. And while hard work is meaningful, we can't waste our time here constantly at the office, much less immersed in strife and conflict. I had to change horses. I heard my father's voice, singing: "Today while the flowers still cling to the vine . . ."

We only get one life. The lights twinkle on the tree, and then . . . it's over.

I can't be contented with yesterday's glory.
I can't live on promises, winter to spring.

Today is my moment. Now is my story.
I'll laugh, and I'll cry, and I'll sing.

I knew suddenly, and with no doubt, that it wasn't my fate to be so unconnected to my fellow human beings. Or to spend my life taking faulty-tire depositions. I was meant for something else. Something more. Now, I just had to figure out what.

9

"Who's Here?" "Me!"

The problem with an epiphany is that, no matter how big it is, you can't necessarily change your life as soon as you have one.

Six months had passed since I'd resolved to leave the law, and here I sat, February in Chicago, frozen in every sense of the word. I knew I wanted out, but I still had to find an escape route. I had to go to the firm day after day, even though my heart was somewhere else.

After some time and consideration, I decided to become a journalist. In making the choice, I thought about the envy I had often felt seeing reporters pursuing careers that seemed exciting and full of purpose. That envy, it turned out, was a gift to me—direction from my conscience on how I could become more fulfilled. I wanted to give it a try. Now that I had nine years of legal practice under my belt, I felt like I had some skills that would transfer. There was only one problem: my only real experience in the field was that two-day internship when I was a teenager. I also wondered if at the ripe old age of thirty-two, I was too old to enter a new profession, especially one with an on-camera component. I started to look for lines on my face.

Dan and I talked about my options. His take was that I should be happy, and broadcast journalism sounded perfect for me. He was a little concerned about the financial hit we'd take (I was making a healthy paycheck by this point, and I'd been mostly supporting the two of us thus far), but he knew that eventually he'd be making money, and that I was a smart bet. He used to say I was the stocks, and he was the bonds. I felt supported in my quest for change.

Still, I couldn't figure out my next move. I tried cold-calling a couple of agents, but none would take unsolicited clients. I called an agent named Kenny Lindner in LA, whose book *Broadcasting Realities* I had just read. The receptionist hung up on me.

Meanwhile, I was trying to improve my life with small pleasures, the greatest of which was a weekly guitar class. At first it was just a stress reliever. Then it became something more.

There were about eight of us, and we met every

Sunday. We'd laugh at our missteps and share tips for nailing the elusive F chord. Sitting around in a circle playing music and singing together is a wonderful way to bond with fellow human beings. It made me aware of how much I craved connection and creativity in the rest of my life.

One day some of us were sitting around talking after class.

"Why weren't you here last week?" I asked my favorite classmate, Meredith.

"I was working," Meredith said. "I'm a freelance journalist. I had to cover the space shuttle *Columbia* disaster."

"Meredith!" I practically shouted at her. "You're in *news*?"

It was like a miracle, a sign from God—or maybe from my dad, whose guitar playing ultimately landed me in that class. Here was this woman I saw every Sunday, and she was the one I liked most in the class. We had never talked about our jobs before—on Sundays it was all about the music.

"I'd love to buy you a cup of coffee," I told her.

"That sounds like someone with a career change on her mind," Meredith wisely surmised.

I told her I was a lawyer, and that indeed I was restless.

Saint that Meredith was, she said yes to my request for a coffee date. And that cup of coffee changed my future. Meredith told me how local news worked— how they hired and assigned, and what kind of training I would need to get my foot in the door.

It was fascinating! I had never heard such things! No résumé needed? Just a tape? What is this magical thing, and how does one get one? Should I get a master's in broadcast journalism and *then* apply for a job somewhere?

"Journalism is more of a trade than a profession," Meredith explained. "Reporters learn by doing, not by reading."

Check, skip the master's. Then she went further: she told me she would help me make that tape. This was huge. *Huge.* How else could I possibly have made one? This was far beyond my wildest expectations. She was like an angel.

Meredith was working freelance at WMAQ-TV, the NBC affiliate in Chicago, and said she'd introduce me to a star cameraman there, Bond Lee. She couldn't promise that he'd shoot my tape, but at least he'd meet with me. It was all happening so fast.

One night she told me some WMAQ folks were going out for drinks. I ducked out of Jones Day early that evening and joined them. Even though I was just meeting people at a bar, I prepared as if I were arguing before the US Supreme Court. I learned everything I could about the station and read all the newspapers cover to cover. What was in the news? What might come up? I needed to be in the know.

When Bond introduced himself to me, I felt as though I'd been hit with a spotlight. This was my close-up. And I was ready.

"So you want to be on TV." He sounded skeptical.

"I think I'd be good at it."

"So does everyone."

"But I really will," I told him.

"Tell me a story in sixty seconds or less."

I thought he'd never ask. I banged out a minute on the preppie murderer Robert Chambers, who was about to be paroled several years after murdering a young woman in Central Park. I did not stumble, the storytelling was there, and I nailed the sixty-second mark. Everyone in the group silently turned to look at Bond.

"You're gonna be on TV," he said, smiling.

Bam, we were off.

He agreed to help me shoot an audition tape. And so for the next few weeks, whenever we could find time, we would go around town shooting footage of me pretending to report live from various scenes. We would set up on a bridge over the Chicago River, and I would talk into a microphone about some story of the day while he shot the tape and gave me pointers.

Meredith also hooked me up with some of the station's reporters, who would let me tag along while they were on assignment. I'd sneak in front of the camera when they were setting up a live shot to give it a whirl before the real reporter took the mic.

It was harder than it looked. In ninety seconds' time I would have to catch the viewer's attention, deliver the information, and come to a conclusion, all without saying "um" too many times and without ever starting over. It required supreme concentration. Looking into a blank camera and trying to speak as though you can see the person listening is absolutely a skill. The pros make it look simple; trust me, it isn't. I had so much to learn, but I was also feeling something I hadn't in years—a sense that I was learning fast and couldn't get enough.

Bond introduced me to a professor at Columbia College Chicago, Roger Schatz, who let me audit his broadcasting class. I was about a decade older than all the other students, who typically sat with their combat boots hiked on the desks, laid-back and half-asleep. I'm sure I drove them crazy with my enthusiasm: "Isn't learning fun? What an opportunity we have here!"

We would go down to the frigid South Michigan Avenue sidewalk at night, look into Schatz's TV camera, and pretend we were delivering real reports— sixty seconds or less. I remember standing out there, freezing from head to toe, holding the stick mic and thinking, *Please, God, don't let anyone from Jones Day walk by right now.*

Every week Schatz gave out what he called the Fendrick Award, in honor of a woman named Fendrick who once became so freaked out doing a sidewalk report that she hailed a taxi and took off. It was given to the student with the best report that night. The award was a baking soda box with a picture of a taxi pasted on the front of it. I coveted mine, and keep them to this day. (On rough days, I admit I look at them and think, *Was that fleeing woman onto something?*)

Thanks to Meredith and Bond, my tape had come together okay. I was convinced it was my ticket to my new life. Then, a curveball: Dan got an offer to begin a pain-management fellowship at Johns Hopkins. For him to take it, we had to move to Baltimore.

I was spending my days working full-time at Jones Day Chicago, and my nights and weekends learning TV journalism and loving it. Between learning from Meredith and Bond and Schatz, some positive momentum was starting to build. The WMAQ reporters were letting me shadow them. It felt like an unofficial internship. How could I find that in another state? Unfortunately, my choices were limited. There was no way Dan was turning down Johns Hopkins, and there was no way we were living long distance again. Jones Day agreed to transfer me to their Washington, DC, office. That light at the end of the law firm tunnel grew dimmer overnight.

Baltimore was challenging. Our place was severely rodent-infested. We killed twenty-one mice in one year. And it was in a rough neighborhood (they shot scenes from HBO's *The Wire* outside our front door). We were new to the town. We knew no one and had no family nearby. I felt removed from the life I wanted, the one I had been building in Chicago.

I looked at the help wanted ads, and every job required at least three years' experience in news. I felt certain I was never going to get hired as a reporter in the Baltimore or Washington, DC, market—they were too competitive. I needed Peoria. I was trying to settle for more, but without a clear path, I felt pessimistic. My new TV dreams felt like they had been dashed.

My friends Andrea and Rebecca from Chicago encouraged me. So did my friend Marla. "If anyone can do it, it's you!" Andrea said. "I know you'll be great, keep at it," Rebecca told me. My mom said the same but wanted me to hedge my bets, saying, "Don't leave Jones Day until you know you can support yourself."

Then one day, home sick from work, I turned on Lifetime TV, which happened to be airing the 1995 documentary *Intimate Portrait: Jessica Savitch*, about a contemporary of Sam Donaldson and Peter Jennings who became one of the first women to anchor a network's evening newscast. Jessica looked a little like me, had grown up middle class, and had reached the top of the TV news business through sheer will and determination. Her father had died when she was young, changing her forever. She had a shell of confidence, with fear underneath.

"I often wish I was perfect," she'd written in her diary. (There were pictures of her personal effects, and some of her diaries were read in a voice-over.) She had a great voice, a compelling on-air delivery, and had made it in what was then almost entirely a man's industry.

I was hypnotized. If she could do it, so could I. Even better, she didn't get her first network job until she was thirty. I felt a bizarrely profound connection to her—like she was somehow messaging me, present-day. As if she knew I was watching that show, and wanted me to do something as a result. I found her story inspiring, except for her tragic end: she had an embarrassing drug-induced on-air meltdown, and later that year died along with her dog and boyfriend in a horrific car accident. But I saw how she had made her own success, and I was more determined than ever to do the same for myself—though, I hoped, with a happier ending.

Armed with my audition tape, I started cold-calling news directors from my Baltimore rodent motel. After a steady stream of rejection, I finally got someone on the phone: Bill Lord, who ran the small local cable station NewsChannel 8 in Washington, DC. I called him, thinking NewsChannel 8 might be an option, and discovered the man ran the damned ABC affiliate, WJLA-TV, too—what luck! The number eight market. I got him to let me drop off my résumé tape in person, a meeting I knew I could parlay into a chance. And that was all I needed. I went out and bought a killer Dolce & Gabbana dress for the occasion.

"Only you would spend a thousand dollars to interview for a job that pays seventeen thousand a year," said Dan, with a laugh.

"It's an investment," I said.

And it was. I went in there, and the interview went great. There simply was no way I was walking out without a job. As Bill would later put it: "She walked in and threatened to put a stiletto in my eye unless I put her on TV." Perhaps it wasn't that direct, but I did think to myself, *I argue for a living. If I can't argue my way into this job, I'm not very good at what I do.*

Sure enough, Bill offered me a part-time position: one day a week at $176 per day. I was over the moon. (I had offered to work for free.) We joked that I was moving from one ill-respected profession to another. I told Bill my next target was used-car sales.

This was starting to happen. At first I worked for Bill just one day a week, and at my law job all the other days. Then Bill offered me another shift, and another after that. Eventually I asked Jones Day if I could switch to part-time.

My fellow lawyers were baffled. The head of litigation told me that I would absolutely make partner barring what he called "this TV thing." He even went so far as to say that if I decided after six months of doing both that I wanted to return to my full-time law practice, he would put me up for partner that year. It was a generous offer, and a good safety net, but I was already gone. I knew I had found my real calling.

I was ecstatic about my budding broadcasting career, and threw myself into it with everything I had. At the station, Bill assigned a staff reporter to show me the ropes. She didn't seem too keen on the mentoring job.

"I had a talk with Bill today about your hair," she told me. "He wants you to cut it off. All of it."

I loved my long blond hair but had vowed to do whatever it took. I got my hair cut in a short bob.

Bill was not pleased. When he figured out what had happened, he called in my "mentor" and chewed her out. I felt betrayed, but not all that surprised. This woman was another Jane: someone I thought of as a friend who was actually working to undermine me.

Fortunately, for every Jane there is a Meredith, who went out of her way to give me a new lease on life when there was no reason for her to do so except generosity and kindness. In my own dealings with other women, I try to be a Meredith. In fact, when I said good-bye to Bond Lee before moving to Baltimore, I asked him how I could ever repay him. His parting words were, "Pay it forward." I've done so many times, and when I do, I think of him and Meredith.

Bill Lord kept finding me work—first on News-Channel 8 mostly, but soon enough on the flagship property, WJLA. My first live report was from Reagan National Airport. At the end, I heard in my earpiece, "Great job." I remember thinking, *Really?* (The truth was, no, not really.) Bill told me I was coming along, that I just needed to relax more.

"What you have, I can't teach," he said. "What you need to learn, I can help you with."

One time in the field, the producer said to me, "Okay, we need an intro and a tag—your standard doughnut in one-twenty. Got it?"

"Yes! Got it!" I responded, wondering what the hell a doughnut was. Thank goodness for the cameramen, who taught me a lot.

Another time my photographer and I were exiting a subway station after wrapping a story when a bunch of cops ran toward the trains, guns drawn.

"We gotta get out of here!" I said.

"We get paid to go *in* there!" he said, pointing toward the danger. And off we went to chase the cops. It was a lightbulb moment for me as a young reporter.

I was excited to feel my TV career coming alive. It was as if it had been waiting for me all these years, lying dormant, and now I'd found it. I was energized getting out of bed each morning. Here, again, was that familiar feeling—the same confidence I'd felt doing moot court in law school: *I got this.* That sense of pride and delight, drained from years of overwork, started to seep back into my life, and I could not get enough of it.

As well as things were going for me professionally, my new undertaking only exacerbated an already difficult schedule for me and Dan. Dan was now the chief fellow at Johns Hopkins, which required—again—a lot of hours at the hospital. Between Jones Day and WJLA, I was commuting from Baltimore into DC just about every day of the week, which meant nearly three hours in the car a day. Two years into marriage, and Dan and I barely saw each other. We were focused on our careers, not on each other—a situation we had both accepted for years.

Still, we held out hope that the end of Dan's residency would bring about a change. In the summer of 2003, Dan finished his fellowship at Hopkins and took his first real job in Northern Virginia as a pain management doctor, and we moved to a small town house in Alexandria. Dan was now working as an attending physician, in a great but demanding specialty. This was what we dreamed of, but it felt much different once the dream came true—the beginning of yet another endeavor in which he had to prove himself (and would), just as I had done a year earlier. We made too little time for each other, and we were too busy to see it for the problem that it was.

Adding to the challenge was the fact that I was in the process of making another switch of my own—one with potentially life-changing consequences. In March 2004, Bill Lord invited me to the Radio and Television

Correspondents' Association Dinner—and a seat at the WJLA table. I had seen this party memorialized in the movie *Broadcast News*, which I'd watched a hundred times. In it, William Hurt's anchorman character approaches his neurotic executive producer, played by Holly Hunter.

"It's incredible who's here," he tells her.

"Who?" she asks.

"Me!" he responds.

I've had that feeling dozens of times since starting in TV, but that night at the Washington Hilton was memorably the first.

I wore a hot pink dress, because I realized no one would know me, and I wanted to stand out. At the bar, I made my way over to a couple of journalists and started making small talk. One of the guys there was Bill Sammon, then a Fox News contributor. We got to talking, and he encouraged me to send my résumé tape to Kim Hume at Fox. At this point I was eight months into part-time reporting, and wasn't at all sure I was ready for a national position. I didn't want to shoot and miss. But I kept Sammon's card.

And then a critical thing happened: a couple of months later, just as Dan and I were moving to Alexandria, Bill Lord made me a full-time job offer at WJLA. It was just the boost of confidence I needed.

A real TV job. It was official: I was going to do this for a living. But rather than simply say yes, I decided to roll the dice. I figured, if I was good enough to be full-time there, maybe I was good enough to be full-time someplace even bigger. I contacted Sammon for Kim Hume's address, sent her my tape, and hoped she would call.

Within twenty-four hours, she did.

10

Lawyer, Broadcaster, Journalist

Meeting Brit and Kim Hume, who were then the managing editor and bureau chief of Fox's Washington Bureau, made me feel like Little Orphan Annie seeing the mansion for the first time. I was determined to work for them. They were gracious and fun but also tough and smart. We hit it off so well that I wasn't surprised the next day when they invited me to meet with the company's then executive VP of news, Kevin Magee, and then with Roger Ailes, the Fox News chairman and CEO in New York—and the person repeatedly recognized as the most powerful man in news.

Magee told me in the interview, "So, you want to be at Fox. Everyone wants to be at Fox now that we're number one."

Holy cow, I thought. *Fox is number one? I hope I get this job!* I hadn't even considered checking the ratings in my overpreparation; I was focused entirely on the news.

He had no idea I wasn't a die-hard Fox watcher, nor did I want him to know. I watched the news, of course. And I had always liked Fox News. In particular, I loved how all of these beautiful female anchors and reporters seemed so strong and smart. I remember admiring Laurie Dhue and her air of authority. Also Catherine Herridge, who seemed to have Audrey Hepburn's face and Margaret Thatcher's brain. I also watched CNN and MSNBC and the networks, but I had not applied anywhere else but Fox at that point. If Fox had said no, I certainly would have.

Soon after my exchange with Magee, I went into Roger's office. Here he was—the legendary Roger Ailes. Heralded throughout the industry as a television genius, Ailes had made people like Bill O'Reilly and Sean Hannity household names. He was well known as a developer of talent. He was also well known as a fighter.

The previous year, after then–Fox News anchor Paula Zahn received an offer from CNN, Roger fired her, sued her, and publicly ridiculed her (saying "a dead raccoon" could have outrated her). The Associated

Press ran a story about the bare-knuckled campaign against Zahn, concluding, "The underlying message seems clear: It's not wise to cross Roger Ailes." *Got it*, I thought to myself. *Not planning to do that.*

Roger and I hit it off immediately. We talked about the news. He asked me if I understood the company's mission statement and what fair and balanced news meant. He asked me how the daughter of a nurse and a college professor understood anything other than left-wing dogma.

I told him the truth: I was raised in a Democrat household but was apolitical. I had been for my entire life. We just were not a political family, ever. As I wrote in my journal in 1988: "Am I a Republican or a Democrat? I seriously don't know."

I also said to Roger that nine years of practicing law had exposed me to other views and taught me how to argue and understand both sides. Contrary to popular belief, he wasn't looking for a Republican reporter—he just wanted someone who was open-minded.

He and I got on the topic of life around New York City, and I told him I enjoyed New York and had actually visited Hogs & Heifers—a famous dive bar on which the movie *Coyote Ugly* would later be based—that weekend. He asked me what I ordered. I told him

Pabst Blue Ribbon in a can. (They yell at you there if you order anything too fancy.) We laughed and challenged each other. I tried not to take myself too seriously. When I walked out, I knew I was getting that job.

Still, Ailes had left himself some wiggle room. While the Humes were pushing hard for him to hire me, Ailes's final message before I left was that he needed to check the budget to see if they could afford a new reporter. I felt certain this was just a formality. I was getting this job.

Then Magee called.

"We're passing," he said. "It's a no."

What?

"Yeah, I have to meet with Roger, but it's a no."

I hung up the phone in disbelief. My exchange with Magee had been fine, but the interview with Ailes had felt like a home run.

Stunned, I got in a taxi to the airport. I was on my way to Spain for a two-week vacation. The whole cab ride, all I could think was: *How could they be saying no? This is not possible. What did I do wrong?* And then the disappointment set in: How close I'd been to national TV! To being on the number-one channel! To working for a boss with whom I'd obviously hit it off! What could I do?

I was at the airport in DC when my phone rang again. It was Magee.

"Well," he said, "Roger definitely wants you." And that was the beginning of everything.

A word on my first contract negotiation: I hired an agent to conduct it for me. Now that I had an offer, it was no problem finding an agent. I told him the number at which I wanted to begin. It wasn't a big number— after all, I had only been a journalist for less than a year. But it was respectable for someone with nine years of legal experience under her belt. The job wasn't about the money for me, but I knew what I was worth.

The agent told me I'd never get it. "Just ask," I said.

"A million girls would kill for this job," he said dismissively. "Just take what they're offering."

Well. As you might imagine, that pissed me off. I wasn't a girl, first of all. And I wasn't like a million others. This wasn't some casting-couch moment where the ingénue is given a chance she has no business getting. I'd been a high-powered lawyer for a decade, on my feet arguing in front of juries and some of the best and brightest and sharpest judges in the country. I'd also spent ten years working harder than just about anyone else they could possibly be considering—an ethic I would clearly bring with me.

"Demand more," I told him.

"You're going to lose this offer," he said.

"Do it," I said. "If I lose it, I lose it."

Sure enough, Fox paid the number I requested.

It's not a bad lesson for young people starting out: trust your instincts. Sometimes even those who are supposed to be looking out for you can underestimate your value. Often you are your own best advocate. I wound up firing that agent right after I started. I hired Kenny Lindner, who was my agent for years (and remains a friend), and for a better-than-usual split, given that his office had hung up on me a couple of years earlier. Kenny and I had a laugh about that.

I have negotiated every contract of mine at Fox ever since.

Once I left the law, I never worried about money again. It wasn't because I had a ton of it. At the beginning of my TV career, I certainly did not. It was just that I had learned—the hard way—to value other things above money, things like time to myself. That's not to say I would ever agree to be paid less than I know I am worth. I'm not stupid. But I saw for myself that being a moneymaking machine is pointless. It pays the bills but leaves no time for deposits into the You Fund, which doesn't need money when it's depleted.

With the offer from Fox, the day had finally come when I had to walk into my boss's office at Jones Day and quit. I felt a sense of relief. I was officially off the path I now knew was not for me, and onto something exhilarating. There was a lot less certainty in news. I'd gone from being on the brink of making partner at a great firm to something far less clear, but I knew it was the right choice.

Even so, when I told my law boss I was leaving, it was hard. It felt like saying good-bye to family and, in a way, to my former self. They had been such supporters of mine, up until the last minute. What other law firm would let its associate become a part-time journalist while still lawyering? I was grateful beyond measure. I was also a bit choked up at the official end of my career as an attorney. I got the words out, and my boss was sad, but understanding.

I'd say the biggest reaction I got from my lawyer friends was deep disappointment, coupled with disbelief that I would leave the law for TV.

"You're leaving the practice of law?" they'd repeat back to me, baffled. "You've worked so hard to make it this far. You're about to make partner!"

"But I get to be on TV!" I would exclaim.

There were a few people who seemed genuinely happy for me and even, in one case, predicted great things. Willis Goldsmith, a partner with whom I'd tried a case, said, "You'll have your own show before you know it. You're a star. I've seen it. Now everyone else will." To this day we've stayed in touch, and he'll e-mail me sometimes, saying, **Remember what I told you?** I do indeed.

I started at Fox News in August 2004. I was hired as a general assignment reporter, which in the DC bureau meant covering mostly politics, but given my legal background, they also assigned me the US Supreme Court. I used to love sitting in the High Court in the media box, watching the attorneys make their cases. A part of me felt a pang of nostalgia, but then I'd remember how much work goes into an argument like that, and I'd be happy I was in a different arena now—still a player, but on another field.

The job brought with it a steep learning curve. I worked hard and got the hang of things fast, but I humbled myself plenty in the process.

I also quickly realized that TV people may be even more colorful than lawyers. On my first day of work in the DC bureau, then deputy bureau chief Bruce Becker showed me around and walked me to the office I would be sharing with Major Garrett, then our Capitol Hill correspondent. Major was on vacation that day. When I first entered the small space we would share for nearly three years, I saw pictures of his kids all over the walls, and a huge stack of *Maxim* magazines with saucy cover girls that had spilled over, covering the entryway to the office. I laughed. Bruce looked embarrassed. He didn't know at the time that I wasn't someone who would find that kind of thing offensive, so he was probably hedging his bets.

Two weeks later, I finally met Major. He was a tall, gregarious, warm guy—quick to laugh and a fantastic storyteller. He has a delicious vocabulary. I used to keep a list of Majorisms. You'd be sitting in the office watching some press conference or roundtable discussion, and you'd hear Major bust out: "Rapacious plutocrats!"

I'd politely laugh and then quietly Google "rapacious plutocrats."

He was finishing up his book *The Enduring Revolution*, about the Republicans' 1994 Contract with America. He used to mess with the summer interns by asking, "How many of my books have you read?" And then he would tell them they should get them at the low, low price of one penny on Amazon.

Major was my sounding board on everything. He knew all there was to know about Washington. He had covered Capitol Hill for *U.S. News & World Report* before starting as a broadcaster. He had no ideological agenda. He'd written for the left-wing *Mother Jones* magazine, and worked at CNN before Fox News. He was the perfect professional roommate for me, and taught me a ton, like how necessary it can be to drink a shot of bourbon at the end of a hard workday.

"It'll put hair on your chest," he told me.

"Think of a different lure," I responded.

My first day of being assigned to a story, I walked into the morning meeting for *Special Report*, a show originally launched and hosted by Brit Hume. Brit introduced me to the group by saying "Everyone, welcome Megyn Kendall: lawyer, broadcaster, journalist."

I loved the sound of that. From day one, Brit and Kim were actively involved in my development. They were kind, but honest. If I screwed up, Brit would tell me. If I did well, he'd tell me that too. In those early days on the air, I was very green, and very stiff. The truth is, I wasn't very good. But I had confidence I *would be* good. TV is like typing: you can't get better without practicing. (I know this because, as you may recall, my mom made me take typing twice.)

This was an advantage of starting in cable: you're on TV all the time. Unlike on a network, where you may have an appearance on the morning show or the evening news, we are 24/7. The first significant story they put me on was the journalistic failure of CBS in reporting a story about George W. Bush's service in the National Guard just before the 2004 election. The program *60 Minutes II* was being humiliated for failing to follow fundamental journalistic standards. Four producers wound up fired as a result of that debacle, and it was effectively the end of Dan Rather's career.[1] In reporting on the situation, I had hits every hour all day long.

It was great practice for a young reporter. My shift for a long time was 5:00 a.m. three days a week and then two weekend shifts. People are so casual and relaxed at those hours. I became close to Kelly Wright, who worked a similar shift and was generous in helping me learn. It was great practice for me. I learned quickly the need to work hard—and fast—in television. Unlike my law days, there was no getting an extension if you needed more time. It was fun figuring out how to work more efficiently. I had to start letting some of my perfectionism go.

In TV, we learn by doing (Meredith was right), and I would try to tape the hours I thought I'd be on so I could go back and review my work. As always, I was my own worst critic. It was hard to see myself on camera in the beginning—you notice only your flaws. But it helped. I would see ways I could improve, tonally or in my delivery or in my general messaging or approach. I also started reading every piece of news I could get my hands on. I wasn't yet steeped in the news, and I soon realized this is a critical job requirement not just for doing a solid report on one topic, but for putting any topic in context and bringing perspective to it. I asked for a lot of advice at this time and wasn't afraid to show my ignorance. Not that hiding it was a viable option.

In those days, I enthusiastically took every shift they gave me. Christmas? No problem. Friday and Saturday night? Absolutely. Work a double? Yes. I'd advise anyone in a new job to do the same thing: say yes to everything. Everything within reason. Until you don't have to. Do it happily and without complaint. These days, I'm more judicious in my choices—I have to be, given the time constraints I'm under. But I'm still a hard worker.

Little by little, I started to get better shifts, and eventually, better stories. Occasionally, I'd get to go on Shepard Smith's *The Fox Report* at 7:00 p.m., which I really enjoyed. He's still my favorite news anchor. And my favorite show to appear on was always *Special Report with Brit Hume*. It was the best journalistic training ground a young reporter could ask for. When our packages would air, we'd watch the so-called Brit cam, a camera on Brit's face that we could see on our internal feed. If he grimaced, you were on the shit list.

If he yelled, you were dead. If he smiled? Well, that was too good to hope for. One night I got a grimace. Damn.

After the show ended, Kim Hume pulled me aside. A sound bite that should have been cut had been in the segment.

"Why was that in there?" she asked.

"I don't know," I said. "I told them—"

"What could you have done differently to prevent it?"

"I don't know. I told the editor not to include it, and he didn't listen."

"Not him," she said. "*You.* What could *you* have done differently?"

This was an important moment for me. She was telling me something bigger than how to make sure a package gets cut right. It was about taking ownership of my own work product. Not blaming someone else. If I had budgeted my time better, I could have been in the edit bay as the piece was being cut. I could have watched it start to finish before it aired. But I hadn't, and a mistake had been made. It felt liberating to realize this, to understand that I was in charge. I still carry this philosophy with me and ask my team to do the same. It mirrors one of Brit's favorite adages: "Winners take responsibility. Losers blame others." It's not just about saying the words. It's about actually doing it.

Kim was an incredible mentor to me—almost as much as Brit, who has had the greatest professional influence on my journalism career.

One thing I love about news is that every day is different, and you learn new things all the time. Not long into my tenure in the DC bureau, what I learned was that then Republican senator Arlen Specter, who at the time was the chairman of the Judiciary Committee, wanted to befriend me. He called me up and invited me to have lunch with him in the Senate's private dining room.

I thought this was a great chance, since I covered the Supreme Court and knew Senator Specter might help me break news on that front down the road. However, it did strike me as odd that someone with that much power was volunteering to give me an hour of his time.

I asked Major if this was unusual. He raised his eyebrows. "Seventeen years I covered Capitol Hill at *U.S. News*," he said. "Another three here at Fox. Never once has anyone asked me to have lunch in the private Senate dining room."

I went to lunch. We were seated at a table for two,

and while I didn't know the men and women around us by face, it was clear they were mostly senators and other Important DC Types (cynics call them Washing-phonians). Senator Specter was obviously well known and well liked, and introduced me to many of his colleagues in the dining room. I found him to be funny, smart, and full of insight.

Senator Specter told me about his time as a young prosecutor in Pennsylvania, and how he was appointed to the Warren Commission. He walked me through what he called their "single bullet *conclusion*"—not "theory"—behind JFK's assassination. After lunch he asked me if I wanted to see his office. I had never seen the office of a US senator before, so I accepted. We swung by his official digs, filled with staffers and paperwork and lots of mahogany and leather furniture. Then he took me to his other office, his "hideaway."

This is a real thing on Capitol Hill. A hideaway office is a rarity among lawmakers, a status symbol, and Specter's was bright and gorgeous, with nearly floor-to-ceiling windows. The white walls were covered with vanity shots of Specter alongside just about every world leader you could think of: Fidel Castro, Saddam Hussein, forty years' worth of presidents and Supreme Court justices . . . He had a copy of the Bill Clinton impeachment papers *signed by Bill Clinton*.

He walked me down memory lane. Every story was more fascinating than the one before. I think he enjoyed regaling a young woman with the impressive things he had achieved, and I felt like a sponge, soaking up new details and facts about Washington. Eventually he had to leave to vote. He asked me to stick around. I started thinking: *Why does he want me to wait? Does he have a great news story for me that he's been saving for hour three?* More likely than not, I figured, he was just enjoying the afternoon and didn't want it to end.

While I was waiting for Specter to return, I e-mailed Major: **I'm in something called his "hideaway"—what is this about? He asked me to stay here while he goes to vote.**

Almost immediately, I received Major's response: **GET OUT NOW! CODE RED! GET OUT! Hideaways are for towel-snapping rights!**

I swallowed hard. *Was I compromising myself? Had I made a mistake coming in here? What would people think? Wait,* towel-snapping?

Within moments, Specter was back. I was already on my feet, saying I had to go immediately. He wondered why I was "off so soon." I said I had work I needed to do and left with many thanks. When I got back to the office, I told Brit about it, and he smiled.

"Welcome to Washington, kid," he said.

For the record, the senator never tried anything inappropriate with me, and he did turn out to be a good source. But those first few months, I was on a steep learning curve.

That same year, George W. Bush won reelection, and I was still relatively new to Fox News. I was sent to cover one of the inaugural balls. Reporters were told to dress in the appropriate attire, so I wore a full-length red satin ballgown. I thought it was a beautiful gown, but—how do I put this? It was very cold in the ballroom, and the material was rather thin.

One of the crew gently let me know what they were seeing on the monitor—"Um, they're asking if you can . . . um . . . cover up."

I about died. I went into the bathroom and put tissues down the front of my dress, which solved the problem, but not before a screen grab of a visibly cold yours truly was all over the Internet. I was humiliated and more than a little disturbed by what people were saying online.

I told Brit about it later, and he said, "Look. Lesson learned. But Megyn, this is a tough business. You're going to need to get a thicker skin."

"Or a thicker dress," I said.

Sean Hannity was great about incoming negativity.

I talked to him early on about how dark a place the Internet was, how much awfulness awaited there, and he said, "Google 'Sean Hannity.' Go to the first website that pops up. It will be IHateSeanHannity.com, and the worst lies and hate will be sitting right there. I never pay that stuff any mind."

"How can you be so calm about it?" I asked.

"It's an acquired skill," he said. "I tell my friends, if someone offered to pay you a million dollars a year if you would allow the most hateful, vile things to be said about you online, would you take it? And they all say yes. Wouldn't you?"

Of course, I was not making a million dollars a year—not anywhere close. But I got the message. Do you love this job, or don't you? Is it worth some unwanted attention, or isn't it?

I'm more like Sean now. I know one of the key lessons of the Internet: a lot of bus exhaust comes with doing what we do. Haters come with the territory, and they will always be louder than the lovers. But in news, there's another rule: ratings reign supreme. If they're ripping you, that's fine, because it means they're watching. There's a saying in television: "It's when they're *not* talking about you that you need to worry."

11

So Long, Little Miss Perfect

The most transformational period of my adult life began early in 2005. I was six months into full-time broadcasting and quickly moving up the ranks. All of the emotional energy I had devoted to the law was now freed up. I was full of ambition and enthusiasm for my new career. Having come from the legal world, I was stunned by how, even as I was working hard by news standards, my new hours were so *reasonable*.

News was shift work. Eight hours on, and then you go home. If you didn't have a hit in your last hour or two, sometimes you could even leave early. That stack of papers on your desk? Throw it in the garbage; it is now literally yesterday's news. What a difference from law, where the paperwork lived forever, and even seemed to breed like rabbits when (if) you slept.

Suddenly I had something quite foreign to me—time. That new gift allowed me to think hard about what I wanted in all areas of my life, and I realized I still had much work to do—on my new career, my friendships, my marriage, and myself.

It all began in January, when Brit pulled me aside and said I "had captured the attention of Mr. Ailes." He said I was "being fast-tracked." I wasn't sure what that meant, but it sounded promising. He also said that he'd told Roger I shouldn't be brought along too quickly—that I should pay my dues in Washington. Brit wanted me to work as a reporter and spend time learning our trade. I was excited for any and all of it.

That summer, around my one-year anniversary at Fox, Roger called me up to New York and told me something: I had an authenticity problem. Roger had literally written the book on how to read people—it's called *You Are the Message.* "Viewers can spot a phony from a mile away," Roger said. He encouraged me not to be so reluctant to show the viewers who I really am. To take more risks. To not try so hard to be perfect. To not fear mistakes. I wasn't 100 percent sure I knew what he meant, but I promised to try.

Sometimes the universe has a way of enforcing a message. Soon after that meeting, I had a nasty encounter with a woman in the DC bureau who clearly did not like me and suggested others felt the same. Brit saw the exchange and pulled me into his office. He could see I was upset.

"Do you know what your problem is?" he asked me. "You're just as vulnerable as anyone else, but you project zero vulnerability."

He meant it kindly, but it was shocking. I began to take an honest look at myself. *Why can't I make friends more easily? Why don't more women want to be around me?* I had been so busy for so many years building up a protective veneer that it didn't dawn on me that I might be alienating others—from viewers to potential friends.

It occurred to me that what I thought I knew, I might not know. What I thought I had, I might not have. I was in a state of flux, of self-examination. I felt both fearful and hopeful that I could improve things, but I needed someone to help me figure out how.

My therapist's name was Amy, and I called her, affectionately, "M'Lady Amy." I met her in late 2005, and she helped me in ways I still cannot fully measure. We didn't spend a lot of time on childhood drama. She just gave me new ways of thinking about things, and I was ready to hear it. When I think of her now, I think of that line from *Titanic*: "He saved me in every way a person can be saved." She did that for me, and gave me a new way of approaching all of my relationships—with women, men, and myself.

With women, she asked me not to assume they did not like me. She suggested that my own preconceived notions about how women were reacting to me were in fact influencing how they did react. That *I* was in control of the responses I was getting. Think about things differently, she said, and you might get different results.

She encouraged me to attend a women's group she ran. At first I was reluctant.

"Am I that screwed up?" I asked Amy. "You want me to go to *two* therapy sessions?"

"It's not about being screwed up," she said. "It's about growing."

And so I walked into a room with six other women who were seeing Amy. I stayed quiet during the first meeting, and the next time I saw Amy, she asked me for my first impressions.

"This one is clearly getting a divorce," I said. "That one needs to get the husband out of the basement . . ." I continued to fire off my judgments.

It was only then that Amy shared with me one of the rules of group—you have to tell the other members your first impressions of them. *Really?*

Sure enough, once we were all back together, Amy

turned to me and said, "Megyn, would you care to share your impressions with everyone?"

"Okay . . . ," I said. I did it. I said what I thought in each case. I held nothing back.

And then the most extraordinary thing happened.

Each woman filled in her story. "This is something you don't know about me," said the woman who I had insisted needed to dump her husband immediately. "We don't have enough money to maintain two places. We're barely able to pay our bills now, much less apart . . ."

One by one, they told me more of their situations, and I realized how arrogant and wrong I'd been on almost every score.

Then they turned the tables and told me their first impressions of me: I was tough, a hot shot, a go-getter. They didn't see any tenderness. Because, of course, I showed none. It wasn't how I saw *myself* at all. It began to dawn on me—the image I am putting out there bears little resemblance to who I really am.

The universe wasn't done with me yet.

One night, a number of my female Fox colleagues went out for happy hour, and I wasn't invited. I could see them gathering outside my office, but nobody came in and asked me to come along. I had been there for about two years, and I thought we liked each other.

I told my women's group about it. I was expecting sympathy. I got something even better: honesty.

"I wouldn't have invited you either," one of the women said.

"Why not?" I asked.

"Because you seem like you have it all going on. You seem so sure of yourself; you are attractive. I'd feel like all the attention would flow to you and none to me. I've never heard you talk about having a bad hair day, or feeling fat. There's nothing in you that I can relate to. I wouldn't want to share the table with you."

I started crying.

"Nothing could be further from the truth," I said. "I constantly feel like I need to lose weight. I don't feel attractive at all without my hair and makeup done. I have the same self-doubts as anyone. But I am an expert at hiding them all."

There it was. In my personal and professional lives, the feedback was the same. I needed to get more honest about who I was—with my friends, my colleagues, my viewers and myself. The Little Miss Perfect act—the very one that law firm had seen and rejected years earlier—was starting to crumble. I found myself re-evaluating the choices I had made, for so many years, about my approach to life.

As I thought about these remarkably similar pieces

of feedback, I suddenly found myself thinking back across the years, coming up with stories like these. Examples from my past when I failed to connect with people. As a young adult, I struggled with what I now see was my threatening personality. At one of my first professional jobs, a couple of women on my floor would eat together every day. When it was beautiful, people would go eat outside on these benches, and I noticed them always choosing benches as far away from me as possible.

Another time when I was living in New York, I met a woman in a bar, and we hit it off. She asked me to join her and a friend of hers for dinner. I sat across from them, thinking, *This feels like an interview for friendship. I must get this job.* And so I felt the need to project all good things. I would never have chosen to show any weakness. The next morning, I sent the woman an e-mail saying, **Thanks so much for inviting me out!**

I never heard from her again.

Women, in my experience, don't want to surround themselves with other women who project only strength and no humanity. I believe men are socialized differently and don't tend to have as much of a problem with this. A tough veneer is considered a life skill for a man, so men do not tend to find the tough-gal routine as off-putting. But women, at least those I have known, tend to demand more emotional honesty in a relationship.

And as I thought back, I ended up where it all began: seventh grade. For years, I didn't think about how that year of bullying had affected me. I figured it was just something I'd weathered; it was terrible, but it was over. But the truth is, it had changed me.

There was one benefit—I'll start with that. I developed empathy in a way I otherwise never could. It affects the stories I choose on my show to this day. I look for stories about survival, about triumph.

That's the upside. But there was a more profound, lasting downside to that middle-school torment. I never dealt with people the same again. When you're traumatized as a kid, it's almost like squeezing a liquid gel over yourself that becomes a hardened shell. It protects you—but it also keeps you at arm's length from other people. I would see that manifest more than once in my life. I wanted to be invulnerable, which I thought meant projecting perfection, strength. I was sabotaging my own ability to form intimate friendships.

Today I am much more open about who I really am, and it has helped me better connect with people. A couple of years ago, at the *Fortune* Most Powerful Women's Conference in Laguna Niguel, California, I was going to be interviewed by Facebook COO and *Lean In* author Sheryl Sandberg, the only person I knew at the conference. The night before the interview, Sheryl—who was not yet in town—had suggested I have drinks with several of her friends. I had never met them, but Sheryl introduced us by e-mail, and the women said they'd be in the hotel bar and I should swing by that night.

Well, I did it. I walked into the hotel bar and walked around a bit. I didn't know what they looked like. No one stopped me. I walked back, twice. Nothing. So I went back to my room and ordered room service. I felt relieved to be alone, but also mad at myself for not having tried harder, and for not being bolder. It's still hard for me to extend myself, to put myself out there. I fear rejection. I fear feeling like an outcast sitting (once again) at the lunch table with no one.

The next day, during my exchange onstage with Sheryl, I told that story in front of hundreds of women. I admitted that even though I feel powerful in my job, I still get insecure meeting new people. I always feel pressure. I want them to like me. I want them to like the real me. And then, that honesty was rewarded. Afterward, several of those women who'd been on the e-mail thread wrote me and said, **We would have loved to**

talk to you! and **Let's be sure to do it next time!** and **We looked for you! So sorry we missed you!**

I learned something: the messages in your head are not always well founded. Because at some level when you fail to make a connection like that, you're thinking, *They don't really want me.* When you take a risk, you find out maybe your instincts are off. M'Lady Amy—and Roger, and Brit, and my women's group— all helped me finally see that. And it was in that frame of mind that I became open to finding true love in my life.

My relationships with women were not the only ones in trouble. The reinvention in my professional life had underscored how little joy I had personally. The truth was, I was unhappily married, and I felt terrible guilt about it. I think when a couple grows apart, there's a part of them that just keeps thinking, *We'll grow back together.* And often they do. The problem was, Dan and I didn't. While it was clear to me that Dan was someone I would always care about, it was also clear that all the hours and work and distance between us had separated us in more ways than one. I spent a lot of time talking it over with Amy, and those who cared about me.

"You can't live like this, honey," my mom said when

I called her for advice. "You have to take care of yourself."

Even though she was Catholic, and had never been divorced, she wanted me to have what she had always had—a deep and fulfilling marriage.

I went on a trip with Andrea and Rebecca, and poured my heart out.

"Dan is a great guy," I told them. "Sure, we've had our problems—each of us has made mistakes, each has hurt the other plenty—but we both know the other person is fundamentally good and kind. So why aren't I happy? How could I consider leaving someone I care about?"

But the writing was on the wall, as you could see in my journal at the time:

I have been asking myself some tough questions. Ones I'm not sure I want the answers to. Leaving the practice of law has shown me the paper-perfect life sometimes isn't. I fear screwing up my life. Why can't I just be satisfied with what I have? Because, in my heart, my soul, I want more. I hope I have the courage to listen to myself. I hope I figure out what settling for more means in my personal life and have the strength to do whatever it takes to have a full, meaningful life.

Dan and I had many honest conversations. He knew we were not compatible. We cared about each other, but it was clear to both of us that we were not meant to be together. We agreed to part ways, and it was amicable. It was also very painful. I moved out.

I bought a town house in the same development. For the first time in years, I was living alone. Dan and I stayed friendly. We shared custody of our two dogs. We both started seeing other people, and that felt strange. It was very sad. I never wanted to cause Dan pain, and he never wanted me to feel it, and yet we both were in pain. I shed a lot of tears that winter and spring. I dated a few people. He dated a few more. I think men in particular find that a helpful way to nurse their wounds, and Dan has never struggled to attract female attention, so this was not a problem for him. (He went on to remarry and have three beautiful children. We remain friendly to this day.)

One day in the Fox makeup room, Brit and I were talking and I told him I was getting a divorce. I noted that we were parting amicably, and weren't doing any alimony.

"And so it's official," I said, making light of the situation. "I am the worst gold digger of all time. I spent years supporting Dan when he made no money. And the second he gets a high-paying job, I'm leaving."

And then Brit said one of the wisest of the many wise things he's told me over the years: "You dig your own gold."

In the wake of my separation, I threw myself into my career, which I found to be a soothing balm. I was covering the Supreme Court for Fox, and a big case came up: Mrs. Smith goes to Washington—Anna Nicole Smith, that is.

She was involved in a lawsuit over her deceased billionaire oil tycoon husband's fortune. The nation—and much of the world—tuned in, riveted, when a dramatically thinner, more chic version of the *Playboy* model we all knew about showed up in person at the Supreme Court.

Every show on the channel wanted my report live from the Supreme Court steps, as did our affiliate service Fox News Edge, our sister company Sky News in the UK, you name it. At the end of a long day, I did my very first hit for Bill O'Reilly, host of the number-one show on cable news. I told him about her travails—how she'd testified that it was very expensive to be Anna Nicole Smith, and she needed someone to continue funding the effort. Bill loved it. We had a fun, robust back-and-forth. One of his producers later told me that he went back to his team after the fact and said, "She's a star. I want her on every week."

That was a big break for me. A regular weekly primetime gig would expose me to a much bigger audience than my mostly daytime reporting had. Not only did Bill introduce me to his audience, he treated me as an authority figure. He let viewers see that he respected me. He asked me to cover big news stories. It was a segment I would do faithfully for the next ten years. Bill was generous with his time and advice. He was always happy to sit down with me and offer his opinion, and I considered him a friend. I helped him too, taking time off to raise money for his daughter's school, helping him promote his books, defending him publicly when he came under attack for this thing or that. We liked each other and had a great rapport.

A month or so later found me covering the Duke lacrosse rape scandal. Brit put me on the case early. Three white male lacrosse players from (relatively) privileged families were accused of gang-raping a poor black single mother working as a stripper at a party. The media had already all but convicted the boys. Brit sent me to Durham, but before I went, he pulled me aside and warned me, "Keep an open mind."

From the get-go it was clear to me that the rape case

was deeply flawed. I developed strong sources, who leaked many significant details to me, and managed to break a lot of news in the matter. Sean Hannity put me on his show almost nightly for months, which again was a terrific platform. He had his own connection to someone close to the case, and the two of us would "bong in" at 9:00 p.m. sharp nightly with new details on the case, the biggest story in the nation.

It wasn't long before some started to question my coverage as racist, and even sexist. Why was I casting doubt on the victim's story? Was it my own "privilege" at play? The DA said it happened. Why would I question that? It must be an anti-black thing. I tuned them out.

Soon enough, the truth came out—the only "victims" in that case were the three accused men. The accuser was a deeply troubled young woman who made the entire thing up. She was taken advantage of by an ambitious DA, Mike Nifong, who was looking to impress a largely black constituency in an election year. He was later disbarred and spent a day in jail. Since then, all three of the defendants' families have reached out to thank me for being one of the only voices to give them a fair shake. I think of them to this day when some media watchers try to pressure me to fall in line with how the mainstream press is swimming on a story.

I learned a lot from my Duke experience—including how many are quick to condemn any coverage involving race that doesn't affirm their own views about what racism is. Fox News anchors are a favorite target for this—another fact of life I don't love, but have learned to live with. It reminded me of the O. J. Simpson case, which I'd followed closely as a law student.

Not long after I arrived at Bickel & Brewer, the O. J. verdict came down. Nicole Brown Simpson was only about ten years older than I was at the time. It was broadcast gavel to gavel on Court TV, and we kept it on at the law school around the clock. Not a student at ALS lacked an opinion. The vast majority of us believed he was guilty. The vast majority of us were also white.

I'll never forget how when we heard the decision was being read, everyone in the office ran into the conference room to watch it on TV—white lawyers, secretaries, and a paralegal, and one black receptionist. When the not-guilty verdict was read, our little conference room was a microcosm of what was happening around the country—everyone's jaw dropped, and we stood motionless, except for our receptionist, who put her arms above her head and cheered.

We looked at her in surprise, obviously missing the dynamic that in retrospect is so clear in that case.

Most African Americans wanted an acquittal, believing the system was rigged against them. Most Caucasians wanted a conviction, having had far more positive interactions with law enforcement. I'll never forget that moment, as it opened my eyes to the reality that two people can see the exact same facts and come to vastly different conclusions about what they mean based on their life experience. As a lawyer, and now a journalist, I find this thought helpful in checking my own bias when reading a case or a story.

In addition to my field reporting, I had great opportunities back in the studio. After Chief Justice William Rehnquist died, Brit, Chris Wallace, and I were on the air wall-to-wall for a week covering the John Roberts confirmation hearings. Then Sandra Day O'Connor retired, and the same team was wall-to-wall, covering Samuel Alito's hearings. I dove into those projects like *I* was the one facing confirmation. I read every case these judges had ever written, every article they'd ever penned. I went to the National Archives and read all of then–Judge Roberts's papers from when he was in the Reagan White House. And when questions would come up at their hearings about a case or their judicial philosophy, I was able to explain it on the air.

We had considerable downtime on the set while the hearings were in progress, and Brit, Chris, and I would chat like teenage girls. At one point Chris asked me whether I would have "even spoken to him in high school." About a dozen male voices popped into my earpiece: "Say no!" . . . "No!" . . . "NO!" In the end I went with, "I would have, but I was in a stroller." We laughed. As is typical for me, I was merciless on myself, watching our coverage back later. I wished I had been smoother. I thought I looked unattractive. I knew I could do better. It was just about then that Brit pulled me aside, telling me how proud he was of me. For a moment I thought maybe I'd been too hard on myself. And then just as quickly, I discarded that thought and resolved to do better the next time.

Seeing that I could hold my own as a reporter, Roger Ailes asked me to try something new: substitute anchoring. I loved field reporting, but by this point I knew anchoring would allow me to do lengthier on-air interviews and to have a bit more fun on the air. He wanted me to sit in one weekend for Geraldo Rivera.

"Are you ready?" Roger asked.

"Absolutely!" I said, thinking, *Not only have I never done this before, I've never even sat in an anchor chair.*

I was so grateful that he was going to let me try. "I won't disappoint you," I promised.

"The only way you'll disappoint me is if you try to hit a home run instead of a single," he said.

That is damn great advice, I thought. It took the pressure off.

But I realized I would need some preparation. Before I headed up to New York, I practiced sitting in the anchor chair on the set in DC and reading the prompter. I realized that if I kept my eyes a couple of words ahead of what was coming out of my mouth, I would have a beat to think about my delivery. I ran through some old copy many times.

Now, I needed to look the part. In New York, they give you The Works when it comes to hair and makeup. In DC you had to do your own hair, and given the seriousness of Washington, they didn't use too much makeup on us either. Often I was short on time and did my own makeup anyway. For a few New York anchors, the hair and makeup room was like a spa. They would sit in the makeup chair for an hour and then in the hair chair for another hour after that. I questioned how I would budget that kind of time into my prep. Before, the whole thing was twenty minutes of my day. Which, for the record, explained the difference between how they looked and how I looked. The first time I saw myself with The Works, I thought, *Wow, the hair is BIG.* And they put false eyelashes on me.

Later, I started refusing the eyelashes.

"Are we doing Hollywood, or are we doing news?" I said to the makeup artist.

The makeup artist said, "Both, honey."

"Get the fucking lashes!" my friend Julie Banderas would yell from the next chair.

A word on hair and makeup at Fox: being on TV naturally plays into a person's insecurities. Everything is magnified on television, and you see things about yourself you never saw before. Thankfully they pay people good money to make us look our best. Between the hair, makeup, and wardrobe stylist, they can really transform a person, and thankfully we employ the best in the business.

To this day, I don't think of myself as some sort of great beauty. I'm not unattractive, but without my makeup I'm not remarkable, and I don't care if people see me without my face on. To crib a line from Trump, what you see is what you see. What you see on the air, however, is a very glammed-up version of myself.

I also have to watch what I eat, especially because I don't have time to go to the gym. After I had my children, something had to give, and I gave up on exercise. I follow the F-Factor diet, from the book by Tanya Zuckerbrot. The *F* stands for fiber, although there's also a delightful section called "F-Exercise." I started after the birth of my first child, Yates. It took off the baby weight right away. This book is a game changer, and no, I'm not getting paid to say any of this.

Anyway, back to Geraldo's show. The moment came. I went out there on the set, and I sat down to anchor my first show. It was thrilling. As always during those first few years at Fox, I went on the air rather buttoned up—wearing my Jones Day business suits and my old fake pearls. My delivery was stilted and awkward, but I was *exhilarated*.

I arrived at Fox News that day nine hours in advance of the show. This is what you might call overkill. As usual, I overprepared for those five segments of television, which has always been my security blanket. I did the show Saturday and Sunday night at 10:00 p.m. I had to return to Washington very early Monday morning. The tryout had gone well. I thought, *Did I just sit in Geraldo Rivera's chair and anchor a national broadcast? I. Did.*

I walked out of my hotel into the heart of Times Square at dawn to catch the train back to Washington. The sun was rising. The sky was pink, and the twinkling lights were flashing against the hazy backdrop. There was no one there. I was in the middle of everything. Being alone for much of this year had felt scary and sad. But on this morning, it felt wonderful. New

My parents met in New York City, where my dad was
studying at Manhattan College, and my mother was in nursing school.
They married not long into their courtship in 1962.

My father had a great combination of intellectualism and romanticism,
while my mom was savvy and whip-smart. He was clever. She was a riot.
They adored each other.

For my mom, laughter is the secret of life. She always was—and still is—a force of nature. When she's there, everyone feels a bit brighter. When she walks out, the room is unhappier.

Nana (on the right) and her sister at my parents' wedding.

My parents' one and only trip to Europe—at the Eiffel Tower in August 1977.

In the summer, my family would drive to Lake Ontario, where we rented a cabin, hiked, and danced around the campfire. My dad would play guitar and sing us John Denver songs, as shown in this photo with me.

Left: Growing up in the suburbs of Syracuse and Albany, attending public school, going to Catholic mass, and, as shown here, enjoying the decor of the 1970s, we had it made.

My family raised me with the core message: Be whoever you are. That person may (or may not) be extraordinary. We're not going to lie to make you feel better, but we'll love you no matter what.

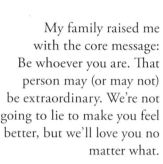

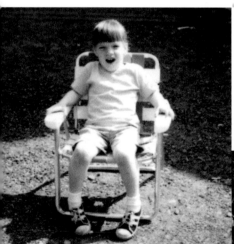

Growing up, I was the youngest, but I still had a voice. We would sit around our dinner table, and Dad would ask, "What's the report?" When it was my turn, I would prattle on, over the complaints of my siblings. "You had your chance," Dad would say. "And now you will listen to her."

The classic Olan Mills photo of my family. I'm sporting my favorite outfit: a black-and-red cowgirl jumper. (My parents did make me remove the accompanying holster and two silver toy guns for the shot.)

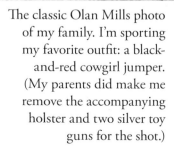

My family on a camping trip. My mother used to say I was the female Ed, minus the beard and mustache; from the eyebrows down—eyes, nose, cheekbones—I look exactly like him.

My high school graduation in 1988 *(left)*.

Mom's graduation from her master's program flanked by me and my brother Pete *(right)*. She would post her grades on the refrigerator next to ours and remark that hers were better. Checkout the Griswold-like family truckster in our driveway.

With Kelly and our boyfriends before the prom.
When I asked my mom what happened to my prom dress years later, she
confessed it had ended up in one of her "all you can grab
for a dollar" garage sales. Classic Linda.

College graduation in 1992. By the time I was a junior at
Syracuse University, I had decided to become a lawyer. It was empowering—
I believed I'd finally found my path.

Winning the Best Individual Advocate Award in a moot court competition while at Albany Law School. I knew, almost as soon as I got to law school, that I could stand up and make an argument. *(Courtesy of Albany Law School)*

The Fendrick Award, given out by my broadcasting professor in honor of a woman named Fendrick who once became so overwhelmed by stage fright doing a sidewalk report that she hailed a taxi and took off. (On rough days, I admit I look at it and think, *Was that fleeing woman onto something?*)

A journal entry from the night I realized I needed to exit my legal career.

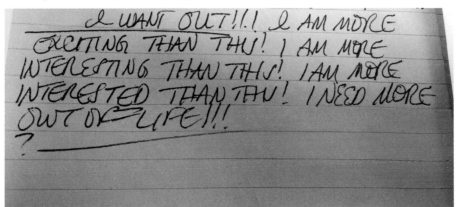

February 2, 2003

I'm taking real steps toward a new career: broadcast journalism. Wow! I think I would really excel @ it—I feel that I will have a real knack for it! I was giving serious thought to getting a Master's in Broadcast Journalism, which I assumed would be the only way in. Unfortunately that would've cost $32,000/year and would've taken a year out of my life.—actually closer to 2 years if you include the application + waiting process. I figured I would be 34 @ the time of my first job. Well, today I asked a woman in my guitar class, Meredith, to have coffee with me. She is a producer for NBC news here in Chicago. I thought I would just "pick her brain" a bit about broadcast journalism + the news in general. What a woman she is! She actually offered to arrange a tour of the studios for me, to set up a meeting between me + her boss (:) fellow

25 June 2004

Full time offer from Channel 7 AND an interview on Monday with Fox News Channel. Wow. Things are really starting to take off for me — it's exciting.

Top: I chronicled my steps toward a new career in my journal, including this entry about my coffee with Meredith from my guitar class, who, in a completely selfless act, introduced me to broadcast journalism. *Bottom:* Getting the job offer at ABC 7 in Washington, DC, and about to interview at Fox News Channel—once I started settling for more, I never looked back.

Reporting at the 2008 Democratic National Convention for Fox News—
there were 80,000 people at Invesco Field to see Barack Obama accept the
Democratic nomination.

My political independence goes back a long time. As this journal entry from
1988 shows, I've never felt a strong call to either party.

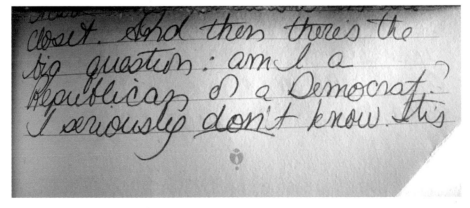

When I look at photos from my wedding to Doug, the ones of us dancing—and dancing hard, as we are to Bon Jovi here, flanked by our brothers and our dear friend—capture the elation of the day. *(Courtesy of Joshua Zuckerman)*

With Doug when I was pregnant with Yates, wearing flag headgear, courtesy of Diane. *Right:* With Yates at the beach, not long after he was born. Becoming a mother is the most profound thing that's ever happened to me. (Doug and I don't publicly share many photos of our children—included here are a couple of now-dated exceptions.)

With Yardley at Newt Gingrich's debate podium during the 2012 Republican presidential primary race. She can use this if she ever runs for president. I propose the caption "Born to Run."

Yardley (on her head) and Yates, letting their full selves shine at a book signing for Doug's second book, *The Means*.

Story time with Yates and Yardley in 2011.

Peter Kirwan, who has been a treasure in my life, here with his granddaughter Yardley.

With Doug and the kids at Disney World. As Doug said after our youngest, Thatcher, was born, "Now everyone's here who's supposed to be here."

After I changed myself for the better, better things started coming to me. I was settling for more. And "more" meant more *from myself*. Finding Doug proved that more than anything else.

In December 2014, six months before he announced his candidacy for president, Donald Trump began reaching out to me—often—with e-mails, phone calls, and things like this forwarded Christmas card.

Trump denied my statement to *Vanity Fair* in January 2016 that he used to send me correspondence, including articles about me signed by him. I saw no point in releasing my file at the time, but here is just one example—a congratulatory note on a cover story about me in the *New York Times Magazine*.

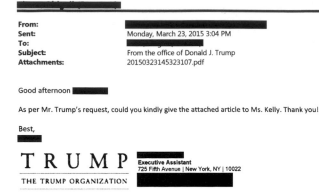

An e-mail from one of Trump's assistants encouraging me to read
a positive article about him from a conservative magazine. The annotations
were added, presumably by him.

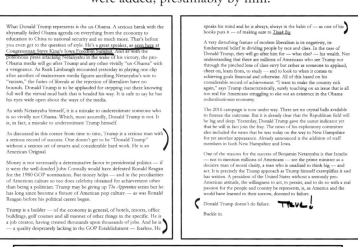

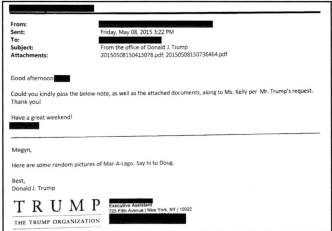

As late as May 2015, just a month before he announced his candidacy,
Trump invited Doug and me to Mar-a-Lago, his oceanfront mansion and
club in Palm Beach. Trump followed up with photos of Mar-a-Lago as well.
It was an invitation I would never accept.

Walking into the first debate in Cleveland after a day from hell. Triumphant.

Most people don't know that the co-owner of Fox News is Prince Al-Waleed of Saudi Arabia here with his sister and with host Mygan Kelly. In case you only watch Fox News and you missed it everywhere else.

GOOGLE IT!

Donald J. Trump ✓
@realDonaldTrump

"@BradCross4: @Drudge_Report_
@realDonaldTrump
pic.twitter.com/Ur1qgG291Z"
8:29 AM - 28 Jan 2016

↩ ⟲ 5,187 ♥ 7,667

Trump skipped the second Republican debate that Fox News hosted in Iowa after complaining about me incessantly. That morning, I awoke to see that Trump had retweeted a fake picture of me with two Saudis, wearing full Muslim garb.

With Trump in his office following the Trump Tower Accords.

My team at *The Kelly File*, who have been with me through it all.

With my mom and Nana at Nana's 100th birthday celebration.

With Doug in Paris—almost forty years after my parents' only visit there.

York, too, had at one point felt cold and alien. Now it felt like it could be home. I felt more alive than I ever had. It was as if the blinking lights around me were in sync with my own heartbeat, flush with blood and pumping away. I was on my own in the center of the world, and the center of the world was where I felt like I belonged.

As I would soon learn, however, the world can be a very dangerous place.

12

Nights of Fear

I'll never forget the first time I was recognized outside of work. I was in Reagan National Airport heading up to New York when a man came up to me and said, "Megyn!"

Not being used to this, I walked right toward him, thinking we must know each other.

"Yes?" I asked.

"I watch you all the time!" he said.

"Oh!" I said. "Thank you!" *Act like you've been there, Meg!*

I told Brit about it when I got back to Washington.

"You're going to be very famous," he told me.

It sounded heady, the way he put it. But as I soon found out, fame has a downside.

About two years into my time at Fox, I began receiving letters from a man who appeared to be a fan. First, they were nonsensical, and I didn't think much of them. But then he started sending letters for me addressed to my colleagues, and—I would later learn from the authorities—leaving them for me around the city. He sent e-mails, too. And the tone grew increasingly disturbing. Then he showed up face-to-face, and it was clear he believed we were in a relationship. For the first time since I could remember, I was genuinely scared.

I had to tell Fox about it, which I hated. It was my habit to keep my head down and work hard. I didn't want to be a squeaky wheel: "Hi! I've been here less than two years and I have a stalker and I need security now and that's going to cost you a lot of money! 'K, bye!"

And then I had to contact the police, too, which meant I also had to face the truth of what was happening: there was a man out there who might try to hurt me.

The police said he was an "erotomaniac," meaning he believed he had a love relationship with me, even though we'd never met. One of the rules of dealing with a stalker (much like dealing with a bully) is to have no direct contact and to offer no response. This stalker, the police told me, was a convicted felon who

was weapons-trained, and had been violent with another female stalking victim in the past.

The letters and e-mails were gibberish, but suggested that he was somehow receiving messages from
me. And that he was receiving messages about me from
other people too. I started doing research on similar
situations. Well, that scared the daylights out of me.
I realized this could go badly. That one wrong move
could aggravate things. I felt adrift, with no one to talk
to, and no one in my life with any relevant expertise.

The stalker kept escalating things, quickly. Fox
News hired me a round-the-clock guard. Then things
escalated more, and Fox got me a second round-the-
clock guard. The guards protected me, but also advised
me on security. I would go to bed at night, and the
guards would be there with their loaded revolvers. I
lived like that for a long time.

Stalking is a deadly serious crime. It is very hard
to shake a stalker. It's like getting a letter in the mail:
"Sorry, your life is now ruined for at least a decade." It
often ends violently. Still, nine times out of ten stalking
is treated as a misdemeanor. And the victim, to get a
restraining order, typically must be present with her
stalker at any hearing, which is insane. Most women
can't afford a lawyer to go on their behalf. And even if
you get the judge to rule in your favor, there are never

any teeth in the penalties. It's not until a stalker does something worse than stalking that the courts finally get interested.

When you have a stalker, you walk down the street differently. A stranger would cross toward me and I would tense up. I was on edge all the time, given the constant threat and his focus on me. I couldn't go through public spaces the same way. There was no feeling better about it. Every movement was fraught with questions: What's my escape plan? What weapon will I use if I'm attacked? Pulling into my garage was a totally different experience. Every hackle was up. Am I returning to danger? When this door goes down, am I trapping myself in?

That was a scary time for me. I kept a fully charged cell phone on my bedside table and took other measures to put layers between me and an intruder. I started to learn how to handle a gun, which felt empowering but also somehow sad. It was one thing to learn to handle a weapon out of interest. It was another to do it out of fear. My journal entry from August 11, 2006, read:

> *Went to the shooting range last weekend. It was kind of stressful. The adrenaline was flowing and when it was all over I felt quite anxious. At one point I became slightly overwhelmed—seeing*

myself there, goggles on, headphones on, firing a
loaded .357 Magnum, a 9mm semi-automatic, even
an enormous shotgun—and I felt teary. What has
become of me? How did I get here?

I took many other security precautions I will keep to
myself, since I remain under threat to this day—by this
man, who is back on the streets after a long imprison-
ment, and, now, others. Suffice it to say, that was not
the last restraining order I was forced to get, nor the
last violent, disturbed stalker I would fear. I followed
every piece of advice my security guards gave me to
the letter. But this man stole my sense of safety from
me for a very long time. (By the way, to all women,
whether you have a stalker or not, read *The Gift of*
Fear by Gavin de Becker. It is life-changing. Please,
just do it.)

Not that there's ever a good time to be stalked, but
I have to say, the timing on this was particularly bad.
Here I'd finally reinvented myself, moved into my
own home, left behind a job that was suffocating me
for one that I loved, and was really hitting my stride,
and then—terror. I began to ask myself, *How much*
do I want this? Am I willing to be threatened to do a
job I love? It's a question no one should have to ask,
and yet there I was. I began to wonder whether it was

worth it. I still loved my job—but I hated the side effects. Still do.

Both of the big decisions I'd made in the prior years—to leave Dan and to leave the law for TV—were suddenly not looking so hot. As I sat by myself in my locked bedroom, the downside to my choices was pretty apparent.

Eventually the stalker was arrested, and I felt liberated. But soon I would become the target of someone else. Around this time, someone started a rumor that my relationship with Brit was more than mentor-mentee. A lie spread that Brit and I were having an affair. Brit was my boss. He was the managing editor of the DC bureau. And his wife, Kim, was also my boss. She'd brought me in to Fox News. I loved them both.

Radar Online started peddling the story. They called me a "Humewrecker." I was upset. I was in the process of divorcing Dan and living alone. I had been working hard to prove myself. I had never even come close to having an affair with Brit—not a single inappropriate or even borderline moment, ever, between the two of us. Brit was Bret Baier's mentor too, but obviously Bret never had to deal with this kind of suspicion around their equally platonic relationship.

Most of all, I hated that people might think I was getting ahead by sleeping my way to the top. Major, my officemate, knew very well that there was no affair. He had a few theories about who might be behind the rumor—a Fox News media relations executive had (at least) pushed it online, and he was caught (and fired in the wake of) modifying my Wikipedia page to add the falsehood. I was too green at the time to realize how egregious that was, but it happened.

Meanwhile, Brit was strutting around the office, proud as a peacock! He was handing out the Radar link like cigars at the birth of a baby.

He walked into my office, chest out, half-cocked grin, saying, "Have you seen Radar?"

I, on the other hand, was not smiling. "Wait, you're upset about this?" he asked, surprised. He was genuinely amused by it, and thought its absurdity was apparent to all.

"Of course I'm upset!" I said. "People will believe it."

"Don't be ridiculous!" he said. "They won't."

"Yes, they will," I said, knowing all too well that people love to dismiss potentially threatening women as "nuts or sluts." Evidently, I didn't pass for a nut, so I was to be branded a slut—never mind that my sexy home life consisted of armed guards sitting in my living room while I lay sleepless upstairs, scared and alone.

"You're Brit Fucking Hume," I said. "Nobody knows me. They'll see that I'm thirty years younger and blond, and they'll just assume that's the whole story."

"They won't," he said, "because we didn't have an affair. Therefore, there will never be proof of an affair. There will never be a text, a photograph, a phone bill, a doorman, a driver, an e-mail, or anything whatsoever that suggests an affair. And people will come to see that it's a lie." And he was right. I think about that lesson to this day when people say false things about me: over time the truth comes out.

Years later, at his retirement party, Brit and I were in a crowded restaurant in Washington. Dignitaries and public figures were there from all walks of life, from Vice President Dick Cheney to Brian Williams of NBC News. Brit stood up to thank his guests.

"I haven't been this honored since that rumor was going around about me having an affair with Megyn Kelly," he quipped. "You know, when that rumor first broke," he continued, "the Fox News PR people came to me and said, 'We've got to tamp this down.' And I said, 'Do we have to tamp it down *right away*?'

"'Well, it's not true, is it?' the rep said.

"'No,' I said, 'but it's not *impossible*!'"

The room roared with laughter. By that point, I could laugh too.

I spent years learning from Brit. He later told me he

knew from the start I'd be headed for big things. "There is no job in this industry unavailable to you," he'd say. He also shared with me the story of what happened when he and Kim had first seen my résumé tape, which included clips of my reporting from WJLA. He said when the last piece of tape rolled, he and Kim looked at each other and high-fived. I always remembered that, because it was similar to the story with Professor Melilli and his assistant coach when I tried out for the trial team. It meant something to me—confirmation that I was supposed to be there.

Would anyone have been doing that if I had auditioned for a job at NASA? No. But I had found what business consultant Laura Garnett calls the "zone of genius," meaning the place where one's top talent combines with one's passion—with what one *really wants.*

I had always wanted to be a broadcast journalist. Way back in 1988, when I was not yet eighteen, I wrote about watching a presidential debate on TV and feeling mesmerized by it even though I couldn't vote. It had taken fifteen years, but my fascination remained, and the more I immersed myself in my new chosen field, the more fulfilled I was.

Well . . . the more fulfilled at *work.* In my personal life, I was still searching.

I'd started dating here and there, but didn't have a strong emotional connection with any of the men. I wanted baby steps out of my first marriage: safe, easy dates—just enough not to be totally isolated. What I wanted more was time to myself, time to be myself again.

I started questioning whether I could really find all the things I wanted in one person. M'Lady Amy—who was happy in her marriage—was forceful in her advice.

"The man I'm looking for doesn't exist," I told Amy.

"Yes, he does," she said.

"You found the only one," I responded.

"Nope," she said. "There are lots of them."

"Bullshit."

"Put this one back on the shelf," Amy said.

She encouraged me to change my thinking as I asked question after question about the men I was meeting.

"You're focusing on the wrong person," she told me. "Put all of this energy back into yourself."

If I had only heard that advice when I was a dieting boy-crazy college student, I wonder how much time and unhappiness I could have saved myself.

Women, I think, have a tendency to obsess about male partners. Whenever I started thinking too hard about this guy or that one—*Is he right for me? Am I right for him? Does he like me too much? Does he like me enough? Will he call? Why didn't he? When will I see him again?*—Amy would bring it back to me. I channel that message often: "You're thinking about the wrong person." It means when you find yourself devoting too much emotional energy to something, try redirecting your thoughts to yourself and how *you* can improve your own life. What is within *your* power to change? How can you make *yourself* more fulfilled?

This strategy is empowering, and results in you becoming a more interesting, well-adjusted person. This in turn attracts better people into your life. For me, it reduced banal worries like *Will he call?* Instead I could think, *He'll call or he won't. I'm going to my guitar lesson.* In my experience, happiness begets happiness, and fulfillment leads to more of the same.

I resumed playing my guitar. I read a lot. I worked out and took long walks. I was taking good care of myself, for the first time in a long time.

It's probably no accident that that's when Doug came into my life.

13

Writing the Wrong Things

I met Doug Brunt in late July 2006. We were set up on a blind date in Washington, DC, by a mutual acquaintance, and it was a date that almost never happened.

A woman I knew e-mailed to say that she wanted to fix me up with a colleague of hers. They'd been flying somewhere and were watching me on Fox News from their seats. She saw that he liked me. He's reserved, but she saw it. She e-mailed me without telling him. I almost deleted the e-mail, and with it, my future children. Something told me not to do it, and instead I hit save. Months later, I saw the e-mail again, and reconsidered. I asked her to send me his picture. She went back to him and said, "Don't be mad, but I did something. Give me a picture."

He did, and he was not mad at all.

Our first date was at Zaytinya in Washington, DC, a trendy spot that had a long, open bar in back.

Because of the stalker I was spooked, so I wanted my girlfriend to wait at the corner of the bar doing recon to let me know when Doug got there, and to make sure he didn't seem sketchy. I had never been on a blind date before.

At 8:00 p.m. I got the first e-mail. **Blue blazer. Handsome. All good.**

I started over, then got another e-mail one minute later. **Abort! Abort! He just hugged and kissed another woman. Not him.**

Then a third e-mail. **Blue blazer. Dark hair. Much more handsome. Think you're going to like this.**

In DC, it turns out, blue-blazer-and-dark-hair is not enough description. I walked into the restaurant, and there was Doug, seated at the end of the bar. He had gone to Duke and knew me from my coverage of the Duke lacrosse rape case, so he recognized me right away. He stood and guided me to the seat next to him.

Doug lived in New York and was CEO of a technology company based in Florida. In those days he flew over DC about twice each week but rarely stopped in.

He said he was passing through for work, and later confessed that he had scrounged up a meeting of no consequence for the following day.

He was generous, funny, and gorgeous. He had a relaxed boldness to the way he talked. Some people wriggle around what they say, worried about what others may think. Doug just talked. He trusted in his good instincts, didn't make attempts to dress things up. He was witty and well read, but not in a showy way. More than anything, what I remember about him that first night is that he listened. Really listened, and followed up. He has a way of making you feel *heard*.

After one drink I dismissed my girlfriend from the other side of the bar. After the second drink, the restaurant announced last call. Washington, DC, is terrible that way, so we left, laughing down the sidewalk like college sweethearts, looking for a late-night bar.

It was all the stuff of a great first date. There were no tearful outpourings of childhood traumas or past relationships. He was inquisitive and perceptive. He offered a new perspective when hearing my old stories, and I liked the way his brain worked. It was refreshing.

When we left the second bar, I said, "You're very tall. How tall are you?"

"Six two."

"You seem taller."

"That's because I actually am six two."

One of the first men I'd met not to add an inch to his height. Also refreshing.

Doug stepped into the street to hail a taxi, and one pulled right up. I walked over to him, and our bodies angled for the approach to a kiss on the cheek to end the night.

My heel went into a pothole. I went forward, almost over, except he was standing right there. I fell into him, and grabbed him out of reflex.

"Hi," he said.

He would later kid me that I literally threw myself at him.

Date one could not have gone better. I started calling him Dream Date Doug. My mom reminded me that "Just Doug" could work out too. It was a happy oasis in an otherwise dark time. We had avoided the personal trauma and grief. I saved that for date number two.

It was in part that I already trusted Doug to hear it. And it was in part that I was overwhelmed. The day before our second date, I had been asked to answer ten questions for a DC politics blog—things like "If you went on a trip and could pack one thing, what would it be?" I'd put the quiz to Doug, and we'd had a great e-mail banter, answering and critiquing each other's answers all afternoon, leading up to our dinner the next night.

One of the questions was, "When did you last cry?" My answer was "today."

Doug saved his inquiry about that one until dinner. "Why did you cry yesterday?" he asked.

What the heck, I thought, and I dropped the old convicted-felon-stalker chestnut on him.

Doug was what I knew he would be: a good listener, and a strong shoulder. He also offered thoughts that helped me process what was happening. He had suggestions on how to keep me safe and well.

We were in Café Milano, another of the swanky restaurants in Georgetown, and among the waiters there was a man in a black tuxedo selling single red roses for the price of an entrée.

Doug nodded to the man.

"Don't, Doug," I said. "That's not necessary."

He still looked at the man in the tuxedo.

"I'm serious. Don't," I commanded.

Doug smiled. Warm, calm. "You're going to have a rose tonight."

Overruled. I loved that. I wasn't used to that, certainly not after I had commanded. It was another refreshing change. He was confident without being showy. Not at all a self-promoter.

Believe me, I've overruled Doug plenty, and that's one of the things that makes us work so well. We each have the strength and self-assurance both to overrule and to be overruled.

It's also nice to be with someone who can make decisions. Especially these days, I make hundreds of decisions each day at work. It's better to come home to a partner who can make decisions too.

Doug knew what he wanted out of life, which was right in line with my own discoveries about what I wanted for myself. He was an intellectual who was quick with a laugh. He reminded me of my dad.

I loved the rose, even though I've never been all that fond of flowers. Nothing against flowers, really. It's just that as a substitute for any real communication from a romantic interest, flowers are a cop-out. Every woman I know would rather have a heartfelt letter.

After dinner we stepped outside the restaurant to a late-summer DC night. I was going home and Doug back to his hotel, so we stopped near the restaurant entrance on the sidewalk.

I was very attracted to him. We'd laughed through

most of dinner, and all the while there was a building romantic connection. A kiss to end the night felt natural.

The problem was that I still had two armed security guards with me, 24/7. They were parked ten yards away and standing outside their car, looking at us.

Anyone could see a kiss was coming, especially two professionals paid to watch me. They might have been trained killers, but they were also gentlemen, and turned their backs.

Doug and I laughed at the situation, and then he came in for the kiss. I was so damn distracted that it wasn't one of my best.

Doug got in a taxi to his hotel, and I got in the backseat of my car, with the security driving. *Damn!* I thought. *Blew it.*

This was fixable, I knew. The next afternoon I had plans to see Doug again. I suggested we meet at his hotel. I was friendly with the security guys by that point. A girlfriend and I had given each of them nicknames. Outside Doug's hotel, I said, "Cougar, Viper, stay here. I'm going in alone."

I marched inside, took the elevator up to Doug's floor, and knocked. He answered, dressed and ready to go.

"Wait," I said. "Back inside the room for a minute."

"What's up?"

"I can do better."

"What do you mean?"

"The kiss. I was feeling self-conscious. I can do better."

Doug was instantly back in the room. "Great. Come in."

That was our first real kiss.

When Doug and I first started dating, Dan and I were separated but not yet officially divorced. Doug had also recently broken up with a long-term girlfriend. We met fresh off the heels of our former relationships. My friends marveled about this at the time. "How do you end a marriage and immediately find a guy like that?" my friend Laura would later ask me.

The answer was that I had gone through a major transformation the past year and a half, and as I changed myself for the better, better things started coming to me. I was settling for more. And "more" meant more *from myself.*

Doug is great looking, but it wasn't just his looks that drew me in. Doug is dignified but also fun. He went to a private boys' school in Philadelphia, where he won an award from teachers and students for being the all-around most decent guy. I probably sound like I'm bragging about him. I totally am.

On our second date, we bumped into a guy from his high school named Dan Murphy, who told me that Doug was good to everyone as a teenager, that he never participated in cliques, even though he was a popular guy. I joked that Dan was a plant, but I would come to see for myself that Doug is fundamentally *good*.

Doug does the thing that every woman on earth wants: if there's something wrong with me, he genuinely wants to know what it is. He never lets me get away with:

"What's wrong?"

"Nothing."

He presses for the truth. Just like my mom.

"Something is wrong," he will say. "What's going on?"

If we've both been busy with work for a while or tied up in our own responsibilities, he'll sometimes sit me down and say, "We need to talk. It feels like there's distance between us." And just as soon as we do, the distance is gone.

Doug is interested in everything. He constantly has his nose in a book. He's expanded my horizons. He is smarter than I am, though he denies it. In the beginning I thought he was too good to be true.

I remember, when we were first dating, saying to Major Garrett, my officemate, "He must be married . . . or gay . . . or a felon. Something has gotta be wrong with this guy." One time Doug sent me flowers at the office—a sweet but rather underwhelming bouquet.

"Well, he's not gay," Major quipped.

The truth was, Doug was unlike anyone I'd ever known. He was so confident but not slick, aloof enough to set me off-kilter but engaged enough to make me want more. I remember M'Lady Amy encouraging me to stay open-minded.

"You asked for something different," Amy said, "and the universe listened. Will you?"

Thank God I did.

About six months into our relationship, we celebrated New Year's Eve in Washington, DC. It was a fun night with a small group of friends, but Doug and I got in a fight—raised voices back and forth, a good old-fashioned argument.

Because we'd been dating long-distance for about six months by then, Doug was staying at my place for that weekend. We went back there in the middle of the fight. Doug went to lie down, but I was too angry for sleep, so I took out my journal and went to the living room to write.

I wrote for about twenty minutes and then heard Doug coming down the stairs. He walked over and sat next to me.

"Put that away," he said.

I was still upset, but his voice didn't sound combative. "Why?" I asked.

"Because," he said, "you're writing the wrong things."

I'll never forget that moment. It sparked the single best, single most important conversation in our lives. We talked from 2:00 a.m. until the sun came up. The next morning, I knew this man would someday be my husband. I had officially gotten the message: more risk, more imperfection, more openness and honesty—in my work, my friendships, and my love life.

Within weeks, Roger Ailes promoted me to full-time anchor, making me the cohost of a new program called *America's Newsroom*. It aired from 9:00 a.m. to 11:00 a.m. and I would be partnered with the highly respected Bill Hemmer. In New York. Where Doug was.

Brit would have preferred I spend another year or two in Washington, but he knew he couldn't stop it—he agreed it was time for me to go. Good-bye, DC, hello, Doug. We kept separate apartments, which we maintained until after (spoiler alert—we're married) our wedding. Doug helped me find a place and lent me some money to cover the ridiculous sums required for the first-last-security-deposit of the New York City rental market. I was still nowhere near my law firm salary range.

I knew living in the same city would make or break us, and I had a feeling that it would make us. I was in the right place mentally. I'd done the work. I'd changed.

For so many years, I'd been approaching my relationships inauthentically. I think my father's death made me determined not to be left again. That meant being "perfect," in my mind. I had to do what it took to maintain a relationship; being abandoned was simply not an option. But spending your life pretending you are something other than what you are is unsustainable. Amy helped me see that I should be focused on what *I* wanted, not on what those around me desired. That helped me make my decision about Dan. It also later helped me see that I wanted Doug, who loved me with all of my imperfections and even, perhaps, because of them.

14

All the Days of My Life

I'd been in TV for about four years when Roger offered me the position on *America's Newsroom*. He began with an invitation to lunch at the Fox News offices in New York. He and his top executives had recently held an off-site meeting to discuss the future of Fox News. Apparently the one thing they all agreed on was moving me into an anchor role, and pairing me with Bill Hemmer, one of the most talented and likable men on TV. Over a plate of chicken, Roger asked me if I thought I was ready for a full-time anchor gig. I looked at the chicken and lied—"Yes, I am more than ready." All I could do was hope he believed it more than I did.

Hemmer and I launched the show in January 2007. We were seated in a tiny studio on top of a tiny oval stage. Our producer was a newsman by the name of Tom Lowell—a rhetorical gunslinger who followed no rules other than Produce a Great Newscast. I was the envy of every woman at Fox, all of whom were hoping to marry Hemmer. Of course, I was madly in love with Doug, Hemmer had a long-time girlfriend, and from the very start we were more like brother and sister. The first day on the air, we popped a big number—unusually big for the 9:00 a.m. show. It was a precedent we'd live up to for three more years. The show was an instant hit.

Much like when I'd first started in TV, being in the anchor chair was moot court all over again—I knew from the first time I sat down that I was exactly where I was supposed to be. And just as I did in law school, I was about to gain an education in very hard work that required very thick skin.

Hemmer and I clicked immediately, and I loved going to work each day. At first I was pretty stiff—I hadn't found my on-air groove yet as an anchor. Nine times out of ten I was happy to let Hemmer handle any breaking news, because it still scared me, and our on-air banter was kept to a minimum. But as time went on, I handled more of the Fox News alerts (Hemmer would offer me pointers, hand me wire copy, or otherwise help me—the man's a prince) and started to take more risks on the air—with conversation and sometimes topic selection.

Possibly my single favorite broadcast was an episode of *America's Newsroom* when we took a hard look at a therapeutic program called Radical Honesty. I'd thought "radical honesty" was something the Kelly family had invented, but evidently no, it was an actual movement. A psychotherapist named Brad Blanton from the middle of Virginia advocated for a world without lies, and A. J. Jacobs had written a must-read, hilarious, impossible-to-tear-your-eyes-away-from article about him for *Esquire*.[1] The rules of the Radical Honesty system were: You have to tell the truth all the time. You may not use a filter.

For the story, Jacobs lived the program for a few weeks. He had to tell a friend he'd forgotten his fiancée's name and was annoyed he hadn't been invited to their wedding. He had to tell his wife he wasn't really listening to her when she was talking, and that he was wondering if his occasional mistake of calling his wife by his own sister's name meant that he secretly wanted to sleep with his sister. At a business meeting, he had to tell an editor he'd looked down her shirt. He veered back and forth between alienating people and feeling elated by how much he was connecting with them. It was spectacular.

I loved everything about that article, and having Brad Blanton on the air made for what is still one of my all-time favorite days of work. Hemmer and I decided that for two whole hours, we would run the show on the Radical Honesty program.

"I thought that guest was fascinating," Hemmer said at one point in the broadcast. "Didn't you, Megyn?"

"I wasn't listening," I said. "I was preparing for my own segment."

We then had a plastic surgeon on, who said of the advice he gives his patients, "I give my patients tits—tips," and then completed the sentence. I burst out laughing.

Hemmer, who is a gentleman, would never ordinarily have commented, but he had to be radically honest, so he acknowledged the slip-up with a devilish grin: "He said tits—tips." We both giggled live on the set. Offstage, the guests asked our bookers, "What is wrong with them?" The bookers tried to explain that this was a one-day thing.

When Blanton came on at the end of the show, I wondered how it would go, speaking live on the air with him, given his hard-core rules of human interaction. Would he insult my looks? Tell me he wanted to sleep with me? Tell me he thought I was stupid? But he was terrific. He later said he was flattered that I'd clearly done my homework on his program. The truth is, I felt like I'd been doing it for about forty years.

Another time I was sitting with Hemmer when Hillary Clinton had a famous exchange in the Congo. A student asked a question that, when translated, seemed to be asking Hillary what "Mr. Clinton" thought about a proposed trade deal with China.

"Wait, you want me to tell you what my husband thinks?" she said.[2] "My husband is not the secretary of state, I am. You want my opinion? I will tell you my opinion. I am not going to be channeling my husband."

For her, it was a pretty serious brushback. She's no Chris Christie.

Hemmer uncharacteristically wanted to talk about our feelings on this. He didn't usually talk opinions, but he wanted to on that one.

"I don't know if that was appropriate," he said.

"What was inappropriate about it?" I asked.

"Stay above it, you know?"

"She's supposed to let people ask her about her husband's opinions when she's secretary of state?"

"I'm just saying," he said, "take the high road."

"Sometimes people get irritated," I said, growing annoyed. "It's happening right now!"

One of the challenges of being an anchor is understanding how and when to bring emotional honesty into the discussion. I used to err on the side of formality, being new to journalism and coming out of the DC reporting ranks. But I soon realized that in some instances—in particular on cable—it's okay to take a risk here or there. If I saw someone speeding down a neighborhood road at eighty miles per hour in some police chase, for example, I never hesitated to call him an idiot. We'd watch these scenarios play out with stupid criminals a fair amount on morning TV, and it wasn't unusual for me to end a segment with "Enjoy prison!"

I'd never be out there calling for the troops to come home from Iraq, or taking positions on policy or politics, but when it was an obvious situation and the audience and anchor were pretty clearly having a moment together, I learned it was okay to share a little of myself.

I think too many anchors fail to realize you can express exasperation or empathy or connect with your audience, without inappropriately oversharing. Charlie Gibson talked about this realization in regard to his coverage of September 11.[3] He was co-anchoring *Good Morning America* that day with Diane Sawyer. When the second plane hit, her response was "Oh my God." He continued reporting the news and said, matter-of-factly, "Now we know what's going on. We're under attack."

Gibson later said he regretted forgetting his humanity in that moment, and that he admired Diane for reacting in a human way, thinking of all the lives being lost. He wished he had taken a moment for that too before immediately charging ahead in journalist mode, going on about the whys and hows and whos. To be too professional in such a situation can be just as inappropriate as displaying emotions full-bore. I try to maintain this balance on the air. If a moment calls for seriousness, I respect that. If it calls for humor, well, I'm your gal.

A very well known female anchor once told me it was "*very* risky" to use humor on the air. She discouraged me from doing it. Thank God I didn't listen to her. I'm no Tina Fey, and I don't need to have people rolling in the aisles while they're watching the broadcast, but I think a flash of mild amusement is gift enough to people trying to get the news. Sometimes my attempts at humor land; often they do not. Either way, I amuse myself, and that is half the battle.

Not long after I was offered *America's Newsroom*, I received another proposal—one that would change the rest of my life. One evening in September 2007, at the shore in New Jersey, Doug asked me to marry him. We walked to the end of a dock where Doug's dad kept a sailboat and watched the sunset with my dogs at our feet (later our dogs, by adoption).

As we watched the sun go down, Doug got down in front of me. My mind raced but was slow to process.

He's going down on one knee. There's only one reason men do that. He's taking off his sunglasses. I'm taking off my sunglasses. Why are we taking off our sunglasses? It's still bright out. He's saying something now. What? It sounds like a proposal. Yes, a proposal. A proposal?

Doug and I had talked about love and kids. Everything was happy and naturally headed this way, but we'd never discussed a thing about a wedding.

I was busy anchoring two hours each day. Doug's work running his company had gotten intense. He was gone every other week to San Francisco, London, or the company headquarters in Palm Beach Gardens. And so I was caught completely by surprise.

"Will you marry me?" he asked.

What? I thought. Images began flashing through my head: marrying this man, having children with this man, growing old with him . . . The answer was and remains obvious.

"Yes," I said.

Apparently it took me a few beats. Doug later told me that in awaiting my response, he had a moment of worry that he'd asked too soon. A few days earlier, he had met my mother and stepfather in secret to ask for their blessing. (It was a miracle my mother kept his secret long enough for Doug to propose.) My mom's first response had been, "Does Megyn know? Is it a little fast?" While I was standing there stunned, Doug was thinking, *Uh-oh. Her divorce is too recent. She's not ready. Maybe it is too soon.* But it's never too soon to start the life you want.

My wedding to Doug, on March 1, 2008, was easily one of my happiest days.[4] We were married at Oheka Castle in Huntington, a gorgeous 1919 mansion on the highest point of Long Island. It was a wintry day. Out the window there were beautiful flurries with fat white flakes slowly drifting in the air. Inside, we had cherry blossoms everywhere. There were fireplaces at either end of the huge white ballroom, which had an elegant crystal chandelier. I wore a long white sheath dress with a deep V in front by an amazing designer named Joanna Mastroianni. All of our closest friends came. Even our dogs, Bailey and Basha, were there.

Every part of that day was magical. My mom and Peter were in the bridal suite of the castle with me, along with my closest friends. Getting ready was joyful—I felt no stress, only excitement for the day and life to come. My mother-in-law Jackie and sister-in-law Diane were also there—two women who would become hugely important figures to me.

Jackie has Doug's quiet dignity. She is gentle, smart, loving, and humble. I have since gone through a lot with Jackie at my side—from childbirth to sleepless nights with newborns. She has never once passed judgment, never offered a harsh or interfering word. More often than not, she was telling me to take a nap, or rubbing my back and telling me I am a good mother. She is my model for how to be a mother-in-law someday to my own children's spouses. I have only ever felt one way about her—I love her and want to be more like her.

If my own mother has given me the gift of a quick wit, Jackie has taught me when to use it. Jackie has shown me that you can communicate more sometimes with the arch of an eyebrow than an entire speech, and that sometimes silence really is golden. On that second lesson, of course, I could probably use some reinforcement. One time Doug and I were interviewing at a school for our son Yates. I started prattling on about this and that. I may have even dropped a harmless swear word. When it ended, and we left, Doug looked at me, eyebrows up.

"What?" I said. "I gotta be me!"

"What if you could be just like—ninety percent of you?" he joked. (He's stuck with the full 100 percent.)

Diane is my spiritual guide. She is a Duke- and Harvard-educated oyster fisherman in Cape Cod. Now there's something you don't hear every day. Like Jackie and Doug, she does not seek the spotlight. The *New York Times* got wind of Diane's situation a few years back and wanted to do an article on her, this brilliant Ivy League graduate oystering on the Cape. She declined. She doesn't need or desire attention. She finds that affirmation in herself. She devotes herself to spiritual growth and education. If I need a different way of looking at a problem, I call Diane. Her philosophy is very empowering—that everything we want or need in life we can have, and we can get for ourselves. (She also believes that you should say nice things to your water if you want to encourage its healing properties, but every sage has a few eccentricities.)

I love Diane's sense of humor and commitment to ritual. She wears a Santa costume to Midnight Mass every Christmas (it is actually a dog costume she bought at Petco, but somehow it works). She makes us all wear antlers or Santa hats at Christmas . . . American flag headbands on July 4 . . . enormous birthday hats on birthdays . . . you get the picture. Every birthday she sends old pictures of the feted person by e-mail throughout the family. Every week or so she sends me a thought of the day or an inspiration. Our kids love their Auntie Di and her partner, Brad. They'll drive down from the Cape and whirl through our apartment with positivity, talking to our children like they are forty (which they eat up)—Diane offering up endless energy for games or projects with them.

Doug's brothers, Ken and Will—both of whom had gone out of their way to welcome me to their family— were also there, along with Will's wife, Leslie, a native Texan full of southern verve. Like Doug, Ken and Will are gentlemen—thoughtful, smart, and funny. Many people wonder how Jackie and Doug's father, Manly, raised four kids who are so well adjusted and so connected. My take on it is that they gave them values but also room to breathe, and prioritized family at all turns. Manly was a brilliant doctor with a photographic memory. He died a few years ago. Shortly before, I asked him, "What was your favorite time with your kids?"

He thought a minute and said, "All of them."

I pressed him with a follow-up: "But if you had to choose one . . ."

"Right now," he said. He was eighty-three.

The morning of our wedding, Jackie pulled me aside and quietly offered me something old, borrowed, and blue: a beautiful embroidered handkerchief that she'd had when she was married nearly fifty years earlier. It brought tears to my eyes. Just about that same time, a staffer at the castle brought me a gift from Doug that completed the prewedding ritual—something new, a strand of pearls, the only real pearls I've ever owned. I held them and thought about Doug and his beautiful family. I remembered the fake pearls I wore in law school and beyond, going into interviews and trying to make my life better. Now I had.

Of course I invited Nana to the wedding. By this point, she was ninety-three years old. When Nana got married in 1934, she was nineteen years old and wore a white linen suit that cost five dollars. She would go on to have two children, five grandchildren, and eleven great-grandchildren. Over the course of her later years, as her health turned a bit, she'd had a mastectomy. She's nearly deaf. She's lost her vision in one eye. But one thing she's never lost is her sense of humor.

"May-gyn, my love," she said, "I got one eye, one breast, two hearing aids, and even dey don't work worth a damn. Ahm just not up to it."

"Nan," I said, "that is a great excuse. I love you. We'll be thinking of you."

It was a beautiful service. Kelly Wright, my old friend from the early-morning shift at Fox, officiated. He is a pastor in Virginia Beach. I managed to keep from crying, except at the very end of my vows—"I will love you, and honor you, all the days of my life."

The passage of time. A beginning, and a promised ending. Life is so bittersweet that way.

I look at the photos now from my wedding, and the ones that make me smile the widest are the ones of all of us dancing—Doug, me, and our brothers, dancing hard. Especially, for reasons that should be obvious to anyone who's heard it, to Bon Jovi's "Livin' on a Prayer," which became our wedding song. It doesn't get more joyful than that.

Doug and I slept at the bridal suite at the castle and then went to Cabo the next day. We were on a cliff overlooking the sea, with a Jacuzzi and a small pool. The place where we stayed came with a butler and a chef. I said to Doug when we got there, "What exactly does one do with a butler?"

Flash forward to the end of the honeymoon—"Oh, Edgar! I've had to refill my own margarita glass again!" It was luxurious and amazing and far too short.

Ten years later, I'm happy to know that Doug wasn't too good to be true. My amazing initial impressions of him were accurate. Somehow, I landed him. Somehow, he saw something in me, too.

I think one of the secrets to our success is that we look at each other through the most generous lens. I know who he is as a man, and I believe in that man's character. Everything he does is interpreted from there. We root for and are unafraid to be honest with each other. We both believe that the harder a thing is to say to your loved one, the more important it generally is to say. We fight, but we never fight dirty. Dr. Phil says of fighting in relationships, "How can you win when the person you love most is losing?" Doug and I live this.

We are generous with each other, and with our support for one another. At one of the presidential debates in 2012, down in Orlando, Doug showed up and surprised me. He came over, kissed me, and offered me a few words of encouragement before I went onstage. My friend and makeup artist at the time, Maureen, said, "Now, that's a man." (More than one woman has said exactly that to me about Doug: "That's a man.")

He's not afraid to tell you how he feels. And yet he's not particularly emotional. I've only seen him come close to crying once in our relationship. He will well up here and there over our kids, but I've never seen him actually shed a tear. And I'm okay with that. I find a certain amount of reserve to be attractive. It's the opposite of how I am.

I recently realized that since I've been with Doug, men have stopped hitting on me. I believe that's thanks to an energy I put off: *Don't even bother, you have no chance.* I have more women friends now, both because of the work I did with Amy and because I think women know when someone poses a threat to their relationship. There was a time I put off a threatening vibe. I don't think I knew what true devotion was. These days women know I don't want their husbands. I'm deeply in love with my own.

15

The Best Line

Early in the courtship, Doug and I were sitting around my living room. He was rumpled, in jeans and a white T-shirt. He looked so good, and I felt such love for him. Turning toward me, he said, "By the way, if you don't want children, you should tell me soon."

It was one of those moments you never forget. Suddenly I felt flush with excitement and love and pleasure at the prospect before me: children. I was in my mid-thirties. Doug looked at me with those eyes, and the idea of my children was born in that moment. I saw the possibility of them and of our family, and it was almost as if we'd already met. As if I had just a momentary glimpse of them—the way when you close your eyes at the end of a long day, for a second your dream from the night before comes back—there they were, but just for a beat. And then, just as quickly, gone . . . for the time being. The next day, I said to my stepsister Liza, "I think I've met the father of my children."

I was thirty-seven when we got married in March 2008. Yates, our oldest, was born eighteen months later, in September 2009. I'd found out I was pregnant with him just before Barack Obama's first inauguration. I took the test early in the morning, and bubkes, no double line. Doug and I had been trying for several months by this point and had one miscarriage already, so I was frustrated at yet another month of disappointment. I threw the test in the garbage, dejected.

Later, after showering and getting dressed, I saw it sitting there in the garbage and—as I had done with about twenty other tests over the past months—picked it out of the garbage just to see if maybe I had read it wrong. And sure enough, there it was: a faint, barely perceptible second line. My first message from my son, delivering the best line any man ever could.

My heart stopped. My excitement soared. I could not take my eyes off it! This little white wand might as well have been the baby itself, the way I cherished it, protected it, and checked and rechecked it about a thousand times that morning.

I took another test. Same thing: an ever-so-slight-but-definitely-there second line. My child! I was meeting my child. That's how it felt. My first knowledge of him. It all happened: the instant desire to take care of him, to protect him, to nurture him, to know him. Of course at the time I did not know if it was a boy or a girl, nor did I care. But I knew I was now a mother, and the world has never looked the same since.

Doug was stunned—he had spent the morning telling me not to worry about the earlier (and, as it turned out, wrong) results, reassuring me that we'd get there eventually. First he wanted to hold the double-lined test, to see it with his own eyes. Then he wanted to hold me.

My friends at work had only positive reactions. James Rosen, a good friend of mine at Fox and a correspondent in the DC bureau, made me laugh with his response. James is one of the most clever, interesting people you'll ever meet. He is obsessed with the Beatles, Watergate, and Woody Allen. His nickname for me is "The Perfect Storm," which has a nice ring to it as long as I don't think too hard about how I've been trying to conquer my desire to be perfect, and about how the story by the same name is tumultuous and sad and they all die in the end.

When I told him I was pregnant, James sent me an e-mail, joking, **Ah! This child will be a grand and glorious testament to the Jewish faith. . . . Oh wait. It's**

Doug's baby? Never mind. Congratulations anyway. He and his wife, Sarah, have two beautiful kids of their own.

I had a relatively good pregnancy, although the nausea was prolonged. My morning sickness lasted through nineteen weeks, and going on the air each day with Hemmer while feeling like I wanted to vomit had its challenges.

Hemmer might very well be the nicest, most patient man you'll ever meet. My general philosophy about him is this: if you don't get along with Hemmer, it's *you.* And let me tell you, in the winter of 2009, it was absolutely me. I used to arrive at the office around 5:30 a.m., feeling terrible. I'd study the news for a few hours and get my hair and makeup done, all the while wishing I could go back to bed and curl up in the fetal position. I remember saying to my makeup artist at the time, "If you could only know the afternoon me—you'd like me so much better."

Bill, of course, was exactly the opposite in demeanor and disposition. I distinctly remember Bill coming out to the set one morning and cheerfully booming, "What's the story, Morning Glory?"

In response, I thought, *The story is "Shut the hell up, Bill."*

Poor Bill. As far as I am concerned, that man is a saint.

I worked up until the very last minute. Thursday night I was doing my weekly *O'Reilly Factor* hit at 8:00 p.m., and Friday morning I delivered Yates. I had all of my children in New York, where my amazing doctor, Elizabeth Eden, personally delivered each child.

When I went into the hospital, Doug and I were bursting with anticipation. We even videotaped the empty predawn New York City streets on the way into the hospital. *"Check out that sidewalk!"* Everything seems more exciting when one is about to meet one's child for the first time. One of the first stops upon getting to the maternity ward was anesthesia. I'll never forget sitting on the table in the OR, waiting for the anesthesiologist. There I was, a beached whale in a gown that covered far too little, when he came bounding in. He saw my exposed rear end first, then saw my front and said, "Megyn Kelly! Oh my God! I love your show!"

"Yep, that's me," I said, thinking, *Don't you have some drugs to administer?*

"I have something for you!" he exclaimed.

An epidural? I thought, hopefully.

"My book! I have a copy for you. You should have me on to talk about how to enjoy your labor."

How 'bout we stop talking about it, and start actually doing it, Doc?

Becoming a mother is the most profound thing that's ever happened to me. It is the point in my life that divided everything into before and after. My friend told me, just before I gave birth, "Now you will know what it is like to have your heart walking around outside of your body," and that has proven to be absolutely right. That feeling I had upon becoming an anchor—"I was born to do this"—was dwarfed by the feeling I had on seeing my son for the first time—"I cannot go on if I don't get to do this." My career change brought me happiness. My child's birth changed my understanding of what happiness really is.

Being a mother helps define me. It also terrifies me—the intensity of this love, the deep, spiritual need to be with my children and to have them be well in a world that is so fickle and unpredictable. It has humbled me, enlightened me, and enhanced my relationship with God.

Maternity leave with Yates was transformative in so many ways. I was learning how to be a mother—by doing it, by reading about it, by talking to my own mother, but mostly by instinct. My mom stayed with us for a bit and gave me some tips. Mostly she cooked—

enough to feed a kingdom—and I was happy I didn't
have to think about it. Doug and I spent a lot of special
time together during those months—we couldn't get
enough of our little man, who we took with us everywhere. Yates never wanted for attention.

Shortly after I returned home, Roger called me to
congratulate me. "I'll be back soon," I assured him, if
soon meant sixteen weeks.

"Don't worry about that," he said, "what you're
doing is more important."

When I finally returned to work, I cried. It was
very hard to leave my baby in the mornings. I remember thinking how bizarre it was to see myself with the
Fox hair and makeup on. I looked and felt like an adult
again. My first time on the air, it was for an *O'Reilly* hit.
I was a bit stiff. I was tempted to speak in baby talk. But
by the second time, things felt more familiar. "There I
am," I thought. And I realized it was actually good to be
back. That there was something important at the office,
too. A piece of me I loved, a piece I needed.

That's not to say it was easy to leave Yates in the
morning. But I knew I needed to go, and that my son
would be getting the best version of me if I could go
and do this thing I also loved to do before coming home
to him and holding him in my arms.

People say Yates is my twin, but I think he's a mini

Doug. He came into this world a sweet old soul and he remains that way to this moment. Once, when he was five, we were walking home in the snow, catching the falling snowflakes on our tongues. Yates looked up at me and Doug and said, "This is my life and I'm loving it."

Doug was very shy when he was a child; Yates is not shy, but he is reserved. He assesses situations if it's a crowded room. But once he's satisfied that it's for him, he isn't afraid to run in. He's also not afraid to play on his own if that's what he prefers. Yates isn't afraid of much, actually. Much like his mother did, he loves monster stories—I'm considering dusting off those old Alfred Hitchcock 45s.

Yates is athletic, with terrific hand-eye coordination. Doug is too modest to say Yates got this from him, but he sure doesn't get it from me. Yates is considerate and perceptive and bright. The responsibility of nurturing that beautiful mind for the next thirteen years is overwhelming to me. (Please forgive me for going on—I'm sure other parents understand.) We're still trying to decide if we should tell him how smart he is. I'm leaning toward yes, since radical honesty probably trumps keeping the ego in check. There will be other opportunities to keep him humble.

For a young child, you would not believe how much he considers the feelings of others. When he was three, he learned to ride a bike without training wheels. Yates saw his friend ride into the playground on a bike with training wheels, which was totally age-appropriate. The friend was delighted to be riding at all. Yates, whose bike was parked nearby, congratulated his buddy and when we were walking away, he said, "Maybe let's wait a minute—I don't want him to feel bad seeing me without training wheels." He wasn't yet four. That's how he is. A lovely boy.

This doesn't mean he never says the wrong thing. Like when I was pregnant with his little sister. Yates came over to me and put his hand on my stomach. "It's getting bigger," I said to him. "Yes," he responded. "And your bottom's getting bigger too."

Recently we flew to visit their Auntie Di in Cape Cod. Yates looked out the window and exclaimed, "I feel like I could reach out and grab the whole world." There's no doubt in my mind, he will.

During my maternity leave with Yates, Roger promoted me. When I came back, I'd be launching my own show—*America Live*, a two-hour daytime program executive-produced by Tom Lowell. It was different not having a co-anchor—no one to play off, no one to help. The humor and reactions had to be done directly to camera—it was a totally different dynamic.

I missed Hemmer. But I also knew this was a great new challenge for me—I had to anchor solo, and help produce my own broadcast. I had to make decisions, handle all the breaking news, and step into a leadership position.

Much as with *America's Newsroom*, Tom Lowell and I worked to turn what was previously a struggling time slot into a tent pole for the ratings. From the start, the show took off—the numbers were strong, and grew even stronger.

I also began to take on more special coverage responsibility. Brit had retired after the 2008 election—a sad moment for all of us, although I was happy he'd still be working part-time. Roger needed an election night anchor, and chose to pair me with my colleague Bret Baier. It felt strange to be taking that baton from him—Brit Fucking Hume, of all people. I think Bret and I had an inferiority complex at first (and probably still do to this day). But we were happy Brit supported Roger's decision, and Bret and I were pals, so the pairing felt natural.

Slowly but surely, I was learning that having a family might not be an impediment to my career. This allowed me to pursue motherhood as enthusiastically as my career without fear that the two were incompatible. Working mothers go through enough as it is; to have a company that makes it easy on you is an enormous boon.

I thoroughly enjoyed my stint in the afternoons. In retrospect, I think I didn't know how good I had it. I was on TV two hours a day, anchoring a show that was succeeding. I had a major role in election coverage, including presidential debates, and was always offered a role on any big story. I was moderately well known, but not to the point where it was life-changing. And I felt like I was succeeding and had balance—an elusive achievement for any working parent.

Relaxed at the anchor desk, I started to take more risks. I battled fiercely with then-congressman Anthony Weiner—who was smug and condescending at times but terrific TV—on matters like the death tax and Obamacare. Weiner liked to fight, and I figured, what the hell. Almost all of these segments went viral. I sparred with former GOP congressman Tom Tancredo, who came on the show and said President Obama should be impeached—"All right, Congressman, that's ridiculous," I said. "How does this raise the level of debate?"

Dr. Keith Ablow came on and tried to say Chaz Bono shouldn't be allowed on *Dancing with the Stars* because watching him could turn kids transgender—a preposterous notion. I told him, "To me, it seems like you're adding to the hate." It felt like another driving-eighty-miles-per-hour-on-a-suburban-street moment—just call it for what it is. While some accused me of over-stepping my bounds, I didn't mind the brushback. I was starting to learn, it's part of the job.

I continued my weekly stint with Bill O'Reilly. We had a few epic battles that made big headlines, particularly over First Amendment issues. For example, O'Reilly had been railing on the vile Westboro Baptist Church, the group that protests the funerals of dead military veterans with posters that read "God hates fags" and include other hateful, bigoted, antigay messages. I forcefully condemned the group's protests, but defended their legal right to do it, explaining to Bill that this was classic free speech. He thought I was out of my skull. I wasn't very popular, defending the right of these hateful people to protest near a grieving military family, but the law is the law, and I called it as I saw it. Ultimately, the US Supreme Court agreed with me, upholding the First Amendment rights of this so-called church, in an eight-to-one decision. In pushing myself to take risks, I'd found a new comfort zone, a growing sense of authority.

And then I got pregnant again—within nine months of Yates's birth. As with my first pregnancy, I became more emotional than usual. I remember sitting in the doctor's office with Doug, waiting to take the blood test to see if I really was expecting. The show *The Price Is Right* was on the waiting room TV. On at that moment was the game where you try to match four items with their prices, then pull a lever to see if you've matched them correctly. The female contestant, an African American woman in her sixties, ran around frantically trying to match the items. With no time to spare, she did it! And she won a new car! She was elated! Doug looked over at me. I had tears streaming down my face.

"I think the blood test is just a formality at this point," he said.

As I grew bolder on the air, I also grew bolder off the air. When Fox PR asked me if I'd want to pose for *GQ*, I said sure. *Well,* I thought, *that would be a fun way to mark hitting forty.* It never occurred to me not to do it. I never considered that I might have to choose between being a serious newswoman and publicly showing a saucier side of myself in a respected magazine.

So I did, and it was fun, though I grew a bit concerned about how much my pregnancy was showing when the photographer said to me, "You're very brave." I was wearing a black slip that looked identical to a dress I'd worn to the Correspondents' Association Dinner a year earlier. The only difference was that in this case, I had a bit of cleavage, which I was kind of proud of—my baby had created something not normally there.

There was some backlash when the issue came out. Some fellow female journalists e-mailed me asking, **Why? Why would you do that?**

I felt no need to justify it. I don't buy into that line of thinking that says we must only be these hard-charging professionals or we sacrifice our credibility. By this point, I had zero fear that people were not going to take me seriously. I wrote back the same thing to all of them: "It's like holding your crying baby on the airplane and looking around at the other passengers. Those who get it require no apology, and those who don't, never will."

I believe I fit into a new archetype for women that thankfully we're seeing more often: multidimensional. Actress Gwyneth Paltrow recently alluded to this when she was honored at *Variety*'s Power of Women event,[1] noting that in modern-day America it's possible for a woman to be "nurturing, maternal, sexual." The same is true for women outside of Hollywood—you can be a tough questioner on a presidential debate stage *and* someone who does softer interviews that play more to a subject's humanity, like Barbara Walters. You can be playful and sexy in *GQ and* sophisticated and feminine on the cover of *Vanity Fair*. You can be a doting mother *and* a tough professional. You can have class *and* drop a good swear once in a while. You can just be you— whoever you happen to be.

I had similar blowback after I went on Howard Stern's show. Journalists from Anderson Cooper to Barbara Walters have done the same, but my appearance was treated as unprecedented by some. Stern is a great interviewer—provocative as hell, that's obvious, but fun and probing and clever. I enjoyed it immensely. That visit, too, was PG-13—even Howard would later say (after Trump and some of his fans attacked my Stern appearance years later) that I had been a complete lady on the program. And being a lady doesn't mean ignoring all aspects of one's sexuality, especially on a show known for its fun, bawdy exchanges.

Now, would I have done *GQ* or Stern one year into broadcasting? Of course not. But I had already established myself as a serious person by the time I took these risks. And I was trying to reach out to viewers who might not normally watch Fox News. Some believe a newswoman shouldn't go chasing an audience; do a great program, and the audience will come to you. But I figured widening the tent was worth a try. And I still feel that way today.

So that was the beginning of my pregnancy with

Yardley. By the end, no men's magazine would have dreamed of photographing me in a slip. I felt enormous—even more than with my first baby—and the viewers watched me expand by the day, sending lovely, supportive messages (it's not all vile on Facebook and Twitter). By the end of my nine months, the director of my show had stopped taking side shots of me at the desk. "It's starting to feel voyeuristic," he explained. When I look back at clips of the show from that time, I am grateful for his discretion.

In April 2011, I gave birth to our daughter Yardley. She is a ball of fire. She could have negotiated a better Iran deal than John Kerry did. She's strong. And she knows what she wants. When she was four, I said, "Yards, come sit next to me on this chair. Let's have a conversation."

"No," she said.

"That's rude," I said, kidding her.

"What's also annoying," she said, "is you telling me how rude I am." Another time, she agreed to stop sucking her thumb. I saw her go for the thumb that night.

"Yards, I thought you were going to work on not sucking your thumb."

"I am," she said, "but not today. Or tomorrow."

Yardley will run around the living room fifty times before sitting down—the same thing she enjoyed as a baby when my mom would visit and stroll a crying Yardley around and around our dining room table into the wee hours. At school, Doug and I have made it clear that we don't want them to discipline that energy out of her. I have very few worries about Yardley, because it's clear she will take life by the reins.

Yards is also very loving, just like Yates. Often I wake up to her gently kissing my forehead. My one friend used to wake up to her child lifting up her eyelids. I thought, *My God, that sounds awful.* I'm grateful that my daughter eases me into the day instead.

Not long ago, she saw me crying at her preschool graduation. "Why are you crying, Mama?" "They're tears of joy, honey." And now when she sees me well up, she'll ask, "Are those joy of tears?" I love that: joy of tears. Because that's true too.

She sometimes reminds me of a pro wrestler. She is freakishly strong, as is my sister, Suzanne. If you need a jar opened or a dresser moved? They are your girls. That trait skipped me, but Yards has the gift. She can pick any of us up, and constantly tries to. Her younger brother doesn't particularly enjoy Yardley hauling him around, but it's his own fault for being so cute and portable.

Yardley and Yates have a special relationship. Once, she asked him, "Yates, are we friends?"

Yates looked over at her. "We're brother and sister, Yards, but we're also friends."

With Yardley, I took another four-month maternity leave. Unlike *America's Newsroom,* this leave was different, because I knew I'd be returning to this anchor post. I worried a bit: Would the viewers forget about me? Would my ratings dip while I was out?

I decided not to sweat that, to just focus on my children and see what happened. Lo and behold, we used fill-in anchors, and the world kept turning on its axis. My job was still there waiting for me after my leave was over. And why? Because I was good at it. They wanted me in the chair. All that time I could have spent asking for opportunities, I had channeled instead into getting *better.* The work paid off. My job was secure.

Returning to *America Live* after Yardley was as it had been with Yates—hard. But I muddled through. One of the things about TV is, you have to play hurt, and you have to do it convincingly. You can't go out and mope on the job.

On my first day back, I had a spirited back-and-forth with radio host Mike Gallagher that attracted a lot of attention. He knew I wanted to discuss his attack on my maternity leave, which he had publicly mocked while I was out. I respected that he showed up, knowing we were going there.

"Is maternity leave, according to you, a racket?" I asked him on air.[2]

"Well, do men get maternity leave?" he said with a jocular smile on his face.

"Guess what? Yes, they do," I shot back with a grin. "It's called the Family and Medical Leave Act."

Indeed, if men would like to take three months off to care for their newborn babies, they can, thanks to the law signed by Bill Clinton. As for women, I pointed out, the United States is the only country in the advanced world that doesn't *require* paid maternity leave. Some companies simply offer it because they know it's the right thing to do. Others are forced to offer unpaid leave, thanks to the FMLA. Still others have no policy at all. A staggering one in four new moms return to work after just *two weeks'* maternity leave.[3] That is seriously wrong.

I wanted to know what it was about carrying a baby for nine months and then giving birth that Gallagher didn't think warranted "a few months off so bonding and recovery can take place."

Having had two babies by this point, I was amused at his notion that maternity leave was somehow a "vacation." Up all night, nursing a newborn, breasts in pain, sleep-deprived, physically depleted, completely exhausted, with zero time to even shower—it didn't feel much like a trip to the Bahamas.

It was a good-natured exchange—Gallagher's a good guy—but he knew I had him. I heard from viewers that the exchange opened a few eyes on the issue. And yet that staunch defender of liberal principles Jon Stewart apparently took offense—can you say Fox Derangement Syndrome?[4]

Stewart went on the air a night later and offered a lengthy hit piece, criticizing my push for better maternity leave for women.[5] To say his presentation was dishonest would be a gross understatement. Stewart played earlier clips of me appearing to question things like food stamps, suggesting that I was against any entitlements except ones that might benefit *me*. This was way off base. For one thing, as a news anchor, I would never take a position favoring or opposing entitlements. I get paid to play devil's advocate. This is my job; it's pretty straightforward.

Moreover, Stewart's assertion that I was pushing for *government-mandated* maternity leave (i.e., an "entitlement") assumed too much. Maybe I'm for that, maybe I'm not—I've never said publicly, and I'm not about to here. But touting the value of "paid leave" does not necessarily mean support for any government involvement; it could mean we ought to pressure employers to voluntarily offer this benefit, as mine does, which has been proven to help families and to attract and retain top female talent.

And finally, the notion that advocating for paid leave would somehow benefit *me* was absurd. I work for Fox News. My deals are by contract. No policies need to be changed for me to get paid maternity leave. Nor is it generally people in positions like mine for whom this is an issue. I have bargaining power, and I'm also well paid. Many are not so fortunate.

Stewart used to attack me fairly often during *America Live*. I spent far too much time worrying about these hits. I was young and still apprehensive of him. I feared that his attacks, however unfounded, were going to hurt me. He was very beloved. And, disturbingly, he was the primary news source for millions of young people, men in particular. Abby grew to loathe him.

"I'm a comic," he would say when people tried to talk to him about his role in the media or his journalistic responsibility.[6] But that was a cop-out. He wanted to be taken seriously on many issues—and *he was*, and *he knew he was*—as when he laudably advocated for 9/11 first responders. But he wanted to deny that reality when it suited him to do so.

One time on the air, I jokingly called Stewart "mean."

He picked up the phone and called me. He had me on the phone for over an hour, wanting to know why I thought he was mean. I told him that he took things out of context.

"We do not!" he said.

"You absolutely do all the time."

"Give me an example."

I gave him the example of the hit piece on my maternity leave.

"No," he said. "I had you on that! Totally self-serving!"

"Absolutely wrong." I pointed out the fallacy of his argument, including the fact that my maternity leave was set by contract and I needed no government mandate to get it.

He did not back down. "You *would* benefit because you would get 'psychic income' from knowing your comments helped people," he told me. It was like arguing with Jell-O.

We agreed to disagree. But he seemed genuinely bothered by the notion that I would think him dishonest or mean-spirited.

"This feels like you've sinned," I said, "and you

want absolution. Well, I'm not giving it. You're like the class bully."

"How?" he wanted to know.

"Because you love to pick on newspeople who can't respond."

"What do you mean, you can't respond?" he said. "You have a show!"

"I'm not Bill O'Reilly," I explained to him. "I'm a journalist. Most of the people you hit are journalists. What are we going to do, take time away from talking about Syria to address something on Comedy Central? Am I going to have my team waste their time pulling more complete clips to prove your cherry-picked clips are wrong? That's not what newspeople do. We don't have the staff or the platforms for that. We're trying to actually report the news."

Stewart and I did have one funny exchange in that call he made to me.

"You are the one person at Fox News I actually respect," he confessed toward the end, in an apparent moment of weakness.

"I hate myself for loving that," I responded in a weak moment of my own.

We talked a bit about our lives, our kids, our spouses. He spoke about his wife and her pregnancies.

"Just so you know," I said, "I was sitting on the couch nursing my newborn baby when I saw your latest hit piece on me. Good times."

"Not listening! *La-la-la-la-la-la!* Don't humanize yourself! *La-la-la-la-la-la!*"

I laughed, and we moved on—not friends, exactly, but not enemies either.

In retrospect, the Stewart bits don't bother me at all. But they were a wake-up call that I was now subject to a whole new level of scrutiny, and that I'd better be ready if I was going to make it in this business. I had put myself out there. Public scrutiny is part of the job. I had two choices: stop actually feeling wounded, or acknowledge the difficulty and not let it "dilute the content of my message." Either way, sitting around feeling sorry for myself was not an option.

I was learning how to do my job under fire. How to be a mother under fire. My children need me, regardless of what's happening in my professional life. And my viewers do too.

Sad about leaving your baby? Smile and do the news.

Worried about Jon Stewart trying to ruin your career? Smile and do the news.

How did I do that? I remembered who I was. These people didn't define me. Nor did they control me. Hell, they didn't even know me. With every hit I'd take, I felt that I was getting stronger. Yep, still standing. Here I am . . . right here.

Functioning in the face of adversity may not be fun, but it is a strength. It wasn't easy. But with practice, and I had plenty, I developed some grit. Hell, I had walked around the Upper West Side of Manhattan with my baby in a Fox News onesie. I could handle *this*.

Stewart's attack on my maternity leave segment didn't hamper my willingness to engage in strong discussions about women. Just a few months after that attack, Bill O'Reilly and I went head-to-head on sexism. He had told Judge Jeanine Pirro to "calm down" on his show as she was making an entirely legitimate argument. I was on a day later. "It's patronizing," I told him. "And it has a special connotation when a man says it to a woman on top of that."

Seriously, few things are as irritating as being told to "calm down." It's paternalistic, like a pat on the head. In April 2016, the Reverend Al Sharpton tried telling me to "calm down."

"Watch it," I warned him, and when he pleaded ignorance as to why, I suggested he speak to O'Reilly.

16

Now Everyone's Here

The first big election event Bret and I co-anchored together was the 2010 midterm elections. It was a big night, as Republicans seized control of the US House, two years into Barack Obama's presidency. However, it was child's play compared to two years later. From presidential debates to wall-to-wall convention coverage, Bret and I were in the middle of it all. By election night 2012, we were ready for anything. Thank God, because, boy, did we get it.

As the show was about to begin, the excitement in the studio built. Fox had rented a helicopter to shoot beauty shots of Times Square, and the Fox News logo lit up the buildings. The presidency would be decided tonight, and we knew we'd have well over ten million viewers watching. Bret and I stood before the cameras as the clock ticked down to the big show open. I looked at Bret and said, "This is quite a moment." He gave me a fist bump, and we were off.

Despite weeks of people like Dick Morris and Karl Rove and some pollsters, like Scott Rasmussen, telling us Mitt Romney was likely to win, it soon became clear that he would not. And yet Rove, a Fox News contributor and former George W. Bush guru, sat next to me at the anchor desk, arguing that the numbers even that night were pointing toward a Romney win. Based on the returns we had at hand, Rove's claim appeared, frankly, impossible.

I had seen Rove do this with the numbers in the past—it seemed he could take any poll and spin it however he liked. It was a skill, really, and he was quite good at it. This is the man who got George W. Bush elected twice to the presidency. Say what you will about him, there's a reason they called him the Architect.

He started pulling that on our set, and I asked him flat-out, "Is this just math you do as a Republican to make yourself feel better? Or is this real?" Stewart and others would make a lot out of that moment, as if I were taunting Rove, but I was genuinely trying to make sense of what he was saying. But the fun with Rove was not over yet.

The time came that evening when the Fox News decision desk was ready to call Ohio. For Barack Obama. Now the decision desk is a group of nerdy, lovable number crunchers who, whatever their personal political affiliation, have one mission and one mission only: to call the race correctly. Calling Ohio for President Obama meant one thing—the election was his, and Romney had lost.

The enormity of this moment was not lost on the decision desk. They told me later they went around the table, one by one, asking each man to raise his hand if he agreed with the call. It was unanimous: Ohio would be called, as would the presidency, and the 2012 race was over.

So imagine our surprise at the anchor desk when Karl Rove challenged the call, suggesting it was too early to call Ohio, based on the results he was seeing. Bret and I looked at Karl. We looked at each other.

"That's awkward," I said on the air, acknowledging the reality of the situation.

It was clear what needed to be done, and we did it. We pulled back the curtain, figuratively speaking, and I marched down to the decision desk and got some clarity. We let the whole thing play out live on the air, inviting the viewers in on the electric moment.

My walk out of the studio and down the hallway was seen by tens of millions of people around the globe. It was easily the most watched, most exciting TV moment of election night 2012, and we knew at the time that it was a big deal. I remember saying to two of the decision desk guys, Arnon Mishkin and Chris Stirewalt, "You realize, of course, this is going to be *everywhere* tomorrow."

They knew. On camera, I questioned them both about the call, and of course they stood by their decision, providing the logic and reasoning behind it. Thrust from a post behind the scenes to a moment on camera before an audience of millions, the guys remained completely unflustered. They had confidence in their judgment: Barack Obama had won Ohio, and had been reelected president of the United States.

It was a big moment for Fox News, and it was heralded by some unusual fans in the press the next day. None other than the *New York Times*'s David Carr wrote about that moment in a story called, "For One Night at Fox, News Tops Agenda."[1] Having worked at Fox News for so many years, I was used to the veiled shots in any compliment from the mainstream press.

We received dozens of requests for interviews with me in the days that followed, almost all of which we turned down. I wondered at the time just how lasting a moment this would be in the national memory of election coverage. Stirewalt and I had a drink later with the rest of the gang at a bar near Fox, debriefing about the night.

"So . . . Obama wins," I said to him.

"*Journalism* wins," Stirewalt responded. We raised our glasses and drank.

Right after that election, I got pregnant with Thatcher. I remember talking about the possibility of having a third child with my dear friend Janice Dean. We both understood it would be tough to manage—three kids, a busy career, another pregnancy on-air. I thought, *Maybe I shouldn't. I am doing well here. Will this interfere?* It didn't matter. I knew I wanted another baby. I said to Janice—and to myself—"We cannot make decisions about our children based on what works for Fox. We have to do what works for us." And what worked for me was to bring my third child into the world. I knew he was waiting for me and Doug to go get him. So we did.

I was newly pregnant when the terrible events of Newtown, Connecticut, happened. It was one of only two times I've ever had to visibly choke back tears on the air. I hadn't revealed that I was pregnant, and that story—oh, that devastating story. It was more than any human being could take. Later that night at home, Doug and I were talking about it. Yates was only three, and I was so thankful I didn't have to explain it to him—that he was too young to understand. Still, he overheard us talking in code. He looked at us, and heard a new word.

"What means hate?" he asked.

I will never forget that moment.

A year later, I would invite several of the Newtown family members onto the show to discuss smart gun and mental health policies. I gave them each a book Doug's own family had read faithfully in the months after Doug's father had passed—it's called *Healing after Loss*, and its daily meditations and prayers can provide some comfort to those in deep mourning.

The months passed, my pregnancy progressed, and I got bigger, in more ways than one. My career was thriving. My kids were thriving too. I felt torn, of course, between my work and my kids, and knew I needed more time with both on any given day. What I definitely did not need was a lecture from three men on how my career was terrible for my kids.

Fox Business host Lou Dobbs had invited two guests—conservative commentator Erick Erickson and liberal pundit Juan Williams—onto his show to discuss a report from the Pew Research Center that said women have become the breadwinners in 40 percent of households with children.[2] These guys were complaining publicly that this trend was one of the horsemen of the apocalypse. They really had been saying some crazy things on Fox Business about how damaging it was for children to have their mothers working, and how women were more the submissive type while men were really the dominant ones.

You can imagine how I felt watching this while at home with two young children and a third on the way. This is, as an aside, one of the beautiful things about diversity in the workforce—in this case, having a working mom as an anchor. The workforce is then not monolithic, and different viewpoints can be aired. I asked them both to come on my show and say that same stupid stuff. To their credit, they did.[3]

My first question, for Erick, was "What makes you dominant and me submissive, and who died and made you scientist-in-chief?" It's good to kick things off with a bang.

Feminists were saying that men's and women's roles were interchangeable, Erick said, and that "isn't healthy for society." He claimed he wasn't judging anybody, but that science supported his view that men should be the breadwinners and women should raise the children.

I told him he clearly *was* judging people. I pointed out that his so-called science was wrong and his facts were wrong, and pulled out a raft of studies to prove it.

Lou spoke for a long time, agreeing with Erick that society's ills had a lot to do with "women in the workforce." I interrupted to ask him if he really meant that. He got irritated. "Let me finish what I'm saying, if I may, O Dominant One."

"Excuse me?" I replied, with a raised eyebrow.

I wound up rattling off study after study showing that they were wrong about children of working mothers. I noted that this was the same thing they used to say about the children of interracial marriages to discourage people from marrying across racial lines—that mixing black and white would be detrimental to the child's success. "Tell that to Barack Obama," I said.

Erickson later said publicly that the exchange really made him think. He admitted that he had been wrong on this subject and believed he should be more careful in what he said, especially as the father of a young daughter. I give him a ton of credit for that—it's hard for any of us to admit when we are wrong, never mind so publicly. He and I have remained friendly throughout the years.

That segment was also the beginning of my friendship with Sheryl Sandberg, who called me up after seeing it and said, "I love you!"

We had a long talk, the first of many, and she has become an inspiring force to me. I love how her brand of feminism highlights the things we can all agree on as women—empowerment, advancement, equality, sisterhood—and steers clear of the more divisive issues.

I told her I am not a feminist. Sheryl—one of the preeminent female role models in America—passed no judgment on my feelings about that term. An example for our younger generation, some of whom openly booed me on Stephen Colbert's *Late Show* for saying I do not consider myself a feminist. I almost scolded the young women then and there. Is there no room for ambivalence about that term? We need more women in this sisterhood tent, not less. Who gives a damn what label we use, so long as we are living a life that supports other women?

My problem with the word *feminist* is that it's exclusionary and alienating. I look at a lot of the self-titled feminists in this country and think, *If that's the club we're talking about, I don't want in.* Feminism has become associated, de facto, with liberal politics. Call me crazy, but Gloria Steinem proudly wearing an "I Had an Abortion" T-shirt[4] might be a little off-putting to some. This is not to take a position on abortion. It's just to ask, why do we have to make the most divisive issues a key part of the feminist platform? Wouldn't we do better to simply unite on female empowerment?

I also reject the feminist messaging that treats

gender issues as a zero-sum game—that assumes that to empower women, we must castrate men. You see the beginnings of this even in the schoolyard, with affirmations like, "Girls rule and boys drool." As the mother of two boys and the wife of a loving, supportive man, I object. I don't want Yardley's empowerment to come at the expense of my sons. Isn't that what we've been complaining about men doing to us?

Sheryl and I talked about everything—our husbands, our careers, and our kids. We'd both taught aerobics in college, it turned out, both married strong, evolved men, and both had high-powered jobs in male-dominated industries. Yes, she went to the actual Harvard and I went to the Harvard of Albany, but why must every detail be parsed?

We of course had no idea that day that Sheryl's husband Dave would die in a tragic accident just three years later. The event would change the lives of Sheryl and her two children forever, and would sadly give us yet another thing in common—the sudden, premature death of a beloved family member. A void that, no matter how much you achieve, how much you have, is always there. Always.

Thatcher came along twenty-seven months after Yardley. I call him my walking cupcake. Not like the cupcakes on our nation's campuses who need safe spaces. Like a walking ball of sweetness. As Doug said when he was born: "Now everyone's here who's supposed to be here."

We knew right away that we were done, that this was our family. Thatcher has been easy and lovely and happy from day one. All he does is bring joy into our lives. I used to laugh when he was a baby about his strategy: "Okay, I'm the third kid. I'll just be as good as I can and hope someone pays attention to me." Wow, has that worked.

Thatcher is smart as a whip, with a great sense of humor. He loves to smile and laugh with us all, and is already picking up his Nana Linda's bluntness. Once, I was putting him to bed and singing him songs. He asked for "something special" so I tried a couple outside my comfort zone (Carly Simon was in there). Let's just say, they weren't exactly in my key. I quickly moved on to an old reliable ("Amazing Grace"). Much better. Thatcher and I shared a loving glance—or so I thought. Then he asked me: "Why were the first two songs not very good?"

He's got the same loving nature as his big brother and sister—he'll let me hold him for five minutes straight in a full-on embrace. He'll bury his face in my chest and comes over often looking for a hug. He looks out for his siblings too. If Yates skins his knee, you'll hear Thatcher say, "You're okay, Yatesey. Do you need a cookie to make you feel better?" (It's possible I am repeating my mother's promotion of emotional eating.)

He's got impressive confidence for someone so young. We had this exchange just the other day:

"Thatch, you were kind of whiny this morning. I know you can do better than that."

"We'll talk about that in one minute, Mom. First I would like you to read me this book." He is two!

I'm still the number-one person Thatcher wants to be with at any point in the day, which makes me feel like I've won the lottery. We have a strong connection.

"Thatcher," I asked him one day, "are you a boy or a girl?"

"I'm a boy," he said.

"What about Yates?"

"Yatesey's a boy," he said.

"How about Yards?"

"Yardley's a grill," which is how he pronounces *girl* right now (love that).

"What about Mommy?" I asked him.

"Mommy's a cowgirl!"

See? The kid gets me.

One quick note on my kids' grown-up names, which people often comment on: Yates was named after his grandfathers, Edward Yates Brunt. My father's given first name was Edward. Manly Yates Brunt was Doug's father's name. We loved Yates as a nickname.

Once you have a son named Yates and you get pregnant, where do you go from there? You can't very well go from Yates to Ann. You have to find a strong name again. Now, I'll confess to being a big fan of the 1945 Barbara Stanwyck film *Christmas in Connecticut*, a movie in which there's a character named Alexander Yardley, played by Sydney Greenstreet. But this isn't exactly the type of character after which you name a sweet baby girl. So I wasn't actively calling upon those memories when I thought of her name. The truth is, it came to me in the middle of the night, late in my pregnancy. I woke Doug up and said, "Honey, I think I have it."

By the time our third child was born, we were pretty attached to the last-name-as-first-name thing. Margaret Thatcher had recently died, so the name was in the air. But I get that plenty of people think my kids' names are unusual.

Not long after Yates was born, this was driven home by an elderly woman who lived a floor below us. One day, as a new mom, I was in the elevator with Yates in the stroller when she got on.

"What's his name?" she said.

"Yates."

"Yates? Is that his first name or his last name?"

"It's his middle name," I said, "but that's what we call him."

She frowned. "It's very confusing."

Fast-forward a year. Now I'm in the elevator with Yardley in the stroller and Yates in the Babybjörn.

"Is that a new baby?" the old woman says.

"Yes."

"What's her name?"

"Yardley."

[*Deep, aggrieved sigh.*]

All I have to say is, thank God we were out of the building by the time Thatcher was born, or she might have called Social Services on me for name abuse.

17

Ready for Prime Time

When I announced that I was expecting another baby, hell if I didn't get promoted again. Roger was offering me the 9:00 p.m. show. It was the first change to the channel's evening lineup in seventeen years—what a chance they took on me. In July 2013, Thatcher was born. In October, so was *The Kelly File*. My executive producer Tom Lowell and I were ready for prime time.

It was the pinnacle of cable news: my own prime-time broadcast. We launched it the way all news programs should be launched: with an impromptu dance party to the INXS song "Don't Change." At first it was just me dancing around my staff about twenty minutes before airtime. Their faces reflected an internal monologue of *Well . . . this is awkward.* But then Abby and

Tom got into it, and pretty soon everyone was on their feet. A few minutes later, I was sitting at the anchor desk interviewing Ted Cruz, asking him my very first question as host of *The Kelly File*: "What's it like to be the most hated man in America?" I think as an anchor I have stayed true to that full playfulness spectrum— the 1980s-rock-to-Ted-Cruz scale.

When I got my own show, O'Reilly gave me advice. He warned me that prime-time cable news is a snake pit, and I would have to gird myself for acrimony. This was unfortunate news, since acrimony was one of the main things I hated about my law job. Of course I had already felt some of it while on *America Live*, but he seemed to be saying, *Brace yourself.* Once my show started, I kept doing *The Factor*, because I was loyal to Bill. It was tough, because Bill tapes his show early in the day, and mine is live at 9:00 p.m., so doing *The Factor* meant leaving my kids at the only time of day I could really see them. Still, I continued my weekly *Factor* appearances for two years after *The Kelly File* began.

Once I got to prime time, things changed between us in that I became his competitor rather than an afterthought marooned in the afternoon. But that's what happens with competitive people—they want to win, and it can create a different dynamic. I know I owe a lot to Bill, and I'll always be grateful for the help he gave me before anyone even knew who I was. Not to mention the terrific lead-in he gives me.

I was thrilled to be able to make my mark in prime time—to spread my wings and do things my own way. I wanted to create a healthy work environment, one where people wanted to come to work each day, where people felt valued, not threatened or ignored. We put up inspirational posters around my team's pod, bought a high-end coffeemaker, set up weekly office hours for the team to come and see me, and created a *Kelly File* rewards program where people would be recognized for outstanding work. Look, it's not exactly Google, but we make an effort. We try to do fun things out of the office together—parties in Central Park or around the holidays, drinks after the show on a particularly challenging night. All of this has fostered a familial kind of relationship among us, and raises the bar for new hires on the show. As my mom likes to say, "Life is too short to surround yourself with unhealthy people."

As for content, we wanted to look and feel different. I am not an ideologue. Nor am I a pundit, like Bill and Sean around me. I am a news anchor who has come out publicly as an independent. I wanted a show that would surprise people. Enlighten them. A show that would be easy to consume but compelling to watch—as we describe it, like "cool water over a hot brain." If we nail an unusually dense segment, we'll say to each other, "Cool water."

One of my goals on *The Kelly File* has been to bring on newsmakers who no one else is challenging. To mix it up. To fact-check people. To set the record straight.

In this vein, one of the most satisfying interviews I've done to date on the show was with Bill Ayers, the domestic terrorist who belonged to the radical-left Weathermen, later known as the Weather Underground.[1] Ayers is married to Bernadine Dohrn, who was once on the FBI's Most Wanted list. (Ayers would later defend Dohrn, saying, "A lot of great people have been on that list." I'm sure she's a peach.)

During the 2008 election, it was reported that Barack Obama launched his career in Bill Ayers's living room. That was a little inflated. They were both in Chicago and in the same social justice circles, and Ayers had a cocktail party for the then aspiring politician. But the reason Ayers was such a good candidate for our show was that he had been all over the news, and no one had really held him to account. Until we came along.

Ayers and his group had terrorized the country in protest against the Vietnam War. They planted bombs in places like the Pentagon, the US Capitol, and the

State Department, and when one went off unexpectedly in a New York City town house, it killed four of their own. They were accused by the San Francisco police union of killing a cop. They terrorized a judge and his family with pipe bombs in the middle of the night. The list goes on.

And then they wound up as college professors, because why not? Who else would these institutions, so offended by conservatives like Condi Rice, Ben Shapiro, and Dick Cheney even *speaking for a night* on campus, invite to teach full time? Folks like Kathy Boudin, who helped kill two police officers in 1981, served twenty-plus years for murder and is now an adjunct professor at Columbia University. Or Dohrn—the Weather Underground leader who celebrated the Charles Manson murders, including that of the nine-months-pregnant Sharon Tate, with "Dig it! First they killed those pigs and then they put a fork in pig Tate's belly! . . . The Weathermen dig Charles Manson!"—who went on to teach at Northwestern Law School, one of the best schools in the country. And her husband, Ayers, spent his post-terrorist life teaching at the University of Illinois in Chicago. Is it me, or is this a problem?

A quick note on what's happening on our college campuses these days. Some in the younger generation today seem determined to shut down any opinions that don't happen to match their own (typically progressive) values. I believe this is not only boneheaded but bad for us as a society. We are becoming what I have dubbed a Cupcake Nation, trying to eliminate offensive or even differing viewpoints and, with them, our grit and resilience.

I am a big First Amendment advocate, and I do what I can to call attention to the attacks on it—whether it's the we-can't-function-if-exposed-to-unpleasant-language college kids who need a "safe space" to discuss any social issue, or the universities writ large who want to banish all speech that doesn't quite line up with their values.

I believe in the right to offend. To insult. Even to horrify. It's not that we're supposed to enjoy it; it's that we're supposed to allow it and then respond in a more persuasive voice. That's the bedrock of the First Amendment—the answer to speech you do not like is not less speech, it's more speech.

In addition to defending the free speech rights of the vile Westboro Baptist Church, I've also defended the free speech rights of Ayaan Hirsi Ali, who comes on *The Kelly File* among very few other shows. She's a Somalian human rights activist who underwent genital mutilation as a young girl, as mandated by her Islamic faith. Hirsi Ali has since become an outspoken critic of Islam, and is under a death threat issued by Islamist extremists. Still, she bravely speaks out. Amazingly, some American universities and critics would like to silence her. Yes, she's said some controversial things about Islam, but the First Amendment exists to protect *controversial* speech, not speech we love that ruffles no feathers. Hirsi Ali deserves her say, and when a critic tried to silence her on my show, I shot back at him, "When you undergo genital mutilation, you may have a thing or two to say about it!"

I was also vocal in my defense of Pamela Geller, a controversial figure who held a "Draw Muhammad" contest and then faced an attempt on her life by radical Muslims. Others (including Trump) blamed Geller, saying she had essentially invited her own attempted murder. I maintained that Geller's behavior was at the heart of the First Amendment, *especially* given its provocative nature.

Unlike Hirsi Ali, Ayers was not banned from college campuses; instead he was revered on them—another reason why my sit-down with him was perhaps the most compelling thing I've done on television. For decades, Ayers had been allowed to pass himself off as nothing more than a Vietnam War protester who set off a few explosive devices and no one got hurt.

Nonsense. He terrorized people, including children.

His group committed murder. Some academic types were so determined to reward him for his opposition to the war that he was given a relative pass for years. But he did not get a pass on *The Kelly File*. Nor was he allowed to dodge and weave with his usual retorts of "No one was hurt."

Yes, they were.

New York Times columnist and all-around ballbuster Maureen Dowd pulled me aside at an event years later and said of the Ayers exchange, "That's when I knew you were a great journalist. Great." Like most human beings, I love positive feedback, especially from people I respect, but what I really loved about that moment was it showed how the Ayers interview had penetrated beyond our typical audience.

Of course, Bill Ayers wasn't the kind of person likely to show up on Fox News. Hannity—to his credit—had been attempting to shine a light on Ayers in the weeks leading up to the 2008 election, because of the alleged Ayers-Obama connection. But those questions were largely dismissed.

Dinesh D'Souza, a guest on *The Kelly File*, had interviewed Ayers for a movie D'Souza had made called *America: Imagine the World without Her*, about American exceptionalism and those who reject it. We had booked D'Souza for a July 4 special, but needed someone to argue against him. He told me privately, "I think I can get Ayers for you." Sure enough, he did it.

I couldn't believe my eyes when Ayers walked in the door. We hid him in the building like he was Justin Bieber at a middle school prom. We knew someone would try to poach him, and we couldn't let that happen, so we stuck him in a part of the basement no one uses at Fox under the dutiful watch of two staffers.

Lo and behold, at the appointed hour, Bill Ayers walked onto my set. He sat down across from me, and what a moment. The next hour between us was extraordinary television. I worked very hard to prepare for that day. I had read up on Ayers, his group, and their crimes—both alleged and proven—for weeks. My team and I had read his books, listened to his radio interviews—you name it. There were many late-night meetings with my staff, who were as committed as I was to making sure we had our facts straight. We'd located riveting clips of him. And he had written about much of it in his book—though he'd clearly forgotten some of what he'd said.

For example, he denied that the Weather Underground bombed the home of Judge John Murtagh, where Murtagh's nine-year-old son was sleeping. I confronted Ayers with a passage from his own book: "Two weeks before the townhouse explosion, *four members of this group had firebombed Judge Murtagh's house* in New York" (emphasis mine).

"I didn't write that," said Ayers, caught flat-footed.

"It's in your book!" I countered, with a graphic ready and on the screen.

There was no way out for him. The audience knew.

We followed up later on in the show with the little Murtagh boy, now all grown up, to describe what it was like to wake up to his home being bombed and to respond to Ayers's claims about no one ever getting hurt.

We also had on FBI agents and NYPD officers who had investigated Ayers's many crimes and who explained why they were convinced he had perpetrated not just the bombings but also many other crimes.

For the first time, Bill Ayers was fully outed. It was a service to the truth. The interview was picked up everywhere. People began clamoring for their own Ayers interviews. He granted one to a far-left website, saying about me,[2] "She's like a cyborg constructed in the basement of Fox News. She's very striking, but very metallic, very cold. Her eyes are very cold."

Ayers was the gift that kept on giving. I responded to that with a humorous bit on our show in which I showed a picture of my eyes looking lovingly at Doug in an interview Doug had done on *The Kelly File*, and then a shot of me looking stonily at Ayers, suggesting that my coldness might have had something to do with the man in front of me. The Ayers interview put *The Kelly File* on the map, as dynamic, different, hard-hitting journalism. It garnered enormous ratings, and Fox ran it and reran it again and again for months.

Not long after that, in September 2014, I landed an exclusive interview with another infamous and reclusive professor, Ward Churchill. Churchill was a professor of ethnic studies at the University of Colorado–Boulder. He'd written an essay in 2001 called "'Some People Push Back': On the Justice of Roosting Chickens," in which he called those murdered in the Twin Towers on 9/11 "little Eichmanns" (Nazi Adolf Eichmann having orchestrated the Holocaust and been executed for it).

Lest you think he was quoted out of context, here's more of that paragraph:

True enough, they were civilians of a sort. But innocent? Gimme a break. They formed a technocratic corps at the very heart of America's global financial empire. . . . If there was a better, more effective, or in fact any other way of visiting some penalty befitting their participation upon the little

Eichmanns inhabiting the sterile sanctuary of the twin towers, I'd really be interested in hearing about it.[3]

This was protected speech, no doubt. The college was a public university, and he was a tenured professor. Except in very limited circumstances, the First Amendment doesn't allow a government body, like a public school, to punish someone for the content of their speech. Still, the school, under pressure from its alumni, found an excuse to cut him loose. He tried suing, but with mixed results.

On *The Kelly File*, I pressed him on his outlandish statements about the 9/11 victims. He did not dial them back, and at one point became slightly threatening. The interview was tense. I was strong with him as he continued to condemn America and to argue that we deserved the 9/11 attacks and more.

"Do you believe the United States ought to be bombed?" I asked.

"I think the United States by its own rules is *subject* to being bombed."

"You can't answer the question."

"Yeah, I have answered the question, I say the United States should comply with law!"

"Yes or no, do we deserve to be bombed?"

"If it does not comply with law, it opens itself up to it."

"Why can't you have the courage to just answer honestly? Yes, or no? Do we deserve to be bombed? *Just say it if you think it's true*," I pressed.

Churchill leaned forward across the anchor desk a bit—slightly, but noticeably, in my space. He lowered his baritone voice. He was angry. I wondered where this was going. I did not budge.

"I *say*, that if you open yourself up, under rule of law, for reciprocation in kind it's quite likely going to happen. I will *say* that at that point, no more than a murderer who's convicted and punished, *you have no complaint*. That's what I *say*."

Again, this was electric television.

For the record, I am not this prosecutorial in all of my interviews—only when someone says something as outlandish as that the 9/11 victims deserved it, or that bombing private homes in which little boys are asleep is a harmless crime.

As I mentioned, I'd also had some epic on-air battles with then congressman Anthony Weiner. I challenged him on his positions, and he treated me with disdain. We had some robust and widely circulated exchanges, including on *The Kelly File*.

In 2011, Weiner was outed for sending lewd texts, including naked pictures of himself, to random women on the Internet. I was on maternity leave with Yardley when it happened. He'd just sent me a handwritten congratulations note on her birth. Despite the contentious interviews we'd had, I felt bad for him.

I typically feel uncomfortable judging what people do in their relationships. That's not to say we should have no moral standards as a society. But I was taught that those standards must include forgiveness; that we are all sinners. You never know what goes on in somebody's marriage.

That's not to excuse Weiner's conduct. An inappropriate Internet relationship is a form of cheating. Beyond that, he had to know in his position as a US Congressman that this kind of intimate exchange with random women he'd met online was an incredibly reckless act. Weiner was nearly ruined by the scandal.

And then, an amazing thing happened: the public seemed ready to forgive him. His wife, Hillary Clinton's right-hand woman, Huma Abedin, stood by him. She clearly loved him. What's more, she took wedding vows, was expecting his child, and wanted it to work. I think her choices helped the public look past his mistakes. But then Weiner ran for New York City mayor, and it came out that he had continued the illicit behavior even after he'd been caught and done his apology rounds and been forgiven. This was a bridge too far, and in the mayoral election he wound up getting less than 5 percent of the vote. There was only so much the public could look past. I understand that, too.

As luck would have it, I was on my next maternity leave (with Thatcher) when Weiner's mayoral race scandal broke in 2013. Even though most people thought I would have loved to cover Weiner's downfall, I felt relieved I didn't have to.

Don't get me wrong, part of me felt a smidge of satisfaction that someone who had been quite rude to me had fallen from grace. Still, I get uncomfortable with the level of zeal our society brings to the downfall of the mighty in this country—particularly when it's due to a personal failing as opposed to a political breach.

This same reticence manifested in our coverage, or lack thereof, of the deeply troubled Canadian politician Rob Ford. We barely covered the story, even when those around us in the TV universe were leading with it night after night. That story, at its heart, was about drug addiction. It was a made-for-TV tale in some ways—the things he was doing were so outrageous. Some TV hosts openly laughed at him.

While I've never tried drugs, I know people who

have struggled with addiction, and it is far from a laughing matter. It is like having a nuclear bomb go off in your life, and your family's lives. What we were seeing was the self-destruction of a man who was failing to conquer a disease that has burdened so many. The ratings gold the story provided simply was not worth it. When Rob Ford died of cancer in 2016, I was glad we'd never added to his public shaming.

I am not naive. I understand that public shaming is often what we do for a living in the news business. A sitting president has an affair with an intern in the Oval Office and then lies about it under oath? Of course the press is going to pounce on that. But the glee the media—and the public—seem to experience in consuming each other's personal embarrassments is disheartening to me. I do my best to avoid these celebrations of destruction where I can. I think my viewers notice. I have received thousands of notes from fans of the show, but only one is posted on my office bulletin board, from a viewer named Linda, written in silver: "Thank you so much. Sharing news that does not create more resentment takes great style."

When NBC's Brian Williams had his fall from grace, we adopted the same approach. His serial exaggerations were a story, no question, but not something we needed to hammer every night. I made sure always to give voice to his explanation when we discussed it, and whenever I was asked about him publicly, I defended the belief in second chances. Did I think he could return to the evening news chair on NBC? No. But should his entire career be over? No. It wasn't as if he'd been actively hurting people. Some seemed to express such glee that he had embarrassed himself. I'm not saying it wasn't a story; I'm saying I hate how we forget about our subject's humanity in reporting these stories.

These are human beings. So many anchors cover these stories and won't even put on a guest to defend the person being attacked—they choose two attack-dog guests, and tear the subject limb from limb, seemingly with glee. I can't stand this—it shows no understanding of the power of our microphones, no appreciation for the responsibility we have.

TV—especially cable news—is not unlike the seventh-grade Group in that way—once a person has been identified as a target, The Group smells weakness and pounces. If someone does something newsworthy or a public figure falls, it's fine to cover it. But we must also remember that behind every story, there are real men and women trying to live their lives. Many have spouses, and often children. Some hosts don't care— they want scorched earth and take-no-prisoners TV. I did that as a lawyer, and that's not how I want to live anymore. Now I want to be curious and honest without transforming myself into a carnival barker.

Years after the Weiner-does-it-again scandal, Doug and I ran into Anthony and Huma on the Upper East Side. They were sitting on a bench outside a coffee shop. She had a big smile—she looked happy, relaxed. The four of us had a great conversation about our kids and New York City schools. I thought: This is the Anthony Weiner she knows. This is the man who wrote me that card after Yardley was born. The man who brought himself into ill repute, but who is still a husband, a father and a human being on this earth.

And then, he did it *again*, sending a woman erotic photos of himself, including one with his sleeping child next to him on his bed. Huma left him. And all I could think about was her smiling face that day on the bench, and the sometimes inescapable cruelty of human nature.

Since launching The Kelly File, which is now the most successful news show in all of cable (O'Reilly is an opinion program), I have been asked many times how I managed to excel in what is still a male-dominated industry. The truth is, every industry in which I've ever worked has been controlled by men—

from retail stores to customer service to health clubs, restaurants, law firms, and now television. So I've had a lot of experience. Generally, my bosses have been male. Generally, they've also been supportive, fair, and more than ready to give any deserving employee an opportunity to advance, male or female.

Having said that, I am an American woman born in 1970. Of course I've also experienced sexism, and even sexual harassment. And I have some thoughts on how to navigate both.

My feeling on the subject of women's equality is that it's better to show than tell. I believe in the Steve Martin mantra, "Be so good they can't ignore you." I have an enormous poster of this saying in my team's pod at Fox. When it comes to living this just-be-better philosophy, Oprah is my role model. In her years coming up, she never made a "thing" of her gender or her race. She just wowed us all. That's my goal: do the absolute best I can, and don't waste time complaining. The less time talking about our gender, the better.

In all the years I've worked at Fox, I have never had to ask for a promotion. I have been asked what I think is the next step for me, and I have never been shy to answer. So many broadcasters line up outside the boss's office, asking for this show or that one. I've spent my time in my own office, working night and day, and opportunity came to me. Most of my own power has come from excellence, not advocacy. My approach is to say to myself, "Just *do* better. *Be* better." That's not to say there's no bias, no sexism. There is, and it's not good. It's just that for me, the solution of *doing better* is far more empowering than lamenting one's circumstances.

It's not that I reject the idea of demanding a place at the table—quite the contrary. But in my own experience, the most effective way to get opportunities is with performance, not persistence. Hard work matters. I really believe that. It can get you on the *Law Review*, on the moot court team, on the partnership track, in the anchor chair. It can improve your friendships, your relationships, yourself. But you can't half-ass it. And sitting around convincing yourself that you deserve more without busting your backside to get it is not only bad form, it's pointless.

I've never worked at a place where some star employee—man or woman—was unknown to everyone, toiling away unnoticed. If you believe this is happening to you, ask yourself if you have worked as hard as possible, studied extensively, and made yourself invaluable. If you can't honestly say you have done all of those things, quit complaining.

"I don't feel valued," a co-worker once said to me.

"That's because you're not," I said. "You should go somewhere else."

I saw no reason to sugarcoat it. Kelly family values in their purest form. Settle for more.

Many people choose to work less hard and to prioritize something else. That's great. My point is simply, if your goal is to rise to the top of your company, and it's not happening, you must look first at your own work ethic and work product before assuming it's gender bias.

Like most American women, I've been interrupted frequently by male colleagues, who don't do the same to the men at the table. I've been checked out physically by more than a few bosses. I've found myself excluded from the boys-only nights out at the bar at which bonding with a superior takes place. Do men sometimes get a leg up at work because they have access to male supervisors that women don't have? Absolutely. You cannot control that.

But you *can* control *you*. Employers want to improve the bottom line. You may not get invited to the bar with the boys. But *do* better, *be* better, and the odds are the hungover boys will soon be asking themselves how you keep getting such great opportunities.

My general approach when hitting a sexist glass ceiling is to try to crash right through it with stellar work product. Bosses tend to be mercenary. If you are great, he'll likely promote you. If he doesn't because of sexism, the options get tougher. Filing a legal complaint is a potential option, but gender-discrimination cases tend to be protracted and very nasty. Some women choose to find a new job, as unfair as that seems. The choices are fraught with peril, which is exactly why many women resign themselves to operating in a sexist workplace, hoping that with time things will get better.

Sexual *harassment* is even more dangerous. Interrupting you because you're a woman is one thing. Trying to shove a tongue down your throat is another. Unfortunately, I've been there too.

When I was sixteen and clueless about the world, Kelly and I took a job at a local sporting goods shop. Our boss was a dirty old man. He used to walk by and look at my ass when I was restocking shelves and say, "Are you sure you're only sixteen?" He was always telling me and Kelly how he was going to "take us back on Old Reliable," a ski waxing machine where one could ostensibly lie down. When we were cleaning up at the end of the day, he would watch porn on a TV in the back. We laughed at him. He was a joke to us. And eventually, we both quit.

I know very few women who don't have stories like this. Remember: I practiced employment law. What I learned was that some men are absolutely still doing the things you heard would happen in the 1950s. You would not believe how many bosses are still grabbing their employees' breasts, or leaving X-rated images on their assistant's chair, or chasing their young female employees around the desk. It happens all the time. And it needs to stop happening, now.

18

On "Having It All"

I own an oversize green T-shirt with I WANT IT ALL emblazoned on the front. One time, while we were visiting my mother-in-law, Jackie, I emerged from the bedroom wearing that shirt and carrying Thatcher, who was still a baby. It was some ridiculously early hour. I had been up late the night before with Yardley, who was sick. I had just come off a week of long hours at the office. My eyes had dark circles under them. My hair was everywhere. It felt like I hadn't slept in a century. Jackie looked from me, rocking my baby, to the front of that shirt and back again and said, "Oh, you've got it all, all right."

And I do: my own show, a great husband, three beautiful kids I love more than words can say. Now I just have to survive to the end of the week.

Sometimes on particularly rough days I say, "Doug, am I going to make it? This might be the week I get the chalk outline around me."

"Eh, you'll make it," he says.

We're in a particularly good place now. Ages six, five, and two are a sweet spot—way better than three, two, and newborn. Way better. Back then, I used to slide into my car and say to myself, "Time to go to that spa they call work!" (Okay, I still do that from time to time.)

We have resources now, which clearly makes things easier. Some moms don't like to admit having a nanny or other support. I don't understand why. Every dollar I have, I've earned. I pay my taxes, donate to charity, help my family, and am saving for my children. My hard work has helped us afford household help, which allows us the luxury of spending time with our children when we are not at work, rather than tending to all of the household tasks, but if we could not afford help, we'd figure it out. I'm new to money. I spent most of my existence without it. I know how to live frugally. If we were to lose it all tomorrow, we'd change our hours, move out of the city, and make other adjustments, just like my parents did. Money removes many stressors, but it has not changed my level of happiness, nor who I am. It changes how I spend my time.

Right now I work at night, so my time with the kids

during the week is mostly during the day. We social-
ize with the parents of our children's friends. I can
chaperone daytime field trips. I go into my son's school
and read to his class during library. I go to most of
the school parties and all of the plays. I miss plenty of
events too, which pains me, but every working parent
makes sacrifices.

Our mornings involve enormous mugs of coffee,
Cheerios, fruit, plenty of stories, and music via Pandora. We dance. We feed the fish, which I did not want
to buy but which, in the absence of any other caretak-
ers, now appear to be "mine." I do not like fish and
take care of them only begrudgingly, but the truth
is, I'm getting kind of attached to the damn things. I
help the kids get breakfast. They eat a lot in the mornings, so Doug and I often feel like short-order cooks—
"One scrambled, one fried with cheese, double wheat!
Coming up!" I help pick out the kids' outfits, although
it's really more of an attempt to block Doug from doing
it. He'll see me cast a disapproving eye at Yardley's
outfit when she's not looking.

"What's wrong with it?" he'll say of the outfit he
chose. "It matches!"

"It does match," I'll say, "in that a polka-dot pair of
pants 'matches' a polka-dot shirt."

It's better just to beat him to the closet. Soon she'll

be in kindergarten, and I'm delighted to say they wear uniforms at her school. Now I can sleep in a few more minutes.

Weekends are all about them. We don't make it to church every Sunday, though we do our best. Doug grew up Presbyterian, but like me, all of our children have been baptized Catholic. Yates will have his First Communion next year. Our priest is Father Jonathan Morris, who is on Fox News sometimes. He's supportive, thoughtful, and good-looking. So handsome, in fact, that his nickname around the studio is Father What-a-Waste (God forgive us).

I'm most exhausted on Sunday nights, because you have to dig deep to keep up with three kids nonstop. Luckily, they're very good kids. That makes time with them very pleasant.

I remember talking to an administrator at Yates's school. I said, "I love spending time with him. He's one of my favorite people. He's the best company."

"Not everybody feels that way," she said.

That was the first time it dawned on me that some parents and kids struggle with each other, even at young ages. Now sometimes I see it on the playground, families who don't love their time together, and it's heartbreaking. I mean, is it hard sometimes? Of course. But I'll tell you, the first time you tuck your baby into his crib and say, "Sweet dreams. I love you," and you turn to walk out and hear back "I love you, Mama!" you know what you're doing on this earth.

One day I was feeling full of self-doubt—wondering if I was doing this motherhood thing right. Just then, Yates looked at me and Doug and announced, "I'm going to marry a girl named Megyn. She's alive and she's five and I need to find her." Thank you, universe.

Balancing motherhood with work has been hugely assisted by having a husband who supports my time at the office and a job that allows for my time at home.

I'll start with the office. First, I have something critical to balancing my dual roles: flexibility in my schedule. Unlike the law, my TV job rarely requires twelve or sixteen hours at the office. Some days I can do six hours, some days a split shift. If I need to come in late, I can. If I need to work from home—except for airtime—it's generally no problem. That's been incredibly helpful to me. Without this kind of freedom, I don't think I'd be succeeding.

I also was fortunate enough to feel supported right after my children were born—I had nice long maternity leaves (by American standards), for which I was not shamed and, to the contrary, was encouraged to take.

I nursed all three of my children for the first year

and exclusively for the first six months of their lives. It took time and dedication, what with all of that pumping and late-night feeding, but I was happy to do it—it was another way to take care of them even when I was at the office.

Now that they're older, the kids come to work with me fairly often, and my colleagues help, especially Abby. We have office picnics. We get pizza and chocolate milk, and they run up and down the long hallways (they're city kids—we have no fields). Everyone greets the kids warmly; it's not uncommon to see people's children at Fox.

My kids love coming to work with me. They love going to the tracking booth. They put the headphones on and speak into the fuzzy microphones for ages, stream-of-consciousness style. Yates and Yards have heard me say lines like, "I'm Megyn Kelly, live in New York!" The first time Yates tried it, he said into the mic, "I'm Yates Brunt! And I'm alive!"

They don't usually come see me do the show, because 9:00 p.m. is too late for them, but if I'm doing a pretape they'll come sometimes and sit off to the side, so long as I'm not talking about anything too dark, like terror. My crew will show them the cameras and let them sit at the anchor desk. My hair and makeup team

Chris and Vincenza will give them spiked hair and painted faces—it's like going to a street fair.

I think it's good for them to see their mother in a powerful position where she's clearly in control. I'm glad they will grow up to understand—inherently—that women loving their work is a natural thing in this world.

When possible, I look for opportunities to take my children with me when I go on the road for work. When Yates graduated from preschool, I took him with me when I went to interview Mitt Romney at a summit he holds every June in Deer Valley, Utah. He tested my microphone at the convention hall. We went on the chair lifts. We went on the Alpine Coaster. He loved it all.

Likewise, I took Yardley with me to the debates in Iowa in 2012. I'd be sitting in the Iowa convention center, pumping in the bathroom stalls—those pumps are so *loud*—and pushing her around the convention center in a stroller. As long as she was moving, she was happy. I'd push her around during meetings, and then my colleagues would take a turn around the debate prep table. I have a picture of Yards at Newt Gingrich's podium before the Iowa debate that I figure she can use if she ever runs for president. I propose the caption "Born to Run."

In December 2013, I was on *The Tonight Show* with Jay Leno. It was his last month on the show. I was still nursing Thatcher, so he (and Doug) came with me. Thatch was being pretty good backstage, but he started to have a meltdown right before I went onstage. So I did what any working mother would do: I nursed him, while sitting there mic'ed and glammed up. Time stopped for a minute, and then I pulled up my dress, handed the baby to Doug, and hurried onstage, carrying a tissue because I had a hideous, hacking cold. Ah, the glamorous life.

When it came time for my second *Fortune Most Powerful Women* event—this one in Washington, DC—I took Yardley with me, and we headed south on the train.

"Where are we going?" she asked.

"This is a gathering of a bunch of women," I said, "who have done amazing things. They are coming together to celebrate their power and how strong they are, and how much they've accomplished."

"Are we two of them?" she asked.

After I gave my remarks, she was running around the lobby of the hotel and I was talking to some women while keeping an eye on her out of my peripheral vision. Suddenly I looked over and she was supine on the ground with her fist in the air—a beautiful symbol of power, solidarity, and sheer exhaustion.

I marvel at my friends who are full-time mothers. I don't know how they do it. One of my closest friends is a stay-at-home mom. I think she has it harder, and she thinks I have it harder. She's always remarking on how "present" I am when I'm with my kids. But to me full-time caregiving is what's truly amazing. If I were with my kids full-time, I couldn't sustain that level of engagement. When Doug and I have the kids all day every day on vacation, I'm wiped out.

If I were a stay-at-home mom, I like to think I could get to be as good as my friends, but it would take time. And patience. The truth is, I always knew that if I became a mom, I would be a working mother. I love that I can go out into the world, and then when I walk into that house, I'm full of excitement and energy. The kids experience it by osmosis. They see that I love my job. They understand that they can find a job someday they will really love. I hope they're really learning that.

I also hope they're learning that one of the best ways to make this work is to find a supportive spouse. Neither Doug nor I came in with any strong biases about gender roles. When we got together, he made more money than I did. Now I make more, and probably that will cycle around many more times over the rest of our lives. He is not threatened because he's secure. It helps that we both now love what we do.

Our kids see that Doug and I support each other's goals. When we got married, Doug was running a company down in Palm Beach. He was splitting his time between there and New York, and he was not enjoying that travel once Yates was born. He was clearly not happy. It wasn't the most productive, healthy work environment.

We went for a walk in Central Park. I suggested he try to figure out what might make him more fulfilled. He's like my dad was, a voracious reader and a master of observation. Doug had been writing a book as a stress reliever on all those airplane rides. He told me he loved writing and thought it was something he could pursue.

"Why don't I read your book?" I said.

It was nerve-racking for both of us. What if I hated it? Luckily, I didn't. In fact, I loved it. It's called *Ghosts of Manhattan*, and it's beautifully written. If you read that book, you'll know why I love Doug. I encouraged him to quit his job and try to become a published author.

Off he went. He sold off a large part of the company, and started writing full-time. And he's never looked back. That book became a *New York Times* best seller.

He cares deeply about his writing, and has networked in the writing community very well. He's in a supersecret book club with some very famous authors and writers. (I've already said too much.) He creates these gatherings like my mom and dad used to do, where they talk about things other than politics—literature, storytelling, possibilities.

Doug's next book, *The Means*, also sold big. The main character is a little bit me and a little bit Melissa Francis, who started out on *Little House on the Prairie* and is now a newscaster at Fox and a good friend. It was funny—when I was reading early drafts, I'd write in the margins, "Hey, that's my story!" So if you've read *The Means* and any stories in here sound like ones in Doug's book, just know they were mine originally.

Now Doug's publishing a third book, called *Trophy Son*, and I have to say, that career has been great for him and for us. Other than for the three weeks after his publication dates, Doug can make his own hours, and usually writes in the mornings after school drop-offs. It allows us a lot of flexibility. He can get the kids to Fox for an office picnic. He and I can meet for a nice lunch. Every once in a while we make a Broadway matinee or take a walk in Central Park. If I have to leave town to cover breaking news, he can cover for me, and I leave knowing my children are with not just a nanny but a parent they love, which alleviates some of the guilt. Thankfully, I don't have to travel much—but I do put in long hours at the office, especially in election years.

We're teaching our kids that moms support dads and dads support moms and the main goal is that the family unit thrive. They are learning the importance of true connection, because they see and feel and live it in our home. They are also learning that being unhappy at the office long-term is not acceptable. We want our kids to think, *I can do better than that. I can find something that invigorates me.* We want them to be excited and challenged by what they do. To find that, you have to get a good education. You have to work hard for good things to happen.

We find ways to inculcate Kelly family values, which thankfully Doug happens to share.

One time Yates and I were playing a game.

"Yates," I said, "you're going to win!"

"Maybe we could all win," he said.

"No," I said, "we cannot all win. There is a winner and a loser. Losing is an incentive to keep practicing."

Doug and I want them to understand that. Right now my daughter doesn't like competition because she doesn't like losing—she's usually playing against Yates, who's got nineteen months on her. I think she also doesn't like to be in a position to make other people lose. I want her to understand the value of competition and winning and losing, but I'm also conscious of not putting my own competitiveness off on her. They can be whoever they are. Our way isn't always right.

We encourage them to do things themselves. Order their own meals at restaurants, pour their own milk in their cereal, clear their own place settings. Inspired by my dad, Doug and I will go around the dinner table and ask, "What's the report?" Each child gets a turn, and sure enough, they go on and on. We try not to interrupt (dinners are long). When we go to the airport, we have the kids get us to our gate. These little things build confidence. This is not to say Doug and I have it all figured out—far from it. This is just how we approach parenthood and find ways to enjoy one another more.

Just like with Linda, we have a lot of laughs. I'll come out in the morning with my hair sticking straight up, my glasses on, and no makeup, and I'll start posing dramatically, like a runway model, telling the kids if they want my styling secrets it's going to cost them big, since I am a *Very Famous Person* and I don't just give these gems out to anyone. Yates will deadpan to me, "That's not your best look."

One thing that was always worth a laugh in the Kelly house growing up was when anyone tripped— usually my mother. There would be a moment's hesitation, just to make sure the person was not hurt—but just a moment—and then laughter would follow. It's built into me to this day, like the response "God bless you" to a sneeze—it's almost instinctual. I cannot help it, and I take no responsibility for it. It's all my mother's fault.

One time Doug tripped coming off a curb and thought he got away with it.

"I just want you to know, I saw everything," I said from behind him.

We both burst out laughing.

Then Yardley chimed in. "I thought it wasn't nice to laugh when other people tripped?"

Doug smiled.

"It's complicated," I said.

Just like in my career, I work hard at motherhood. And I have to because motherhood takes practice. It's trial and error.

Once, my mom and I were out with Yates when he was a baby. I was gazing at him lovingly in his stroller. After a while, my mom got exasperated: "Talk to him!" she said.

"What?"

"You should talk to him!"

"Oh!" I'd been so busy admiring him, it hadn't even occurred to me. Good idea.

A few months later, we were out at the Jersey shore, staying with Doug's mother. Yates was about nine months old. It was a rainy day, and so I took him to the arcade. I thought he'd like the stimuli. Sure enough, he loved it, and then he fell asleep.

I didn't have anywhere to be, so I decided to play Skee-Ball while he slept in the stroller next to me. I was doing really well. Like, *really well.* I kept hitting 50s and the 100, which is hard to do. It was a rush. (I was a new mother. I had very little excitement in my life.) Then Yates woke up and started crying. I had four balls left. What would you do? It was a question of maybe thirty seconds, tops. I decided to finish my game. So there I am, rolling Skee-Balls, saying to Yates, "Mommy just needs one more second . . ."

At that exact moment, a woman comes up and says, "Excuse me, aren't you Megyn Kelly?"

"No," I said, rolling the last ball and picking up my baby. "Who?"

Now that they're older, I take all three of them with me and let them roll right alongside me. It's utopia.

With practice, I have gotten better—at both Skee-Ball and parenting. But just as you get the hang of taking care of one child, you have two and then three and you realize, usually the hard way, that the old tricks are not working. What I know now is that the moms who make it look easy also had to learn.

Once, when Thatcher was a newborn, I took him in the stroller and went to pick up my two older kids at preschool. It was cloudy, but I didn't bring an umbrella. You can't take the stroller into the school, which I forgot, so I got to the school and had to wake up Thatcher to carry him upstairs. So now I had a crying baby and my two little ones, and it started to rain. The stroller wasn't collapsible, so I couldn't get a taxi even if I could find one. I thought, I'll take the subway, but I couldn't get down the stairs with the stroller and a baby and two little kids.

So what did I do? I exercised my advanced problem-solving skills. I sat on the church steps across from the school with the three of them and cried. In the rain. That, as it turned out, was not really a solution. So I stood up. We walked ten blocks in the rain. We got soaked, but we got home, and everyone was fine. I knew I needed to do it differently next time.

Once I was dry and sitting at the kitchen table, I thought, *What was I trying to prove?* I had a nanny. She could have watched Thatcher while I picked up the older kids. But I was trying to prove that I could do it all, and so I took the baby even though it made my life more difficult. And for what? My baby would not have cared if his mom wasn't there for an hour of his nap.

As mothers, we tend to put pressure on ourselves, especially as working moms, even if we push ourselves to the point of frustration. I realize now that it's better to take a forty-five-minute nap if you can and be present for your kids with calm or positive energy thereafter than to power through and be a miserable version of yourself. Live and learn.

I am still learning. Not long ago, I went to the park with Yates and another boy and the boy's mom, who stays home and seems to me like an excellent mother.

I left the house with two things: me and Yates.

The other mom brought a backpack to the playground, and while the kids were running around, she took it out.

"Mom, I'm thirsty!" her son said.

Out came a juice box.

Ah, juice boxes! Smart move.

"Would Yates like one too?" she said.

He would. Thank you so much.

Then the boys were hungry. Out came some dried fruit and nut snack.

Ooh, snacks! Right. Well played.

And after that, sidewalk chalk.

Chalk? A brilliant idea!

And then, how about a ball?

Soccer, yes! They like soccer.

I went home laughing at myself, but I knew, too, that while all of those things from the backpack were nice, to have a good day, all Yates and I really needed was time with each other.

Finding that time is perhaps my greatest challenge as a working mother.

Most American working moms have been asked at some point, "How do you balance it all?" Many say the question is sexist because we would not ask it of a man. I suppose that's true, but the reality is, some things *are* different between the sexes, and in my experience, guilt at being at work all day is often one of them.

Every working mom I know—from part-time freelance consultant to killer Wall Street hedge fund guru—has guilt about missing out on her kids' day. I don't hear this as much from my male friends, although there are exceptions, like my executive producer Tom, who's devoted to his son and often expresses those pangs of missing out. In general, however, most of the men I know seem to be in a better place when it comes to leaving in the morning and coming home in the evening and being informed about the child's day as opposed to having been there for it.

To me, some of this is inherent. The reality is that mothers have a biological need to be with their children, especially when they're young. To be strong women, I don't think we have to reject that reality, that particularly special bond between mothers and children. That's not to say that women working is the calamity Lou Dobbs and Erick Erickson were suggesting. It's just to acknowledge the emotional toll on mothers who choose to do it all. Sometimes it's hard. In my view, the way forward is to be honest about this fact and to better support new mothers, rather than to guilt them about their choices.

Our society also bears some of the blame—it rarely reinforces the message to women that it's okay or expected, much less admirable, for them to go out and earn the money it takes to sustain a family. Too often, shame still attaches to maternity leave (or to getting pregnant at all as a working mother), to taking days off when a child is sick, to slowing down one's work flow when one's children are very young or having a difficult time. These are important things for a mother to do, and yet the American workplace remains reluctant to embrace them. In addition, the failure to celebrate working mothers is similarly damaging. Dads are given credit for supporting their families; when was the last time you heard a mother praised for working all day?

I believe in what billionaire Charles Koch's dad referred to as the "glorious feeling of accomplishment." There is no reason to feel guilty about enjoying hard work, or pushing yourself at the office, just because you are also a mom or a dad. A job well done at work enhances our self-worth, brings joy and satisfaction, for women and men. And it has the added benefit of teaching that value to our children when we go home to them at the end of the day.

In my little circle of the world on *The Kelly File*, I have resolved to build a better environment for parents. I encourage our working mothers to celebrate and not feel guilty about their work, just like the dads. (I'm not saying this always works, but we do try.) But we are realistic. When the women get pregnant, I also try to make sure they don't feel pressure at the office. I'll say, "I know that once the baby comes, you may need more flexibility for a while, and we will help make that happen." If they are feeling overwhelmed, I tell them, don't just quit and give up the struggle—come to me and Tom first and see if we can help. Similarly, if our guys need extra time with their kids, we all work to accommodate that. We are a team.

If filling these gaps requires a temporary extra head count, or additional hours for those who didn't just have a baby, or some adjustment to people's work responsibilities, so be it. It's to the employer's benefit. If you support new parents' need to be with their children—during a decent parental leave, and then within reason thereafter—you are far more likely to keep them long-term.

And that is probably one of the reasons why half of the people on my staff have babies or are pregnant. One producer whom I love moved to damn Canada and had a Canadian baby. "What the hell, Deb," I told her. "We'll work out some arrangement." And we did.

It's not that we have unlimited resources. It's just that only women can have the babies. If society wants the human race to continue, they're going to have to help us out here. Also, we're talking about a time-limited situation. There are very few Duggars out there with nineteen children; it's unlikely the women on my team will be having babies every year for the next twenty years. We're talking about a few years when we need to get some backup. We can do that to hang on to our top talent.

And to the employers of the world thinking, *This is insane—it'll hurt the bottom line,* just remember: if you force a woman to choose between her work and her child, and she has any choice at all, she will choose her child. And then you will lose her, and all the money you've spent training her, which you will then have to spend again on a new person, when the cycle will likely continue unless you hire all men or postmenopausal women, which happens to be illegal.

For me, the balance between work and home has gotten both better and worse over time. Better because when I first became a mother, I worried about two things: that my children would not feel bonded to me if I wasn't there all day, and that I was somehow shirking my responsibilities in choosing to go to the office. Wrong on both counts, as it turns out.

As for my fear that our bond wouldn't be as strong—I now know that's nonsense, at least if you put in the effort. Seven years into motherhood, I love my children and they love me. Our relationship is fully intact and secure. So I no longer worry about them being confused by our setup or estranged from me as a result.

As for shirking my responsibilities, I've been able to let that go. At first I felt sad—and yes, guilty—about not being the one doing all the baths and meals and drop-offs. But soon I realized that even if I can't do "it all," what I really need is good time with them where we feel connected—playing, talking, sitting together. I don't need to get them from point A to point B each day to prove a point. One day I was getting ready for work, and feeling a little sad. I did not want to go in; I wanted to stay with my kids. Our occasional sitter, who's from Bolivia, was there. She's a hard worker. She cleans houses. She's a full-time nanny for another family. Her husband drives a cab. She has two kids of her own. She saw me changing Yardley's diaper at the time with tears in my eyes and put her hand on my back. She said, softly, "There are many ways of taking care of them." And she was right.

But the thing that still haunts me, the thing I *do* still worry about, is that I'm missing too much of it. That's what keeps me up at night. It's not that they're not going to turn out well—they are. It's not that they won't love me or appreciate my efforts on their behalf—they do, and they will. It's that I'm missing large chunks of their childhood—like most working parents do. Settling for more right now for me means pushing myself to improve this balance. Keep my job, and spend more time with my kids. That's the next reinvention.

I love my job and the excitement and challenges it offers. But my job does not define me. If this job ended tomorrow, I'd find another way to find that glorious feeling of accomplishment. No employer or career choice "made" me. I made me. And Linda and Ed made me. And my children made me. And they, and Doug, are the people—the only people—who have true power over me.

19

Election Season

My family knows that election season brings big demands on my time. What it also brings is vitriol—a tidal wave of it. Even as a news anchor, you have to gird yourself for battle. During the lead-up to the 2008 election, Doug and I were at a cocktail party in Park Slope, Brooklyn. As soon as I was introduced as a Fox News anchor, the couple we were talking to turned and walked out. Four years later we were at a dinner party in Manhattan, and the woman next to me asked, "You work for Fox? How do you sleep at night?"

"Like a baby," I responded. "The check clears every week, and we provide a service to the nation. And you?"

The point is, things always get tense as presidential politics fire up. That makes elections the best and worst thing to cover. I love the excitement, the competition, the high stakes. The anger, accusations, and demonization I could do without. Never do I reassess life on the political front lines more than during election years.

The truth is, it's always far more than just a year, and, entering the 2016 presidential race, I knew the process would require endurance. The first Republican candidate, Ted Cruz, announced in March 2015, more than nineteen months before the election. Babies would be born on Election Day whose parents had not yet met when the race got started. We were going to be with these guys for a long time.

For the first few months of the primary season, our show was like a revolving door for the Republican candidates. We asked for the Democrats too, but they generally chose not to come on Fox News. If they wanted to ignore the largest cable news audience in the country, there wasn't much I could do about it (other than incessantly ask them to reconsider, which I did). Virtually every one of the Republicans came to *The Kelly File* within twenty-four hours of their official announcement, and we'd talk about their bios, their policy, and the race. Slowly but surely, we were helping America get to know them.

By the time we got to the summer of 2015, the GOP had seventeen candidates. Seventeen! It was an absolute mob scene. I understood why a lot of Republican politicians thought they had a shot. We were coming off of eight years of the Obama administration, and America tends to want a change of party after a two-term president.

With so many candidates, the debates were going to be key, and Fox News was lucky enough to be hosting the first one. It was scheduled for August 6 in Cleveland, on the same stage where the GOP victor would accept the nomination one year later.

There were so many candidates that not all of them could possibly participate in one debate. We discussed the problem at length. Should there be two debates, with the candidates mixed up randomly? Just one, with the top-polling candidates only, and nothing for the others? In the end, Fox settled on two debates—one for those with the highest poll numbers, one for the lower tier. The Fox management team would choose five national polls and take the average to figure out the ten who were polling the highest. Most of the folks relegated to the undercard debate were not happy, and some complained. But in no world did it make sense to put seventeen candidates on the stage. We felt comfortable with our approach. Voters needed help figuring out what distinguished each candidate from the other, and that's where Fox News came in.

I had moderated presidential debates four years earlier, so I knew the drill. The debate team would be spending many, many hours meeting with one another and preparing for the big night. I was not looking forward to the extra hours away from Doug and our kids, but I was also mindful of the importance of the work. It's the most rewarding thing we do—the biggest professional responsibility we have. We take it very seriously.

One person dismissed by all of the pundits at first was Donald Trump. When Trump had announced just a couple of months earlier, his poll numbers were dreadful, in the low single digits. No one thought of him then as anything more than an entertaining diversion. For the first half of the summer, everyone was just enjoying the show.

The smart money back then was on Jeb Bush. Jeb was seen as presidential. He was smart and had experience. Maybe it's that he is from American royalty, which the Bush family certainly is—he looked and felt like other presidents. And yet, he didn't have that special *thing* that presidents usually have, the unbridled confidence, the moxie.

He gave his first television one-on-one to me after a speech at Liberty University. It did not go particularly well for him. He told me the Iraq War was not a mistake. I asked him, "Knowing what we know now, would you have invaded Iraq?" He said yes.

We went back to his team for clarification before the interview hit air, because the exchange was a little confusing. His team was steadfast: "We have nothing to clarify." We put it on TV, and it made headlines everywhere. Jeb spent days trying to clean it up, until he finally reversed himself on the answer. Many who had thought Jeb the odds-on favorite suddenly started to ask, *What if he's not?*

Chris Christie was seen as a straight-talking tough guy and was always fun to interview. But he was dogged by an exchange he had with President Obama prior to the last election, in which Christie appeared to fawn over the president, who had fast-tracked Hurricane Sandy relief funds to New Jersey. Republicans were having a hard time forgiving the governor for that display, or maybe it was just that Christie had been out-Christied by Trump.

Marco Rubio was also a contender at that early point. He was someone with a great personal story, conservative credentials, and Hispanic heritage in a party looking to increase its performance with Hispanic voters. But he'd co-sponsored the immigration reform bill a couple of years back, and in the 2016 Republican party, that was anathema. Rubio has a good-looking, boyish face, but for some reason he struggled to connect the way an Obama or Clinton or George W. Bush had. His promising run never quite soared.

As for who I suspected might take the nomination, going into that first debate? I told Doug, "Watch Ted Cruz." Cruz, as I mentioned, was the first guest ever on *The Kelly File*. I liked having him on—he was interesting. He had come to my office a year before his presidential announcement with his press person. He spent an hour and a half with me, just chatting. I knew he wasn't there because he loved my tiny office, and assumed he was laying the foundation for a presidential run. He's not a particularly well liked guy, as you may have heard, but I found him perfectly affable one-on-one. He is the smartest man in almost any room. That was borne out as we saw him navigate the primaries.

During the run-up to the first debate I noticed which of the candidates—like Cruz, Rubio, Huckabee, or Carson—could sit for a tough interview and roll with it, and which ones would throw a fit. They shall remain nameless here. Suffice it to say that many would call up my bookers after the segments and complain about what I'd asked them. "They want George Washington's job," I'd marvel to my team, "but they don't want to deal with tough questions to get there." Some interviews call for a punch between the eyes—

especially if the candidate's been saying controversial things. Others allow (or even require) a softer touch. Over an election cycle, it all balances out.

As for Trump, believe it or not, he and I were once mutual fans. The beginning of our relationship was perfectly friendly. I used to watch *The Apprentice* and thought he was entertaining. I never interviewed him much, but I saw him on Fox News a lot. And during the lead-up to the 2012 presidential election, I had him on *America Live* once.

In December 2011 Trump wanted to moderate a Republican primary debate, hosted by Newsmax, in Iowa. Most of the candidates declined the invitation. Trump pulled out, and the debate was canceled. I went over to Trump Tower and interviewed him about it.

"I would be the best debate moderator ever!" he said.

I joked with him: "Do you really think you'd be better than *me*?"

"Oh no," Trump said. "I could never be a better moderator than you, Megyn."

Someone cleverly dredged up that exchange once he started going after me for my moderating in the 2016 election.

There was actually a funny moment in that interview where he let me run my fingers through his hair to prove that it was his own. Yes, I touched the famous hair. He had a sense of humor about it—he was not afraid to be playful.

Following the launch of *The Kelly File* in October 2013, I had Trump on a total of twice in the next twenty-one months. I enjoyed interviewing him. He was fun to watch, irreverent, and you never knew what he was going to say. Apart from that, I had no contact with him.

Then, in the winter of 2015, six months before he announced his candidacy for president, Trump began reaching out to me—often. At the time, I figured he liked my show. In retrospect, I see that he was attempting to charm me in advance of his presidential bid. Starting around February, he began calling me and sending me personal notes.

When the *New York Times Magazine* ran a cover story about me by Jim Rutenberg called "The Megyn Kelly Moment," Trump mailed me a copy of the article, which he'd personally signed. The accompanying note read: "Great article, especially from the source."

Once, he forwarded me a Christmas card he found amusing.

Another time, he sent me a note about his high speaking fees.

I thought, *Why is he telling me this?*

"And to think," I wrote back, "we can get you for free!"

He would call me up to chat about a segment after it aired, to compliment how I'd handled a guest.

One time Trump invited me and Doug to Mar-a-Lago, the historic oceanfront mansion and club he owns in Palm Beach. He followed up by sending me pictures of the seventeen-acre property and estate. It was an invitation I would never accept, though plenty of others who hold themselves out as journalists have.

"It's Mr. Trump again," Abby would say, pointing to the phone on my desk.

Why is he calling? I would mouth to her. We would look at each other as if to say, *What's going on here?*

In April 2015, Abby knew I was going to be at Trump Soho, Trump's downtown NYC hotel, for a weekend vacation with my Chicago friends Andrea and Rebecca. Abby was friendly with Trump's assistant from all the calls he'd placed to us, so Abby asked her for a restaurant recommendation near the hotel.

Apparently, the assistant told Trump about it. She called Abby back and said, "Mr. Trump is going to take care of Megyn's girls' weekend."

"Oh, no," I said, realizing that he may have thought I had been angling for that. "Abby, call right back and say thank you so much, but I cannot accept that."

She did, but the next time he came on my show, he told me directly, "I'm gonna take care of your girls' weekend."

"Thank you," I said, "but you know I can't accept that."

"I'm taking care of it," he replied.

"No," I told him.

"I've got it," he insisted.

"Mr. Trump, not only am I not permitted to accept gifts like that, I certainly can't accept them from someone who might run for president." This was not long before he announced his bid.

Trump started to sense that I wasn't going to play, and he seemed slightly irritated by my refusal.

"Abby," I said when I got back to my office, "e-mail them and put it in writing that I am paying for everything that weekend." And I did. I paid for every last cent.

When I went onstage at that first presidential debate in August 2015, I had a printout of that e-mail under my debate papers, just in case Trump tried to discredit me. By that point, I'd seen him slam countless other people who had accepted his gifts and then fallen out of his favor.

This is actually one of the untold stories of the 2016 campaign: I was not the only journalist to whom

Trump offered gifts clearly meant to shape coverage. Many reporters have told me that Trump worked hard to offer them something fabulous—from hotel rooms to rides on his 757. The few reports that have been made public—veteran reporter Wayne Barrett says Trump offered him an apartment;[1] writer Mark Bowden says Trump tried to win him over with a book deal[2]—are from years ago, but make clear Trump's history of trying to buy positive media coverage.

In addition to gifts, Trump used praise. This is smart, because the media is full of people whose egos need stroking. Trump would flatter certain people on Twitter—singling them out for their "incredibly fair," "smart" coverage—one was even teased with a possible role on Celebrity Apprentice. Trump's Twitter followers would respond with accolades, and occasionally you'd see the commentator respond with gratitude. Trump tried to work the refs—and some of the refs responded.

One pro-Trump host called up a conservative writer who had been critical of Trump and told him: "You understand where this is going, right? He's going to be president. It's not too late for you to get on board. Get behind him."

This host tries to pass himself off as unbiased, as

objective. But his behavior raises the question: How many other phone calls like that took place?

When it became too obvious that some media figures were in the tank, certain TV hosts actually took to gaming out with Trump in advance the hits they'd have to do on him occasionally to make themselves appear unbiased. I have been told this directly by more than one TV executive, at more than one network.

One news star would go over the subjects—and even the questions—with which he'd be challenging Trump just before their interviews. "I have to give you a hard time on X," the host would explain, softening the on-air blow so the candidate would not get angry and cut off access.

Another very well known host would call Trump up before criticizing the candidate and warn him: "I have to hit you. I'm getting killed on credibility"—and Trump, the famous counterpuncher, mysteriously didn't hit back after those pre-gamed attacks. Why do you think that was?

This is an egregious breach of journalistic ethics. It's absolutely inappropriate, whether they consider themselves "journalists" or not. You don't "act" the part of an independent, objective host and secretly rehearse your exchanges with a candidate. Ever.

If neither gifts nor praise worked, Trump would use insults or threats. Commentators like Charles Krauthammer, Brit Hume, George Will, Jonah Goldberg, Dana Perino, Rich Lowry, Steve Hayes, Marc Thiessen, and Chris Stirewalt were derided as "dummies" or "losers" or "lightweights" or "failures" for offering their honest, albeit unflattering, analysis of Trump. Anyone who didn't fall under the Trump spell was fair game.

Plenty of straight news reporters were hit too. The *Des Moines Register*'s journalists were banned from Trump's campaign events because the paper's editorial board had harshly criticized him. The *Washington Post* was later banned for similar reasons. So were Univision, the *Daily Beast,* and others. The message was clear: cover Trump "nicely," and good things happen. Hit him too hard, and suffer the consequences. He'd been laying the groundwork for that basic strategy for months before he launched his campaign.

In June, Trump announced his candidacy. Weeks before that, he had appeared on my show.[3] As we sat on set, getting ready for the segment, he could hear me discussing with my producers in the control room which polls I needed. Trump did not approve of my choices.

"I really hope you won't discuss those polls," Trump said.

"Oh, we have to," I told him. They were terrible for Trump back then.

"Well, you should mention this other poll," he protested, naming a far less reputable poll in which he was doing a little bit better. He was trying to manipulate my coverage.

That's fine. People try to do that all the time.

"Mention that if you want to—that's for you to do, not me," I told him. "I'm going to talk about the latest poll from Bloomberg."[4]

He was not happy with the segment. As I said, politicians are often unhappy with their appearances, or at least pretend to be so that you will feel you owe them one. It never bothers me. It's not my job to please them, only to be fair to them.

A month or two later in July, after Trump had formally declared, we had him on again. It was a rough time for Trump in some ways. Macy's and NBC were ripping him for comments he'd made about Mexicans being rapists ("and some, I assume, are good people") in his campaign announcement. Macy's broke up with him. NBC ended his Miss Universe deal. It was a crazy story. Major companies publicly battling with a presidential candidate? When does that happen? Tom and I knew this was a big story.

During the pretaped interview, Trump kept going off topic to talk about China and trade, which he knew would play well with his base. As the world would later see, Trump would come to talk about China and trade every chance he got in the primaries. You could ask him, "How's the weather?" and he would respond, "We need to get tough with China!"

Months later, Bret and I were on set one primary election night. Trump had won and was giving a speech about his victory, saying, "We never win anymore. We're going to start winning again." A man in the audience yelled out, "*Chy-nah!*" Bret and I marveled at Trump's messaging prowess. He had his supporters marching in lockstep with him.

At the end of the lengthy pretape on Macy's and his NBC dispute, I thanked Trump, and he said, "I hope you'll keep all of my remarks."

"We won't be able to do that," I said. "It's way too much for one block."

"I really hope you'll keep the whole thing."

"We can't," I said.

Again, he seemed annoyed.

We did leave in some of what he said about China. Any candidate will get mad if you never let them highlight some of their own message. But he'd mentioned it a dozen times, so most of it got cut. I heard later that (again) he was not happy.

Two things stand out about that appearance in retrospect:

1. He was already trying to control my coverage of him; and

2. He was already remarkably adept at pushing a few core messages. And he had a read on the American electorate that few if any of the other candidates—not to mention party bosses or journalists—did.

From the beginning, Trump knew what made good TV. I remember the first time *The Kelly File* took a Trump campaign event and put it on the air. It was July 2015. Trump went down to the Mexican border and held a presser, and we aired it. It was riveting. It was one of the most compelling political events we had seen in years. And no news came out of it. It was just Trump being Trump: unscripted, unguarded, and fun to watch. We couldn't take our eyes off of it.

The next day we saw the ratings, and there had been a huge pop. The viewers felt the way we did—this was great TV.

Trump held another campaign event not long thereafter. We took that too. Same result with the ratings. It

was then that Tom and I looked at each other and realized something was going on here.

We knew we had made a questionable choice. This
was television crack cocaine, and while it might feel
good in the moment, we felt guilty afterward. Tom
and I had a talk about the Trump coverage we were
seeing in the cable news universe (and, soon thereafter, broadcast news too). Trump was amazing TV, but
what was the cost of giving him all that time, when we
knew damn well we weren't about to do the same for
Jeb Bush or Scott Walker?

Tom and I agreed: no more gratuitous Trump coverage.

This was not a directive to cover Trump negatively
or to ignore him. It was a call to remember our journalistic duty, to provide balance and be judicious in our
coverage, not to sell our souls for ratings or for our own
entertainment.

"When the postmortem is done on the Trump campaign," I said, "let's make sure we're on the side of the
angels." We would wind up rather lonely in that place.

Some other television executives and anchors made
different choices. The amount of free TV time Trump
was given dwarfed all others.[5] In the first few months
of his campaign, he received close to $2 billion worth
of media attention, roughly double the haul of the next

best earner, Hillary Clinton. In one month, he earned in free media about what John McCain spent on his entire 2008 campaign. Of Trump's run, CBS chairman Les Moonves said, "It may not be good for America, but it's damn good for CBS. . . . Man, who would have expected the ride we're all having right now? . . . The money's rolling in and this is fun."[6]

Like many things, Trump *was* fun, until suddenly he wasn't. In late July 2015, my relationship with him took a turn for the worse.

The week before the first Republican primary debate, a report about Trump broke in the *Daily Beast*.[7] A reporter named Tim Mak had dredged up the divorce proceedings between Donald and Ivana Trump, in which Ivana had testified that Trump raped her.

According to her sworn deposition testimony, Ivana had encouraged Trump to have surgery to cover a bald spot. She claimed that he came home in great pain and was angry with her for encouraging him to do it. She described a violent assault, in which he held back her arms and tore out pieces of her hair, then ripped off her clothes and raped her.

On one hand, this was under-oath testimony.

On the other, it was a divorce proceeding, and it was from thirty years ago.

I thought about ignoring it, but the story had gotten

a ton of pickup, and so I decided to bring Tim Mak on the show to press him on his reporting.

"You are under fire for writing a piece about a man's divorce—allegations made in it—from three decades ago," I said to Mak by way of opening. "Why did you think this was relevant?"

He said it was relevant because Trump had accused Mexican immigrants of being rapists. I suggested that was hardly a strong connection, and I continued on.

"Having practiced law for ten years," I told Mak, "divorce proceedings are notoriously ugly. Spouses often say things that aren't true and that they live to regret. How did you account for that reality in your reporting?" I also pointed out that Ivana had later recanted her testimony.

Mak struggled a bit but handled himself all right. Unlike Trump's attorney Michael Cohen, who responded to the *Daily Beast* article with threats and thug tactics. First, Cohen publicly defended Trump by saying, "You cannot rape your spouse. There's very clear case law." This is untrue, as any lawyer from this century should know (he was later forced to walk this back).

In between bouts of misstating the law, Cohen managed to find time to threaten Mak for reporting on the story at all. I quoted a bit of Cohen's strong-arm statement on the show, but this is the full text of what Cohen said:

> I will make sure that you and I meet one day while we're in the courthouse. And I will take you for every penny you still don't have. And I will come after your *Daily Beast* and everybody else that you possibly know. So I'm warning you, tread very fucking lightly, because what I'm going to do to you is going to be fucking disgusting. You understand me? You write a story that has Mr. Trump's name in it, with the word "rape," and I'm going to mess your life up. . . . for as long as you're on this frickin' planet. . . . You're going to have judgments against you, so much money, you'll never know how to get out from underneath it.

This seemed significant enough to me to mention with Mak. I didn't dwell on it, but it was notable, so we noted it.

The next day I got a call from Roger Ailes.

"What did you do to piss off Trump?" he said.

I learned that Trump was, to say the least, not happy

that I had given this story any oxygen and had called my boss. He had come to think of Fox as his friend. He is, in fact, friends with Roger and with many people at the network. He and I were friendly as well. And so when I did that segment, he felt like I had broken some kind of covenant. Trump was booked to come on my show soon after—Monday, August 2, which was the Monday before the first presidential debate. But that Monday morning Trump refused to come on unless I called him personally.

And so I called him up from the back of my car. That phone call was the beginning of the most bizarre year of my life, my Year of Trump.

"*How could you?*" he said instead of hello.

"Mr. Trump," I said, "that story was everywhere. I did you a favor by having the reporter on and telling the other side."

"Oh no," he said. "That story never should have been on your show. O'Reilly didn't put it on his show."

"Well," I said, "Bill is not my editorial gauge."

He was especially enraged that I hadn't mentioned on the show that in addition to recanting, Ivana had said she thought Trump would make "an incredible president." That had not been relevant to the propriety of Mak's reporting, which was the topic at hand.

"I read Ivana's statement rebutting the rape allegations, Mr. Trump. That's what was relevant to the story we were discussing."

"You had no business putting it on your show!" he said. "Oh, I almost unleashed my *beautiful Twitter account* against you, *and I still may.*"

"You don't control the editorial content on *The Kelly File*, Mr. Trump," I said.

And that was when he snapped.

"That's IT!" he shouted. "You're a disgrace! You should be ashamed of yourself. You should be *ashamed of yourself!*"

He hung up on me. My driver looked at me.

"That went well," I deadpanned.

Needless to say, Trump canceled his appearance on *The Kelly File* for that night.

I called Roger, as well as the head of the debate team, to alert them to what had just happened. The debate was in less than four days. And Trump was not happy.

He hadn't pulled out of the debate, but it was conceivable that he might. So much of what he'd done so far had surprised us. I considered that Trump just might be nervous about his first presidential debate, and I tried not to worry about it.

But there had been something more in that phone

call. I believe Trump had realized, once and for all, that he could not control me. He had failed to woo me with his offerings. He had failed to threaten me into submission. And I believe this made him anxious. When I said he couldn't control the editorial content of my show, it appeared to finally dawn on him that it might be true. So he launched a campaign to bring me in line before the coming debate.

20

The First Debate

The Fox News debate moderating team had been set for months—Bret Baier, Chris Wallace, and me. At that point, the moderators were hoping the Fox News management would limit the debate to just the top six candidates, so there would be more time for give-and-take between them. But we were already under fire for cutting it down to ten, and ten was about as small as the Fox News brass was willing to go. We knew that with ten candidates, they would have very little time to engage with one another, so it would be on us, the moderators, to hit them with the toughest questions.

Meanwhile, Trump, having realized in our phone call that he could not control me, tried to go over my head to try to get others to do it for him. In the days leading up to the debate, Trump called more than one executive at Fox in an attempt to rein me in. No one suggested to me that I should go easy on Trump at that debate. Nor would that have worked even if they had.

Trump called our then executive vice president of news, Michael Clemente. He called Bill Sammon, the head of our debate team and at this point our DC bureau chief (Kim Hume had retired years earlier). He called Roger. He wanted assurances about me, although no one ever told me exactly what they were. To my knowledge, Trump wasn't pushing to have me removed from the debate team, but he did want a message sent. I was starting to wonder where this was leading. I had pointed questions for Trump—but my questions for all of the candidates were tough, as were Bret's and Chris's. I wasn't about to dial back on one candidate just because he was complaining in advance.

The day before the debate, Trump called Bill Sammon again, clearly anxious about the debate and me in particular. He said he had "heard" that my first question was a very pointed question directed at him.

How could he know that? I wondered. The debate prep is sacred to the five of us on the debate team—Sammon, Chris Stirewalt (part of our decision desk on Election Night and our digital politics editor), Bret, Chris Wallace, and me. I knew no one on our team would ever have breathed a word about our questions to anyone, much less to one of the candidates. But Trump was extremely agitated, and Sammon tried to calm him down.

Trump was not appeased. I spent a lot of time pacing the Fox News hallways on the phone. Folks were starting to worry about Trump—his level of agitation did not match the circumstances. Yes, it was his first debate. But this was bizarre behavior, especially for a man who wanted the nuclear codes. Though I usually tried to find humor in any situation, I didn't find much to laugh about here—he seemed very anxious about me. Given the number and nature of his calls, it seemed like I was his chief concern, rather than the competitors heading for that stage.

Meanwhile, the question that he hated so much in the debate had been written weeks earlier. Before the Ivana story. Before the "beautiful Twitter account" threat. We'd been working for two months on debate prep. My research assistant Emily Walker had prepared a huge binder on every candidate for me, and having read Trump's cover to cover, it was clear that his Achilles' heel was women. I went to the woman place with Trump because it was obvious this was an issue he would eventually have to face, especially if he were to run against Hillary Clinton.

And so, under this cloud, we flew to Cleveland. I wasn't out to kill Trump, but he wasn't going to have an easy time, either. (Some would later claim the tough questions for Trump were pursuant to a Rupert Murdoch directive. Nonsense—there was zero interference in our debate questions by anyone in Fox management.) I was a bit on edge about asking the question, because I knew Trump was already focused on me. I also knew I had to ask it—these guys were running for president, for Pete's sake.

I talked to Tom Lowell, who was not involved in my debate prep but is always a chief adviser to me, as well as the entire Fox News debate team. The five of us had gone over each of our questions dozens of times. We finessed and toughened them. We eliminated parts of them, added to them, got rid of some, and in some cases wrote new and better ones up until the last minute. We did have a debate about the propriety of the line in my question about Trump telling a contestant on *Celebrity Apprentice* that it "must be a pretty picture" to see her on her knees.

We talked first about whether the line was taken out of context. It was not. There was video.[1] Brande Roderick, a contestant on Trump's show, was sitting across a table from Trump. Bret Michaels, sitting next to her, mentioned that Roderick had begged on her knees to be project manager.

Trump smirked. "Excuse me, you dropped to your knees?"

"Yes," she said.

"That must be a pretty picture," Trump said, "you dropping to your knees."

The camera cut to a laughing Piers Morgan.

It was not out of context.

The next issue was whether or not it was appropriate for a prime-time debate audience.

"Do you think it's appropriate for the decorum of a presidential debate to make a reference to oral sex?" asked Bill Sammon.

"The very fact that you have to ask me that is the reason I have to ask it," I responded. "This guy is seeking the highest office in the land, and he said it on the air, on national television, to an aspiring female professional. It's fair game."

After the debate, Roderick would come out and say she hadn't even remembered him saying it. "I don't condone men being derogatory," she said on MSNBC,[2] "but he's on television. He's trying to be funny. I don't think he meant anything horrible by it."

Fair enough, but the truth was, this wasn't about

Brande's feelings. It was about Trump's history with women and how it might affect his electability, running against a woman.

One of the things we addressed in debate prep was what to do if Trump went after me once I asked the question. I said to Bret and Chris, "If he does, don't try to help me."

They both said variations of: "Oh, don't worry. We'll be behind you—*way* behind you."

They knew I could handle myself, and anyway, they had no particular desire to inject themselves into that back-and-forth.

On the last day of debate prep, once the questions were set, Bret, Chris, and I looked at each other. I said, "This is it. If anyone has a problem, speak now or forever hold your peace."

Mine were not the only tough questions, not by a long shot. Chris was going after Trump on his four bankruptcies.[3] Bret was going to open the debate by asking the candidates if they promised to support whoever the Republican nominee was. It was a controversial, dramatic way to start. I was hitting Scott Walker on abortion and Ben Carson on foreign policy. The first round of questions, in particular, was the Olympics of questioning. No one has gone harder on the candidates than we did in that opening round.

It was electric. It was journalism. And it was spectacular. We were all in.

To figure out who would open the debate, the debate team huddled in the Cavaliers locker room. Stirewalt went to get a coin to flip and came back holding one with a queen on the front. They looked at me and said, "Call it."

I said, "Gotta side with the queen."

The queen won. I opened up the debate. (Bret opened the next one, and I did the third.)

The moment backstage before we went out in the arena, we were like a sports team putting all hands in. We walked out together. I knew I had the support of my co-moderators and the network. Even Brit had been in our debate prep the final day, for which I was thankful. I read him my opening question to Trump about the women. "It's a great question," he said. So I went out to the stage feeling fine about it.

However, physically of course, I was not feeling fine, since I had been violently ill for most of the day. Moments earlier, as I walked from my dressing room to the debate stage, surrounded by my team—my research assistant Emily Walker, Abby, Chris, and Vincenza—I felt my mojo start to come back. I started to feel less shaky and ill, more geared up and focused. The endorphins began to flow.

Bill Shine, our executive vice president of programming at the time, was in the hallway just outside the debate stage entrance. He pulled out his camera and shot a picture of me. In it, I am walking toward Shine, pointing at the camera, ninja-like. If I could caption that photo, I'd call it "Triumphant."

And I was off.

The debate began, and it was raw, pure, all-encompassing excitement. I had a blanket on my lap and an empty trashcan at my feet in case I threw up again, but I was confident I wouldn't. Now my adrenaline was pumping.

The opening round boiled down to: "Are you electable?" Republican voters may like you a lot, but if you're too extreme or uninformed or inconsistent, it could pose a problem for the party. We are here to find out: Can you win? This was a process of elimination. Each opening question was an A-plus-level question. Three Fox News anchors, no holds barred.

The drama started immediately when Bret asked the candidates if anyone was not prepared to say they would support the eventual nominee of the party. We weren't sure how many hands we would get. We assumed Trump and Rand Paul might stand out. Only Trump raised his hand. In doing so, he sent a clear message to the millions watching at home that he was a different kind of candidate, one not concerned with pleasing the party elders. While Trump handled himself just fine in the moment, I now know he was very unhappy with the question.

Moments later, I asked Trump the women question, and he became even more unhappy.

"Mr. Trump," I said, "one of the things people love about you is you speak your mind and you don't use a politician's filter. However, that is not without its downsides. In particular, when it comes to women. You've called women you don't like 'fat pigs,' 'dogs,' 'slobs,' and 'disgusting animals.'"

He interrupted halfway through with the line: "Only Rosie O'Donnell." The audience erupted in laughter. There was no way I was going to laugh. It would have been inappropriate, for one thing, and for another, what he said wasn't true.

By that point, I was well aware of everything he had said about Rosie O'Donnell, and what she had said about him. And in Trump's defense, Rosie gave as good as she got during her tiff with Trump. That's why I was determined, in crafting the question, to include more than just his references to Rosie. My question has been fact-checked many times since then, and every part of it has been verified by every publication to look into the matter. Trump had a long pattern of attacking women for not being, in his view, pretty or sexually appealing enough.

In fact, there was so much material that I left most of it on the cutting room floor. He'd talked about wanting "a young and beautiful piece of ass" by his side,[4] and said of his approach with the opposite sex: "You have to treat 'em like shit."[5] He'd rated countless women's looks on a scale from one to ten. He'd lamented how "unattractive" Bill Clinton's alleged lovers had been. Just to name a few.

So when he tried, somewhat predictably, to say it was only Rosie O'Donnell, I was prepared to fact-check him on the spot.

"For the record," I said, "it was well beyond Rosie O'Donnell." Even Trump had to admit that was true in the moment. Then I continued: "Your Twitter account has several disparaging comments about women's looks. You once told a contestant on *Celebrity Apprentice* it would be a pretty picture to see her on her knees. Does that sound to you like the temperament of a man we should elect as president, and how will you answer the charge from Hillary Clinton, who is likely to be the Democratic nominee, that you are part of the 'war on women'?"

Trump responded that we've gotten too politically correct in this country—and on that I agree with him, as do many voters. Whether that excuses his comments about women, well, that was the voters' job to decide. My job was simply to shine a light.

"What I say is what I say," he continued. "And honestly, Megyn, if you don't like it, I'm sorry. I've been very nice to you, although I could probably maybe not be, based on the way you have treated *me*. But I wouldn't do that."

I noticed the shot but moved on, glad the exchange had gone relatively well. After that, I was relieved. I knew the hardest part of the night was over, and the rest felt like downhill skiing.

When the whole thing was over, I was elated. I believed the debate had gone very well. It was riveting. Everyone was on their game, and the ratings the next day would confirm it. Bret, Chris, and I exchanged congratulations, and I hightailed it off the stage.

Immediately after we wrapped, I had to do my show live from what they call Spin Alley in the convention center. At 11:00 p.m. sharp, I rushed from the debate stage to my set, perched in the middle of a swarm of reporters. During that live broadcast, with reporters wall-to-wall around him, Trump walked by my set. He yelled out, "Megyn Kelly is *not nice*! She is *no good*!" I chose not to acknowledge it.

The media saw how angry he was, and he did not

mince words in interviews that night, describing my woman question as "nasty" and "unfair."[6] I saw my fellow reporters eating it up, apparently reluctant to challenge his characterizations.

Trump's annoyance built from there.[7] He retweeted followers, calling me "overrated," "angry," and a "bimbo" and he directly called me "not very good or professional!" He said I "really bombed tonight. People are going wild on twitter! Funny to watch." Some reporters openly speculated about whether Trump himself could be sending these tweets.

Being accustomed to politicians unhappy with their coverage, I wasn't particularly concerned with these criticisms. They usually got over it quickly. In fact, I understood Trump's anger. He was new to the political process, standing up there next to a bunch of political pros who had been through dozens of debates in their careers, and he didn't know what to expect. He said repeatedly that we were "not nice" to him. No one ever promised we would be nice. Debates aren't cocktail parties. However, all of this was new to Trump, who thought he had a good relationship with Fox News (which he does), with these moderators (which he did), and that his presence on that stage would help drive huge ratings (which it did). He felt betrayed. I get it. I don't agree with it, but I get it.

By the end of the primary debate process, Trump would be far more savvy. He understood that these things could be very tough, and he was more up to the task. He learned to project "I'm a winner" instead of "I'm a whiner" after the debates were over. That shift did not, however, include moving on from what happened with me.

The next morning, at the airport in Cleveland, sitting with Abby at a café, I scrolled through my phone. Half of what I saw were great reviews and kudos. The other half were incredibly nasty messages from Trump and his supporters. He was repeatedly ripping on me in interviews and on Twitter. "Beautiful Twitter account" indeed. *Holy shit*, I thought. *He's really going for it.*

At that point, I figured that he'd wear himself out. I still believe it would not have been nearly as big a deal if Trump hadn't reacted the way he had. Every one of the candidates got extremely tough questions that night. But Trump was the only one to complain. Trump's extraordinary reaction was enough to draw millions of eyeballs to the woman question, over and over and over again. I wondered whether that was a smart tactical move on his part.

Having been on TV for over a decade, I had seen

plenty of on-air exchanges go viral on the Internet. But this was in a league of its own. It was everywhere. *Everywhere.* Broadcast, cable, talk radio, print, Twitter, Facebook, Instagram, every online site known to man, domestically and internationally—Peru, Brazil, Italy, and beyond.

My brother Pete texted to see how I was holding up. My sister wrote me, "Put on some *Willy Wonka*— and remember, you can run circles around any of these people."

"I have every confidence in you, honey," my mom said. "You never met a man you couldn't handle."

As soon as we arrived in New York, I headed into Fox News. I had agreed to do a pretaped interview that day with Howie Kurtz, Fox's media watchdog, for his Sunday show. In the on-camera exchange, I told him, "I'm sure nerves were high, as they were for all of the candidates. Trump felt attacked. It wasn't an attack. It's okay with me that there's some consternation. He'll get over that, and we'll be fine. I'm a big girl. I can take it."

Everyone in the Fox building did one of two things when they saw me: congratulated me or asked if I was doing okay. Such an odd combination of celebration and sympathy. I would get very used to it in the months to come.

Most nights, *The Kelly File* is live at 9:00 p.m., but

that day we pretaped it with a studio audience reacting to the debate. When I was done, it was almost 9:00. I sat at my desk in my office and flipped around the channels to see what the coverage looked like. Every channel was wall-to-wall debate coverage, with most talking about my question and Trump's attacks on me.

On CNN, Don Lemon was anchoring, and Trump was doing a phoner. I heard later that Trump had insisted his interview with Lemon air opposite our show at 9:00 p.m., as opposed to at 10:00 p.m., when Don usually anchors. CNN acquiesced and gave Trump a thirty-minute phoner, commercial-free. (For what it's worth, *The Kelly File* crushed them in the ratings that night.)

Lemon asked Trump, "What is it with you and Megyn Kelly?"

"Well, I just don't respect her as a journalist," Trump said. "I have no respect for her. I don't think she's very good. She's highly overrated. But when I came out there, what am I doing? I'm not getting paid for this. I go out there. They start saying lift up your arm if you're . . . I didn't know there were going to be twenty-four million people. I knew there was going to be a big crowd because I get big crowds. They call me the ratings machine. So she gets out and she starts asking me all sorts of ridiculous questions and you could see there was blood coming out of her eyes, blood coming out of her . . . wherever. In my opinion, she was off base. And, by the way, not in my opinion—in the opinion of hundreds of thousands of people on Twitter. . . . She's a lightweight, and I couldn't care less about her."

My *wherever?*

I e-mailed Irena Briganti, Fox's top PR person.

Did you see that? I asked.

She had indeed.

Fox News is very good at responding when one of its people is attacked. But we were in uncharted territory. We had to be careful. This was a front-runner in the campaign. I certainly did not want to get down into the mud with him, but I was also stunned at the tone of his attacks. And yet I don't think I realized the magnitude of what had just happened or where those comments would take us.

I texted Don Lemon, with whom I'm friendly: **Cannot believe the latest.**

Continue taking the high road, he responded.

I like Lemon. I enjoy his approach to the news. Some people would later give him a hard time for not calling out Trump on the blood comments in the moment. I don't think Lemon understood the comments to be a reference to a woman's menstrual cycle. There is still debate about whether that's what Trump meant—

Trump would later say he meant my nose or ears—but I was fine with how Lemon handled it.

I was heading to the Jersey shore that night to be with Doug and my kids for the weekend. It was Friday. Getting into that car was like getting into a warm bath. I was done with the debate and the months of preparation that went into it. Bret, Chris, Sammon, Stirewalt, and I all felt great about it, and were exchanging e-mails about the strong reviews. Frank Bruni's in the *New York Times* was particularly memorable. The debate was "riveting," Bruni wrote. "It was admirable. It compels me to write a cluster of words I never imagined writing: hooray for Fox News."[8] Once again, the insult tied to the compliment.

I was finally on my way to my family . . . my happiness . . . the heart of what I truly am.

It was in the back of that car that everything seemed to explode. Staring at my phone, I saw the Internet lose its mind over those blood comments. And I knew, as that car sped through the dark night, phone glowing in my hand, that things would never be the same again.

21

Fallout

The shocks came one after the other. Within hours of the Lemon interview, Erick Erickson disinvited Trump from a conservative gathering he was about to host. Erick Erickson! The very man I had publicly castigated for his sexist views on women was castigating a different man for his comments about me. I couldn't believe it. I could not keep up with all the e-mails, texts, and notifications coming in, many with the hashtag #IStandWithMegyn. I felt uncomfortable. The story was growing, and I wanted it extinguished.

The exchange was catching fire in a way I had never seen before. My head was swimming. It is truly bizarre to cover the news for a living and then to see yourself actually become the news from coast to coast and beyond. I felt like Alice through the Looking Glass. I was used to talking about politicians; all of a sudden, politicians were talking about me.[1]

On Twitter, Carly Fiorina wrote,[2] "Mr. Trump: There. Is. No Excuse," adding "I stand with @megynkelly."

Scott Walker wrote, "There's no excuse for Trump's comments. . . . @MegynKelly is a tough interview. Being POTUS is tougher."

John Kasich, Rick Perry, George Pataki, Jeb Bush, Lindsay Graham, to name a few, weighed in with similar condemnations, and some called for Trump to drop out of the race.

It was clear now that this story wasn't going away anytime soon. At first, I felt gratified that, to the extent people felt the need to comment on it at all, they appeared to be saying enough is enough—that Trump should stop the nonsense. But in twenty-four hours I would feel very differently. This was the beginning of a cycle I would go through many, many times with Trump. A master at manipulating the media, he would find a way to reset the public's perception of an event within days or even hours. The media was, of course, eager to give him the platform.

Someone asked me later if I felt embarrassed that the nation was discussing my menstrual cycle. I didn't. It was more like disbelief. What was happening? Every show in the nation is leading with Trump talking about my period? I mean, who the hell has a file for that one?

Trump denied that those comments meant what many thought they meant. He said in a statement that "only a sick person" or a "deviant" would think that he was referring to menstruation—a line that would wind up the subject of considerable mockery, especially by Jimmy Fallon. He would do the same thing later after mocking Carly Fiorina's appearance. "*Look* at that face!" he said on the trail.[3] "Would anyone *vote* for that? Can you imagine that, the face of our next *president*? I mean, she's a woman, and I'm not s'posedta say bad things, but really, folks, come on. Are we *serious*?" Trump would later dismiss this as an innocent comment about her "persona." Fiorina later addressed that at a debate, saying,[4] "I think women all over the country heard very clearly what Mr. Trump said." It was a mic-drop moment for her.

I found it curious that no one was asking Trump about his retweets of people calling me a "bimbo," which were unambiguous and continuing around this same time. Blood apparently trumps bimbo on the scale of offensive rhetoric; indeed, "bimbo" didn't seem to carry much shock value. Trump also continued saying that I was terrible, unfair, a lightweight, and so on. People were calling it a "feud," or a "war," when in fact it was a one-sided offensive. I had neither baited him nor fought back. I just sat and watched, and waited for it to end.

Looking at the constant ongoing barrage from him and the vitriol coming from so many of his supporters, I realized for the first time, *He's not stopping.* I'd seen angry politicians before, but usually they wore themselves out once they got a complaint out of their system. Trump seemed to be gaining steam. Later I would return to work to find a litany of voice mails—someone had released my number on the Internet—calling me a "cunt," "bitch," and "fucking whore." This wasn't particularly enjoyable to listen to, but didn't really upset me—again, unfortunately, it can be part of the job, as virtually anyone who upset Trump during his presidential run found out. One caller reamed me for raising the women issue at all, saying, "No one gives a damn about misogyny. This country has real problems."

One of the greatest ironies was that with every new comment, Trump was proving the point of my question. I had asked about how he would combat the likely Hillary narrative that he is part of the so-called war on women, a meme used rather effectively by the Democrats in 2012. With each new blow against me, I thought, *She's going to hit you with that one, too.*

Late that Friday night, I arrived at the shore and slipped into bed with Doug. The next morning, I told Doug about what had happened. He was angry about the blood comment and wanted to know what Fox was doing about it. I told him the truth: "Nothing for now."

What could they do? Roger was talking to Trump daily, trying to calm him down. But it wasn't working. Many in the press questioned why Fox wasn't hitting back hard at Trump, given Roger's infamous love of fighting and the nature of the attacks on me. I understood Roger's decision, however. None of us wanted a fight with Trump—what we wanted was to cover his fight with his opponents.

It was that morning that I saw Trump's attorney and executive vice president of the Trump Organization, Michael Cohen, getting retweeted, over and over and over again, with a message directed at me. He had retweeted a Trump supporter who said **#boycottmegynkelly @realDonaldTrump we can gut her**.

Gut her.

For the first time, I felt alarmed. Michael Cohen is the same man who had threatened *Daily Beast* reporter Tim Mak with the line, "What I'm going to do to you is going to be fucking disgusting." At the time he was Trump's main surrogate, his top message man, and is to this day a loyal soldier in the Trump army. Now, as tempers were already at fever pitch, he was telling his 40,000 followers to "gut" me? This went too far, and was easily the thing from Team Trump that most bothered me in the days after the debate. As if on cue, the threats skyrocketed.

"Fox has to do something," Doug demanded. Trump may have been polling well with white men across America, but not so much with those inside my apartment.

I later found out that Fox *was* doing something. Bill Shine called Cohen directly and tried to make him understand this kind of irresponsible messaging had already led to death threats. Cohen—a frequent guest on Fox News—was not particularly moved.

Shine, exasperated by Cohen's indifference, tried to explain it in terms Cohen might understand: "If Megyn Kelly is killed, it's not going to help your candidate."

Sean Hannity also worked behind the scenes to lower the temperature among Trump's more prominent supporters, including some on talk radio and online who were ratcheting up the anger. He didn't have to do it, but he had my back.

I was growing concerned—with the threats, the misinformation, the battering ram being used on my reputation and my relationship with my viewers. I realized that my pretaped segment with Howie Kurtz was going to air Sunday morning, and it occurred to me that I should contact him. I wanted to be sure that, given the "gut her" tweet and the amount of threats pouring in, he made it clear that my "No big deal" reaction was taped prior to the weekend's events. Having lived under threat years before with the stalker, I didn't want to give the impression that threats to my safety were fair game.

Howie understood completely, and agreed to make that point.

I went back to work that Monday and Tuesday, as previously planned. I would then start a ten-day vacation at the shore.

When I got back to New York for my Monday-night show, things were strained around the building. So many of my colleagues were incredibly supportive, but there were also plenty who had no idea what to say to me. Was I a heroine or a victim? Or a villain? Should they high-five me or hug me—or hate me? I think it was unclear to many of them. A few were vocal Trump supporters who, like Trump himself, appeared to be somewhat angry with me.

I toughed it out for two days, heartened that a break was coming my way. On *The Kelly File*, I announced that I was going on vacation: "It's been an interesting week. A long six months, without a vacation for yours truly. . . . So I'll be taking the next week and a half off, spending some time with my husband and my kids, trying to relax. . . . Have a great week."

The statement fell on deaf ears. By the time I arrived at the shore in the wee hours of the morning, Trump's supporters were already celebrating the fiction that I had been suspended. Trump fueled the rumor with more tweets, saying I should "take another 11-day 'unscheduled' vacation,"[5] and that my show was better without me. His Twitter brigade rejoiced.

Of course it wasn't true. You don't get suspended for moderating a debate watched by nearly 25 million people and asking all the candidates hard questions. Even from the shore, I spoke to Roger often. We wrestled with what to do, since the company couldn't control Trump, but didn't want to aggravate him (or his supporters) further. To its credit, Fox came out and publicly ridiculed the suspension nonsense as up there with alleged UFO sightings. Later, they would also issue a strong statement defending me and my debate questioning.

My time at the beach was otherworldly. I tried to ignore the insanity, but everyone I knew during my vacation asked me about it whenever I saw them. I started to feel like someone with a bad medical result, the way people would react to me: "Are you okay? How are you? You hanging in there?"

Going online was an exercise in self-flagellation. Angry, threatening messages were everywhere. This was well beyond the typical "You suck!" that any tough questioning of a candidate might get you in 2016 cable news. It was, "Fucking die, bitch!" And "If I see you, you better run." And "I wouldn't be sleeping too soundly if I were you. Watch out." There wasn't one in particular that stood out; it was more the uncontainable level of rage that was surprising and disconcerting.

Fox informed me that they too continued to receive threats to my life. I would spend many days of the coming months accompanied by security. A word on these threats—despite their number, it bears noting that I wasn't walking around constantly in fear. I didn't actively worry that I might get attacked; it was more of a recognition that the risk was heightened, that I needed to be careful—to take precautions, and be aware—especially when with my children.

Most disturbing were the overwhelming number and violent nature of the messages we were receiving—and the way Trump's anger was evidently seen by some as a call to action. Trump told his supporters that Mexican immigrants were bringing drugs and were rapists, and shortly thereafter, Hispanics were attacked by Trump fans ("My supporters are very passionate," Trump later rationalized). Trump told his crowds they should punch protesters in the face; sure enough, they did. Trump called the media disgusting and openly shamed them to his fans; the media then got physically attacked at Trump rallies. The point is, some of Trump's supporters took his word as gospel. And Trump's word (and that of his lawyer) on me was clear: *Megyn Kelly is no good. Gut her.*

At times I wondered if I had done something other than ask a tough debate question. Had I attacked Trump while in some rogue dream state? What else could possibly explain this level of anger?

Doug insisted that I step away from the iPhone: "You have to leave your phone at home when we go out," he said. "Look at it once in the morning, once in the afternoon, once at night. That's it." Then he put it in a drawer. It helped.

Every time I turned my phone back on, it practically exploded with hundreds and hundreds and hundreds of messages. One nice memory of that time was that, for every nasty incoming note, I received many supportive e-mails from friends at Fox and elsewhere: **We love you!** or **This is wrong! We stand behind you!** Janice Dean and Dana Perino, my two closest friends at

Fox, were particular standouts. Stirewalt, too, was such a good friend to me. My old pal Kelly texted me **Bat Shit Crazy**, which summed it up perfectly. My sister-in-law Diane wished me via text **the courage to continue being big and brave and beautiful**.

Katie Couric, whom I've always liked, reached out to me. She had been through her own public backlash after she had the nerve to ask Sarah Palin, in the run-up to the 2008 election, what newspapers she read. **Are you okay?** she wrote me. **Do you need some Tampax?** Doug and I appreciated the chance to laugh.

Even Harvard's David Cutler, a mild-mannered guy who helped craft Obamacare and with whom I used to argue on the air, e-mailed me and said, **I hope you're okay. Let me know if there's anything I can do.** That e-mail stood out as especially sweet.

Janice, her husband, Sean, and their two boys came to visit us at the shore. They helped take our mind off the threats as much as possible. But things were tense. Our neighbors reported seeing strange cars casing our home. Another neighbor spotted a photographer in our backyard. Then one on our front porch. We kept the blinds closed most of the time, wondering where this would go. Would people be trying to catch me in a compromising position, similar to what happened with Erin Andrews and that Peeping Tom? Word spread of

still more unfamiliar characters on or near our property, and the police stepped up their patrols.

I talked to my mom about it, and she was angry
at Trump and incredulous at his willingness to play
the victim. The main thing she wanted to know was
whether Roger was behind me. I told her the truth,
which was that he had many considerations to factor in.

The last day of vacation, Doug played in a doubles
tennis match. He and his friend Matt play in this tournament every year. It is held at the summer club Doug
grew up a part of, where he learned to sail and play
tennis years ago. Matt and Doug are both very well
liked guys—tall, fit, friendly, and handsome. They
had made it to the finals of the tournament, where they
faced off against two men who were a bit older, shorter,
and, as it turned out, better tennis players that year.
The opponents wound up beating Matt and Doug in
the third set.

One of the men had complained about the rules
for much of the match, to the point where the crowd
began openly booing him. His partner said very little.
It was crowded on the club balcony above the court. I
was there, along with Janice and Sean, the wives of the
other players, and other family members, cheering our
guys on. Our children were with me.

When the match ended, I made my way over to the

gate leading off the court so I could see Doug. The complaining player was over at the umpire's chair, showing him a rulebook. His silent partner made a beeline off the court—not toward his wife or kids, but toward me. When he got to me, he was silent no more. He pointed his finger at my face, looked me in the eye, and boomed, "*Trump* 2016!"

This was his first reaction to his own victory. He wasn't celebrating or hugging his family; he was pointing at me and angrily yelling, "TRUMP!"

Doug hadn't seen the incident, and when he saw my face, he asked me what was wrong. I told him what had just happened. Immediately he turned around, grabbed the man by the shoulder, and threatened to hurt him if he said another word to me. Then he stormed off the court. The player would later complain that *Doug* had broken the club's etiquette rules by threatening him. He was particularly upset that Doug had done this in front of the man's wife, which struck me as ironic.

It was jarring to see Trump's anger manifest so personally in my own life. I wondered if this was my new reality—angry Trump supporters yelling at me (and indeed it would happen many times over the next year). On the bright side, I told Doug, "You are definitely getting action tonight." Why should there be no silver linings?

Doug's mother, Jackie, had been at the beach with us. She had to return home to Philadelphia, and on her way home, she pulled over to the side of the road. She and I hadn't gotten the chance to really talk, and she wanted to see how I was doing. She didn't want to half-ass it, talking while driving or not giving the discussion her full attention. She sat in a parking lot and did something she rarely does—gave advice. She told me the country could see who I really was. That this man was not convincing any reasonable person of anything about me. That I had handled myself with dignity. That I was loved. I held on to that talk for a long time.

I returned to work ten days later, on August 24. I met with Roger, Irena, and a friend of Roger, attorney and counselor Peter Johnson Jr., in Roger's office that day. Peter had been a vocal Trump defender on the air for some time and I wondered what he was doing there. We had agreed over the previous weekend that I should offer an on-camera statement upon my return, and we were there to discuss a draft. The overall goal was for me to stay above it all, not to get drawn into a fight.

We discussed Trump's blood comments, the "gut her" tweet, and the attempts to get Trump to listen to reason during my vacation. Roger felt reasonably certain that he had calmed Trump down for now, even though Trump had not let up during my break—tweeting out my *GQ* photos and calling me a "bimbo."

"He'll do it again," I said to him.

"We fight tomorrow's fight tomorrow," Roger responded.

This was the first time we had all sat down together since the debate, and I shared with the group the story about what had happened the morning of the debate—my sudden illness, my doctor, and so on. Peter Johnson Jr. heard mention of vomiting and asked whether there might be a "different, happier" reason I'd fallen ill, suggesting I may have been expecting.

I looked at him and deadpanned, "Haven't you heard? I'm on my period."

That first night back on the air, tensions were running high. I felt a little nervous, and I don't really get nervous about doing TV anymore. It seemed like the eyes of the world were on me. The air in the studio felt heavy. I could feel the energy of people tuning in, waiting.

Moments earlier, Trump had been on O'Reilly for two blocks—an interesting choice by Bill for my first day back. They had not discussed Trump's bogus suspension claims, or any of his comments about me.

I went out and sat down at my desk in the studio.

This is normally where I feel most powerful. That desk has a way of transforming me into a stronger version of myself. When in that spot, I feel in command. That night, however, I just felt anxious to get it over with.

Now, I love my staff and my crew—my audio guy and stage director and my cameramen. I think of them as my scarecrow and lion and tin man, times a few. Every night I'm with these guys. These are my guys. We talk about the guests, the news, our spouses, our lives, Fox, everything. They're like brothers to me. They all greeted me warmly and asked how I was.

"Hanging in there," I said. I sat down. It was 8:57. My statement was loaded in the teleprompter, and I practiced it one time, which I almost never do. I wanted to make sure I could get it out clean. I could see the red numbers counting down on the bottom of my camera. It was 8:59:53. We were about to "bong in" with the open. My shoulders were inched up a little higher than normal. Tension. My stage manager, James, locked eyes with me and nodded his head. He started counting me down, "Seven, six, five . . ."

It was at that moment that Dion, our audio guy, yelled from offstage, "*We love you!*"

I still can't think about that moment without tearing up.

It had not been an easy time. Off the set, we don't

really know each other all that well. I mean, I throw a party for the gang at Christmas. And we have fun. They know I would do anything for them. But I could feel the support in that room. When I read that statement—"Mr. Trump has attacked me personally. I have chosen not to respond"—I was thinking about my crew. *I don't need to prove anything to anyone. Those who know me know who I am.* I believed—hoped—that would be the end of it with Trump, whom I promised to cover without fear or favor.[6] We now know it was nowhere near the end. There's no modern historical precedent for a mainstream political candidate targeting a journalist as Trump targeted me. Nor was there any example to follow.

If I had one guiding principle, it was to take the high road. Brit Hume understood, and would observe to me months later, "The policy of dignity has served you very well."

I consider myself lucky, because I have a big platform. I get to show the world who I am every night. Truth drowns out the unmoored lie; I really believe that. I used my platform at times to defend other women Trump went after, including Katy Tur of MSNBC, CNN's Sara Murray, and Heidi Cruz, who was the subject of a nasty Trump retweet comparing her looks unfavorably to those of Trump's wife Melania. But I never responded to Trump's personal attacks on me.

I think that frustrated Trump. He began to mock the fact that Fox News would occasionally respond to him, but I would not. It was clear that Trump was baiting me, that he wanted me to engage with him, which only shored up my resolve not to do so. I'm guessing I seemed to Trump like the women he could usually charm. When I was not charmed, perhaps he felt confused. I think he didn't know quite what to do with me.

With a bit more hindsight, I think Trump was bothered by me not necessarily because I'm a woman but because I'm a woman with power. I had the 9:00 p.m. show on Fox News, his favorite channel, and I couldn't be brought to heel. I think he believed I could help or hurt him more than Anderson Cooper or Chuck Todd (both of whom also covered Trump with skepticism), or just about anyone else in the media. That's why he repeatedly demanded a boycott. And wanted me pulled from future debates. And his supporters petitioned to have me fired. They wanted to remove me from power.

People often ask me, given the number of Trump's tweets and barbs, "How did you keep from responding to him?" One thing I remembered came from my mom. She always said that parents can project one of three things to their children: the Good Me, the Bad Me, or the Not Me. If a child can't get attention for being good, he'll try being bad. Any attention is better than none. The worst thing for a child is the Not Me, to feel that he's not worthy of a response, no matter his behavior. That's how you deal with a bully. A bully wants your attention. Give it to him, and you're feeding the fire. You stay focused on your game. As I always tell my team in times of controversy: head down, shoulders back, forge forward.[7]

22

Relentless

During the nine months following the August debate, Trump's poll numbers rose steadily. It didn't matter what he said or did. Republican primary voters were angry, and they liked that he was angry too. Trump remained angry with me, which made it tough to extract myself from this strange space. I was still covering the news, but I was also *being* covered. Although I did nothing to stoke or even respond to it, the Trump vs. Me storyline was still regularly in the press. At times I felt as if I had been dropped into a shark tank—watched by slightly horrified passersby as I tried to get out and get back on solid ground. Every appearance I made on other shows or in public venues, the interviewers asked me about Trump, and not much other than Trump. I did my best to politely move on.

As his campaign continued to dominate, more reporters ultimately started challenging Trump—on his call to ban all Muslims, his reversals on substantive issues, and his attack on *New York Times* reporter Serge Kovaleski's physical disability, to name a few. If Trump believed anything he said or did might be problematic for him, he would simply deny he said or did it, and throughout the primaries the media usually gave him a pass—often because almost instantaneously (and, some believed, intentionally), he was on to the next controversy. He attacked many journalists who pressed him on his vulnerabilities, but he never went after other reporters in the same way he did with me.

Meanwhile, his focus on me was incessant:

I refuse to call Megyn Kelly a bimbo, because that would not be politically correct, he tweeted. **Instead I will only call her a lightweight reporter!**

And then: **If crazy @megynkelly didn't cover me so much on her terrible show, her ratings would totally tank. She is so average in so many ways!**

Just as I would think the onslaught was over, he would again go on the attack. Then he would quiet down, and then start back up again. In just a few months' time, Trump offered scores of insults about me on television and on Twitter.[1] The word was *relentless*. Every time he started in, I'd get a call from Roger (who was getting calls from Trump). Was I being fair to Trump? Was I being too hard on him? He felt the bar for skeptical Trump coverage should be higher. Tom and I disagreed. The pressure was intense internally and externally.

There was often no discernible trigger for Trump's attacks. Something that seemed of no consequence would set him off without warning. For example, after *Vanity Fair* profiled me that winter, Trump popped up to complain about it. There was a line in the story that mentioned he'd tried to woo me before he announced his presidential bid with notes and calls and by sending me articles written about me that he had signed. In response, Trump denied it, saying "The last person in the world I would try to woo is Megyn Kelly" and claiming that he'd never sent me anything other than polls.[2] I didn't say anything more at the time, because it did not seem worth ginning it up again. For the record, some of the many notes he denied sending can be found in the photo section of this book.

Over the 2015 holidays, tragedy struck our family. My stepbrother Patrick died. Patrick, Peter's son, was a gentle and loving man. He managed a Rite-Aid. He supported his children. And one week before Christmas, he had a sudden, massive heart attack at age forty-seven, just a few months before he was supposed to walk his daughter down the aisle. Patrick led a quiet life—he loved his kids, his dogs, and going on day trips with his wife. His Facebook page was filled with sweet animal videos and pictures of his kids. He never had anything but a kind word for people.

Peter was distraught. Liza had to take a leave of absence from her nursing job. And a dark pall was cast over our family. We spent the days leading up to the holiday burying Patrick and saying good-bye. As we dealt with the loss, and I saw my family—especially Peter—in such pain, I was reminded of how little all of the political nonsense meant. Of how much value there is in simply being a good man, even if not a powerful one.

It was around this time that I first considered reaching out to Trump. I'd been thinking about the pointlessness of being mired in conflict, of what a waste all that emotional energy was. My mom had taught me this from an early age—that conflict resolution is a gift to yourself. I learned it again when I decided to leave the law, in part because of the constant acrimony. This was not how I wanted to lead my life. Some controversy is unavoidable, but constant brawling is not good. It's just not how you want to spend your time.

I asked some colleagues at work who were close to Trump if they thought I should reach out to him. To a person, they told me that Trump was too angry, that his hatred for me was too deep-seated. I decided to give him some more time.

I returned to New York to more vitriol—messages calling me misogynistic names or people returning their signed head shots of me, writing the word TRAITOR across the picture. I wondered what kind of person spends the Christmas holiday sending hate mail.

I received a nice message from—of all people—Dr. Phil, and it lifted my spirits. He reminded me that bullies who poke you with a stick want to see you jump. Not long after that, he came to Fox for a promotional appearance on *The Kelly File*, and an incredible thing happened—we became friends. It won't surprise you to learn how much that meant to me. He told me about an interview he had given shortly after one of Trump's tirades against me. He told the reporter, "Successful lawyer, top journalist, wife, mother of three children—if that's a bimbo, I hope all of my granddaughters grow up to be bimbos." I loved that, and I am still floored by the fact that the man who changed my life from the *Oprah* set is now someone I can call for advice.

We spent most of January preparing for the next Fox News debate in Iowa. Trump was firing off nasty tweets about me here and there, but nothing too incendiary, until the Saturday before the debate, when out of the blue, he threatened not to come.

He went on Twitter and asked his followers if he should go to the debate at all. He accused me of being unfair. For the first time I thought, *Is this real? Or is this for attention?* With Trump, you just never know.

Sunday, he kept at it. Tweet, tweet, tweet.

At the same time, Trump's campaign manager, Corey Lewandowski, made a phone call to Bill Sammon and tried to get me booted off the debate team. When Sammon told him that was out of the question, Lewandowski threatened me, saying I'd had a "rough couple of days after that last debate," and he "would hate to have [me] go through that again."[3] The tone was unmistakable. Sammon warned Lewandowski that he was out of line. I was far from the only woman or reporter Lewandowski had threatened during Trump's campaign. Trump fired him many months later. Then CNN hired him for a reported $500,000 a year.

That Monday, January 25, Trump went on CNN to say he might not show because of me: "I don't like her. She doesn't treat me fairly. I'm not a big fan of hers at all." I was at a loss—why would he allow me to have so much of a role in his campaign? He told CNN he might be the best thing that had ever happened to me, saying no one had ever heard of me before my dust-up with him. Obviously not true, but typical Trump.

There were some editorials about the sexism of this

claim,[4] but that wasn't my reaction. My main thought was how ironic it was for him to suggest he had made my career while he was in fact trying to destroy it. And how ironic of him to suggest that I was the one who needed a man's help to succeed, given our relative backgrounds and fathers.

On Tuesday, Trump kept at it—he put up an Instagram poll asking his followers if he should participate in the debate, given my involvement. He was upping the ante.

Later Trump posted a video of himself with the caption, "Should I do the #GOPdebate?" In the video, he says into the camera, "Megyn Kelly is really biased against me. She knows that. I know that. Everybody knows that. Do you really think she can be fair at a debate?"

I was in disbelief. Doug joked, "Should we vote?"

Trump's taking to Instagram was the last straw for Roger. He fired off a statement dripping with sarcasm. It read in part, "We learned from a secret back channel that the Ayatollah and Putin both intend to treat Donald Trump unfairly when they meet with him if he becomes president."

Within a few hours, Trump bailed from the debate, citing Roger's statement as his sole reason. It was, once again, the lead on every national news network, and once again many in the media seemed to be taking at face value Trump's explanation—too lazy to look back at the preceding days and Trump's crescendo of complaints about me.

Roger canceled a couple of interviews Trump had scheduled on Fox, including—I was told—one set for twenty-four hours prior to the debate on *The O'Reilly Factor*. But O'Reilly refused to cancel Trump. Sure enough, Trump appeared and went on the attack, over and over again. There was no context offered for how we had gotten here: that Trump had spent the previous six months attacking Fox and me, including another "bimbo" tweet just that morning. Instead, O'Reilly apologized to Trump, extolled the virtues of "forgiveness," and asked Trump to consider turning the other cheek. *From what?* I wondered. O'Reilly ended the interview by joking about all the milkshakes he and Trump had shared together.

I was sitting in my makeup chair in Iowa, getting ready for my show, when I saw it. To me, it was the culmination of so much that had taken place since Trump began his tirade six months earlier—the unchallenged attacks, the misinformation, the tension in my own work environment. For the first time since August, I felt a surge of anger, and then—finally—a surge of tears. I put my hand over my eyes.

"It's too much," Vincenza said softly. And that was how it felt to me: like too much.

While I wasn't happy with that interview, the truth is, Bill has done far more good than bad for me over the course of my career. And he, too, was in an awkward spot that night. I believe he was genuinely trying to get Trump to reconsider his decision to skip the Fox News debate, and did not want to antagonize him. In time, I let go of it and moved on.

Debate day arrived, and I awoke to see that Trump had retweeted a fake picture of me with two Saudis, wearing full Muslim garb. Abby tried to keep it from me, concerned it was some sort of dog whistle to those who might be anti-Muslim, and that it might lead to even more aggressive post-Trump threats than usual. I had security with me, and tried to put it out of my mind.

The Trump-less debate went great. Many commentators remarked afterward on how refreshing it was to watch the candidates define themselves on their own terms, rather than in relation to Trump.[5] Some also noted my new, much shorter haircut.[6] I loved cutting my hair off. It felt empowering—like saying, "Here I am. Have at it."

I had actually cut my hair a couple of months earlier, just before Halloween, but this was a big night, so more people noticed. It took some of the wind out of our Halloween costumes—Doug and I, happy to make fun of a ridiculous situation, went as Donald Trump and Megyn Kelly. (When Doug went into the costume store to buy a "Make America Great Again" hat and a wig, the checkout girl actually asked him, "Does your wife need a Megyn Kelly outfit?") We headed out on Halloween, and a stranger—seeing the new hair—dropped a line on Doug straight out of the movie *Dave*, in which a presidential look-alike tries to pass himself off as the president, going out in public with the actual first lady: "You're good; she needs some work."

So that was that. The second Fox News debate was over. I was relieved. We stayed to cover the Iowa caucuses, which Trump lost. He later blamed his loss in part on his decision to skip the debate—his final job interview. We covered the results, and then went home.

Even though Trump lost Iowa, his poll numbers continued to rise. I couldn't say whether the attacks on me (or others, for that matter) were directly helping him, but they definitely generated media coverage and kept Trump in the news, which is just where he loved to be.

I marveled at how women were flocking to Trump notwithstanding the nature of his attacks, which by this point had expanded to Carly Fiorina (over time, his numbers with women would crater). But I also understood their anger at the politicians in Washington that had so let them down. In Trump, they had found someone they believed was a fighter, someone who would go to bat for them whether others liked it or not. He said our elected leaders were losers; that we never win anymore; that with him, we would win so much we'd get tired of winning. He sold his candidacy as something bigger than regime change—he pitched it as the chance to feel good about ourselves again, to feel *strong*.

After Trump lost Iowa, he went on to win New Hampshire and South Carolina. *This is happening*, pundits started to realize. My mom called me up and said, "He's right about one thing—I'm getting tired of the winning."

No sooner did I arrive back in New York than we had to start preparing for our next debate, which was just thirty days away, on March 3, in Detroit. *Again?* Debate prep is the most intense work we do. The researching, fact-checking, and question-writing process is meticulous and thorough. That alone requires dozens of hours—but the added layer of "What's Trump going to do next?" was an extra stressor, and an unwelcome distraction.

·

Through all of this I was doing my nightly show, which was full of Trump news. I was determined to live up to the promise I had made months earlier, on my first day back from vacation, to cover Trump fairly and without fear. I asked my team to help: if they saw the show tilting too far in any direction—too hard on Trump, out of a desire to punish him, or too soft, out of a desire to appease him—they had an invitation and an obligation to speak up. Night after night, we did our best. These are seasoned professionals—they care deeply about the viewers, and the product we put on air each night. Trump and some of his supporters felt we were too hard on him. I would argue we merely stood out by comparison.

Doug and I were raising our children. I was writing this book. I was starting to work on a special for Fox Broadcasting, a Barbara Walters–type in-depth interview show. There was a lot going on. I wasn't seeing enough of my family. When I go too long without spending ample time with my children, my heart aches. I am not happy. Abby usually guards my schedule to protect my family time, but Abby suddenly had a family issue of her own—her first baby arrived, two months early. She and little Aubrey were fine, thank God, but just like that, Abby was gone, much earlier than expected. My friend, my confidante. I missed her terribly. Her fill-in, Emily Jeffers, fresh out of college, got a jaw-dropping introduction to life in cable news.

It started to feel like my law days again. Acrimony. Long hours. Too little fun. That's okay for a while. Work doesn't need to be fun at all times. Work pays the bills, and in the case of TV news, it's also a public service. But if something that was good morphs into something that's not good—and is not changing back—one has to stay conscious of that too. Settling for more is not an endgame—it's an active process. It means staying aware of one's surroundings, because "more" is a fluid concept. Life changes, and requires that we change too.

Before I knew it, it was time for the third Fox debate in Detroit. Trump would be at this one.

I spent debate day in a makeshift office at the fabulous Fox Theatre, reading up on Trump University, which I knew would come up that night. Just before I headed down to the stage, Yates and Yardley, fresh off a plane, burst into my office with Doug. What a perspective setter. *Just in case you were thinking this debate mattered to your life at all, Mom, we're here to remind you that it doesn't.* Being in their presence is grounding. They're like an elixir in times of stress.

Yardley said she was a little nervous.

"Why?" I asked her.

"I'm afraid of Donald Trump," she said softly. "He wants to hurt me."

"No, he does not!" I emphatically corrected. Doug and I exchanged a shocked look.

"Well, he wants to hurt you, so he wants to hurt me too," she countered.

"No, honey. *Never.*"

Doug and I had never discussed—and never would discuss—threats in front of our children.

"Donald Trump does not want to hurt Mommy. We just had a little disagreement," I said. "We're friends now," I lied. "And he's a good daddy. He would never, ever hurt you."

Doug and I looked at each other again, eyebrows raised. Yards seemed to feel better.

As surprising as this exchange with my child was, there were plenty of other contenders for most memorable moment of the Trump absurdity, like this one:

"Mommy, what's a bimbo?" Yardley asked one day upon returning from school.

"*What?*"

"What's a bimbo?"

I could not believe my ears. We certainly had never told Yardley, nor any of our children, that Trump had used that word about me. But she lives in this world, and sometimes well-meaning people, or kids, can say things, not knowing the effect they will have.

"It's a not-nice word for a woman," I said.

What a moment. The same girl who the previous summer, surrounded by the most accomplished, powerful women in America, believed she was one of them was now afraid of the man who might be president, and asking me what the word *bimbo* meant. To this day I think about that juxtaposition, and the loss she suffered, which she doesn't yet realize.

Bret, Chris, and I took to the stage. Trump was directly in front of me. I didn't speak much until about thirty minutes into it. Then it was my turn. We were both polite.

"You're looking well," he said.

"As are you," I responded.

The Q and A went fine. Bret and I shot each other a look that said, *That went well. Off we go.*

That debate was raucous. Rubio's campaign was flailing, and so was he. He tried getting crass with Trump, and it did not go well for anyone. Trump infamously used his time onstage to tout the alleged size of his manhood. Bret, Chris, and I kept our cool. When the cameras weren't on us, Bret and I again looked at each other: *Did he really just say that?*

I hit Trump with a videotape question, getting right

to the heart of some of his many position reversals. Wallace pressed Trump on his economic arguments, and hit him with a fact-check that would make big headlines the next day. Still, no signs of anger—so far, so good.

As predicted, Trump University did come up. This was a school Trump had started for aspiring real estate moguls that resulted in a class action for fraud. A court compared the plaintiffs to the victims of Bernie Madoff. The school was ultimately closed. At the time, it had a D-minus rating from the Better Business Bureau. As he had done before, Trump denied this fact at the debate. I challenged him, which led to a contentious exchange between us. Trump was clearly irritated by it, but after the debate, he seemed just fine—he told reporters that everyone did well, that he believed I had been fair.

I did my show that night from inside the Fox Theatre. Doug came over moments before and gave me a long hug. It said more than *Congratulations*. It felt more like *You made it*.

It had been a long eight months. Doug and I had been in the bunker together. He had weathered every Trump attack right by my side—in fact, the experience had been harder for Doug in many ways, as sometimes it is more painful for someone to watch a loved one get attacked than to be directly on the receiving end. Many times Doug had wanted to respond to Trump: to call him up, to write an op-ed, to track him down and let him have it. But he knew that wouldn't help anything. We had to stay quiet and let the storm pass.

Vincenza captured that hug on camera. When I look at it now, I remember the exact feelings I had in the moment—love for my husband, and such gratitude that I have him.

I felt like we had finally turned a corner, that this thing with Trump was finally over.

I should have known that when it came to Trump, it was never over.

On Tuesday, March 8, Trump won the Michigan primary. The following Sunday, he started in again on me. He let loose on *Fox News Sunday*, complaining about our Trump University exchange. What happened in that week after the debate? To this day, I do not know.

A week after Michigan, Trump won Florida, ending Marco Rubio's presidential campaign. In the wake of his victory, he celebrated by ramping up his attacks on me. As the *Washington Examiner* put it, "GOP front-runner Donald Trump took aim at Fox News' Megyn

Kelly Tuesday evening with a flurry of insults over Twitter, just moments after he was declared the winner in Florida's Republican primary."[7]

He fired off a slew of tweets: **Crazy @megynkelly is unwatchable. Can't watch Crazy Megyn anymore. Talks about me at 43% but never mentions that there are four people in race. With two people, big & over!**

Many anchors were quoting the same poll numbers, but hearing it from me was always different for Trump. Or maybe I was just part of his game. *Here we go again,* I thought.

Tom Lowell and I worried at times that the calls for a boycott would have an effect. Roger put my mind at ease. "In forty years I've never seen a call for a boycott work," he said. And he was right—my numbers remained very strong throughout the Year of Trump.

But Trump's campaign against me did have serious ramifications. Every time Trump acted up, so did his supporters. Every time he tweeted about me, it was like he flipped a switch, instantly causing a flood of intense nastiness. The number of harassing tweets, Facebook messages, online comments, articles, and even negative face-to-face public interactions would increase exponentially. There would be more strategy meetings at work, more stressful calls from my boss at all hours. There would be heightened security issues when I left

Fox News at night, and when I arrived home. One night, after a Trump attack, a suspicious man showed up in the lobby of my apartment building close to midnight, demanding to see me. When questioned by the doorman, he turned and ran. How did he know where I live? Where my kids live?

Paparazzi and other unfamiliar men started showing up—a first for us in New York—on the sidewalk outside of our building, taking pictures of me and Doug and our children. Part of this was laughable. We imagined the photographers watching our every errand with bated breath: *There they go! To . . . Petco! Extra, extra! What's in the bag? . . . Pet fish! Stop the presses!*

Thankfully we managed to keep the pictures of our kids from being published, or at least to have their faces blurred. (We don't publicize or post online pictures of our kids, due to security concerns, and out of respect for their privacy.)

The voice messages, hate mail, and online attacks would also spike after each Trump tweet. I had perspective on them—I realized this wasn't fighting in Syria—but it wasn't a day at the beach either. A sampling on a typical day:

You're a real cunt!

Fuck off you slut, I will beat you up so bad I will force you to support trump you slut.

YOU BITCH! . . . [A] twisted Bitch!!

This whore @megynkelly will get hers sooner or later. Media slut, biased unfair and no professionalism. Bitch.

[T]he bitch from Rupert Murdoch News? No thanks #cunt

You suck and you're a hack . . . you're not all that, you LOSE, Trump WINS.

You really need to stop bashing Trump. You must be a democrat or a liberal. Don't watch your show anymore . . . won't watch it again until they fire you.

I could go on.

What confused me was that by this point, Trump was winning the race for the nomination. He had vanquished everyone but Ted Cruz, who was at least as disliked by Republicans as Trump was and way behind in the delegate count. The prospect of Trump as the nominee was getting more and more likely, and yet he maintained his focus on me. If winning couldn't distract him from coming after me, would anything? *This will keep going until he chooses to stop or he loses*, I thought. But he wasn't stopping, and he wasn't losing. That meant I likely had months—or even months plus eight years—more of this.

Over and over I thought surely things had gotten as absurd as they would get, only to be proven wrong.

One day my mom told me a strange man had contacted her, trying to dig up dirt on me. Two friends of mine reached out, saying much the same. Was it a tabloid? A private investigator? Was I *in* this race, or a journalist covering it? The Trump army seemed not to care.

Two weeks later, on March 21, Fox News was supposed to have a Republican debate in Salt Lake City. Trump decided not to come. "We've had enough debates," he said. It got canceled. Frankly, I was relieved. I didn't want to deal with the nonsense again.

We flew to Florida for a Disney vacation—our family, and our security guard. Yes, we took an armed guard to the Magic Kingdom. More guns, more guards. My Year of Trump.

"Why is Mike here in Disney?" our kids asked. We'd all seen a lot of Mike that year.

What do you say to your children when they ask you that question? We didn't want to scare them, especially given Yardley's existing concern.

"He's here to help us, honey," I said. I think my kids were a little confused about how he could be helping us by standing next to us on line for It's a Small World, but luckily they didn't press the question. We did have a couple of nasty encounters, but nothing violent.

Worrying about physical harm at Disney World was definitely new territory for me and Doug. We kept thinking we'd encountered the darkest moment, only to find a new one right behind it—from strangers at our house to security at Disney to our four-year-old daughter asking what the word *bimbo* means. But the lowest point for me was something much quieter.

The Fox PR folks and I had spent many late nights in the office, watching the tweets roll in, staying steady at the helm, refusing to respond. But when Trump started up again in March out of nowhere after his Florida win, Irena Briganti was not pleased. She told me she believed that he had crossed a line. She felt it had become abusive, and she issued a statement defending me and calling Trump's "vitriolic attacks . . . his extreme, sick obsession with [me] . . . beneath the dignity of a presidential candidate who wants to occupy the highest office in the land."

"Irena," I said to her, "this is just my new reality. I've come to accept it."

As soon as the words left my mouth, I heard the resignation in them—the defeat. When I got home that night, I couldn't stop thinking about what I'd said: "This is just my new reality." *That doesn't sound like me*, I thought. *I sound like a sad little martyr.* Biding my time until things improved was one thing; pathetically resigning myself to the never-ending antics of a bully was another.

And that, right there, was the sound of me hitting bottom.

Because that wasn't me. My commitment to myself is to settle for more. Yet here I was, ready to accept a life of stress and attempted bullying that could go on for years. A life that acquiesced to being what Maureen Dowd described in a column as "Donald Trump's chew toy."[8] In that passive, resigned stance, I didn't recognize myself. My low point didn't come from the threats or the hate. It wasn't the shots at my credibility or the lame insult of "crazy." It was the moment when I no longer felt I was being true to who I was, to the person I'd worked so hard to become ever since that late night in Chicago, watching *Oprah*.

I knew where the feeling of resignation came from, of course. The previous nine months had taken their toll. The security scares, the harassment, the threats, the guards, the pressure at work and on the air—it was all-consuming. I'd long since stopped being able to find any kind of humor in this mess. Laughter wasn't a coping tool, because this wasn't funny. It was deeply unsettling, and appeared to be never-ending.

And in that moment I knew, once and for all, that I must put a stop to this. Roger had tried. Hannity had tried. Bill Shine had tried. Time had passed. Trump wasn't stopping. And I was done sitting back and taking it. Way back in seventh grade, I'd made a promise to myself not to tolerate bullies. Now I had to honor it. I would take control of my own life. I would get back to a normal state of affairs, one where I was reporting the story, not part of it.

"You can't respond to irrational behavior rationally," my mother always says. Trump has an irrational love of controversy, of acrimony. He clearly liked the idea of our "fight," of the drama. He enjoyed it as a storyline, and if it were up to him, I believe he would have kept it going and going. Which meant it would be up to me to write the two of us an ending.

Then I saw an answer staring me in the face. I knew he wouldn't come on *The Kelly File*, but I was preparing for my Fox Broadcasting Special, which was by its nature a more casual, less aggressive venue. Trump would be a natural lead interview—he had already done Barbara Walters's *10 Most Fascinating People* series three times. ("A record!" he once told me.) Talking to him face-to-face could reestablish a sane relationship. If my year of death threats was a highway, that sit-down looked distinctly like an off-ramp.

The question was: Would he do it? I thought he might. He was inches away from securing the nomination, but he was looking at a possible contested convention and a bare-knuckled general election. And he hadn't spoken one word to the 9:00 p.m. host on Fox News in nine months, which he had to see as a liability. My ratings were stronger than ever. His calls for a boycott hadn't made a dent. Millions of women and independents—two groups Trump needed badly—watch *The Kelly File.*

So there were good reasons on both sides for the meeting.

I reached out to him through two different people and asked for a meeting.

First he said no. And then he said yes.

23

The Trump Tower Accords

The morning of the meeting I woke up around 7:00 a.m., poured myself a cup of coffee, and got Yates and Yards off to school. Normally at home I am happy, and certainly when I am around Thatcher. But that day I was anxious. I did not know what to expect. I believed, sitting face-to-face, Trump would be cordial. My goal was simple—to put a stop to his behavior and remove myself as a storyline from the 2016 election. If I could also secure an interview, great.

Chris and Vincenza came over to help me get on my hair and makeup. Typically, when they get me ready at my house, it's a lighthearted hour. We play music, drink coffee, tell stories, and laugh with the kids. That day we didn't speak much at all. They knew I was preoccupied.

"Do you want me to keep it natural," Vincenza asked, "since it's daytime?"

"No," I said. "I need my game face on."

I went in my bedroom and put on my black Gucci sheath dress with a belt. A pair of black pumps, and I was ready to go.

Thatcher was feeling sad about my leaving that day, saying, "Mommy, don't go. Mommy, stay here."

While those moments usually kill me, I was in an entirely different place that morning.

"Thatch, Mom's gotta go," I said, "I'll see you later. I love you."

I kissed him on the head, took a deep breath, and walked out, with the gals waving and blowing kisses at me as they packed up their gear.

Doug insisted on coming along in the car, and I didn't object. We planned on getting lunch together after, and I knew I would be glad to have him there to debrief when it was over.

Many people offered to go into the meeting with me: Doug, Fox anchor Brian Kilmeade (who had successfully brokered the meeting), and Bill Geddie, who was producing the Fox Broadcast special. But it was clear to me I needed to do this by myself. Just me and Trump. No one to distract us, no one to screw it up.

I think they all wanted to protect me somehow. But I needed no protection.

The texts from the few people who knew what was about to happen came in:

This is like waiting for the kickoff in the Super Bowl! wrote one friend.

I have heart palpitations right now, texted Janice Dean. **Sending all my love and energy to you.**"

We got there right at 11:00 a.m.

As I got out of the car, Doug said, "Babe, when you get in there, just pretend it's your desk and your studio." He knows how the anchor desk makes me feel.

"I'll be fine," I said, and closed the door.

The newspapers the next day would say that I entered the building "incognito."

Not true. I was wearing my black dress with a black coat on top of it—with no hat, wig, or sunglasses, as fun as that would have been.

I entered on the residence side of the building. The doorman opened the door for me. His eyes grew to the size of silver dollars when he recognized me, now just twenty stories away from Trump.

"Hello!" he said warmly. "Wow! Good to see you!"

Trump's security guard, Keith, a former NYPD detective, was waiting in the lobby for me. He gave me a nice greeting and said, "Right this way." We walked together to the elevator, got in, and Keith directed the elevator operator where to go.

When I walked into his office, Trump was sitting behind his desk, smiling. He got up immediately and came around to greet me. I moved in for a handshake, but he held out his arms for a hug, and the next thing I knew, we were hugging hello.

We are hugging, I thought. *Donald Trump is hugging me and I am hugging him.*

There was a part of me that felt like I was betraying myself by hugging this man who had insulted me so publicly and had created such security and privacy concerns for me and my family over the past nine months. But it felt like a kind gesture on his part—an effort to say, if not "I'm sorry," perhaps "Let's move on," which was what I was there for.

"Hi," I said.

"Hi, how are you?" he responded.

"I'm good, how are you?"

"I'm good too. Proud of you in a certain way. Please, sit down."

This was going well so far.

Wait—proud of me?

I sat down in the chair across from Trump's desk. His office is large and spectacular. Huge windows wrap around two of the four walls, overlooking Central

Park and Fifth Avenue and the high-end shops below. The walls were lined with memorabilia and photos of himself with other celebrities. On his desk were stacks of magazines with him on the cover: *People*, *Time*, and about a dozen others, with several copies of each one per stack.

I told him that I had felt a little nervous, coming over.

Why did I say that? Radical honesty. Damn.

"Don't be nervous!" he said. "It's good to see you."

And we were off. The conversation was off the record, and I will respect that here, but suffice it to say that we had a friendly talk about the race so far and in general the dynamic between us. We did not discuss the specifics of his antics toward me. I had zero trust in him. I had known only his erratic, volatile behavior for months. And yet at no point did it get tense. In fact, to a fly on the wall we might have sounded like friends who hadn't seen each other in a long time. With total detachment, we chatted as any reporter and candidate would. I felt no anger toward him, only confusion. How could he be so affable, given the level of anger he'd sustained for so long? I tried to reconcile the person in front of me with the person I'd seen on Twitter—one warm and kind; the other—very different. They didn't seem to match.

I tried not to let the strangeness of the moment distract me; I was laser-focused on the mission—get back to normalcy, personally and professionally. For months on end, Trump had been everywhere around me: night after night, on for the full hour with Greta or Hannity . . . on with O'Reilly on virtually any night he attacked me. He was the GOP front-runner—of course he was going to be on TV—but at times the pure saturation got tiring. Once he went on *Hannity* and criticized me, and I cluelessly drove our viewers to the interview: "Don't miss Donald Trump coming up on *Hannity!*" Perhaps that best conveys the professional oddity of my Year of Trump: he went after me—in an interview I promoted.

After we'd been talking for a bit, Trump brought in his son Eric, who was also friendly. Then he called for Ivanka and Melania to come and meet me, but they weren't in the building. He did get Ivanka on the phone, and we had a lovely exchange. I like her a lot—she and his other children reflect well on Trump. Before it was over, I asked Trump for an interview for my upcoming Fox Broadcast special, and he seemed agreeable, but did not give me a date.

As the meeting wound down, I felt relief, like I'd set down something heavy I'd been carrying for most of the year. Sitting at Trump Tower having a conversation with Trump felt strange, but not totally insincere. There was kindness between us in the moment. Distance, too, but kindness. I felt a bit like a hostage whose hostage taker was seeing her as a human being for the very first time—who needed to believe that he would let her go.

As I got up to go, Trump asked me for my cell phone number.

I hesitated.

"You're not going to use it for evil, are you?" I said.

"No! No!" he said. "I promise!"

"You're not going to 'Lindsay Graham' me, are you?" I asked him—a reference to the moment Trump publicly disclosed Senator Graham's personal cell phone number after Graham criticized him in the early primary season.

"No, no, don't worry!" he said. "Everyone's afraid to give me their cell phones after that!"

"Of course they are," I said.

We laughed. I gave him the number.

Trump suggested that we take a picture together. I said yes. It felt historical to me somehow. It wasn't exactly Reagan-Gorbachev in Reykjavik, but it belonged in a time capsule for 2016.

Later I studied the picture on my phone. In it, Trump has a big smile and is flashing a thumbs-up—

his standard pose. His arm is around me, and mine is around him. And yet we look like two people in very different places.

Despite his nine-month rage against me, Trump seems to have immediately let it go, if it was ever real to begin with. His smile appears completely authentic. He had bigger things to worry about: a pressing presidential campaign, and a business to run. I, on the other hand, am smiling, but it's a forced smile. I look rather like a person who's been through some sort of trauma and is waiting for the Coast Guard helicopter.

When I walked out of the office, a group of people had gathered—about seven or eight of them—clearly staffers for Trump. The only face I recognized was that of Michael Cohen, who had retweeted "Gut her" after the August debate. That tweet, more than any other, really bothered me. It was so visceral.

He shot me a somewhat cold look.

"Good to see you," I said.

"You too," he said, and at the sound of his voice, my skin crawled a bit.

He loves his boss, I told myself. *That counts for something.*

Trump walked me to the door of his outer-office suite. We shook hands good-bye, and I walked out with Keith.

When I left the building, Doug was out front in the SUV.

"How did it go?" Doug asked. "It must have gone great for you to be in there that long."

"It did," I said. "It went brilliantly."

I looked at my iPhone. It was lit up: text messages, Twitter notifications, voice mails. The news had broken of our meeting while I was inside. A producer from MSNBC had apparently seen me enter Trump Tower, and the Internet was going crazy. So was my office. I hadn't told any of the management at Fox—including Roger—that I was going to this meeting, and they knew nothing about it in advance. Some later reported that Roger orchestrated the meeting; the truth is, he knew nothing about it. Roger was none too pleased that he found out from MSNBC.

But I didn't care. Having the meeting take place at all, and then go well, had been too important to me to do anything that might screw it up. I had hoped to get in and out unseen and to be the first to tell Roger about it, but the risk that someone else might break the news was worth it if I could be sure the meeting took place without anyone getting too much in my head or in Trump's in advance. I was glad I'd kept it quiet. And the bottom line was: it worked.

I was out of the shark tank.

Not long after my meeting with Trump, Doug and I were at our favorite restaurant when we overheard the women next to us talking about me. One of them asked the other, not realizing I was next to her, "Why would she meet with him? That Megyn Kelly! What could she have been thinking?" *Why wouldn't I meet with him?* I thought. *I host a news show and he's the Republican nominee. Am I supposed to let his behavior prevent me from doing my job?*

I mean, I understood the objections. While many Trump fans would later tell me they appreciated my reaching out to him, some who didn't like Trump wanted me to keep the "battle" going, because they believed it was hurting his campaign—in particular, his numbers with women. I think some also enjoyed the gladiatorial nature of it, and so they delighted in every flare-up. A few people felt that by asking for a meeting, or an interview, I "caved."

The way I see it, I rose. I made a decision to change the story, to restore my proper place in this election, and I followed through. I was not a scorned lover, intent on making a man bow to me. I was a reporter trying to cover a presidential candidate. The nature of that relationship is one of pursuit.

Trump ultimately agreed to sit with me for my Fox Broadcast special. As we waited for him to arrive to the interview in a conference room at Trump Tower, you could hear a pin drop. The lighting guy told me he'd been so nervous he couldn't sleep the night before. I think everyone realized this could go badly. In fact, it went very well.

I pressed Trump on his temperament. On the responsibility that comes with power. I asked him about his attacks on Heidi Cruz, John McCain, and others. About whether he would own up to the mistakes he'd made. I refused to let him downplay his disparaging language about women. I asked him how American parents could teach their kids not to bully, tease, taunt, and name-call when the GOP front-runner does all of those things. I asked him if he had ever been bullied or emotionally wounded. I found his answers fascinating.

He said he really had been angry all those months. He admitted—almost too easily—that he'd never really boycotted *The Kelly File* despite his insistence that his fans do so. He claimed not to know he had retweeted messages calling me a bimbo. It wasn't a cage match. It was a chess move in a complex game—not a policy interview, but an interview focused on Trump the man that would publicly end this months-long spectacle.

Trump was pleased with how it turned out, and seemed to finally recognize that it was time for our story to come to a close. He tweeted out, "And they all lived happily ever after!" Sure enough, he stopped his relentless attacks.

Some critics were disappointed. They wanted me to take down Trump. But that was never my goal, or my job. Others wanted to see me play the victim, to hold him to account for what he'd done to me. They didn't know me at all.

By this point in my career, while I didn't enjoy the media attacks, I was largely able to dismiss them. My feelings about them had matured considerably. I now generally feel that they can only help me. Sometimes the media builds a figure up too much. When that scale gets tipped too far in favor of such a person, there's something delightful about pulling them back. I believe that if the country needs to knock you down a little, it's probably best to let them. It lets some steam out of the pressure cooker. And more humility is always good.

Many people assumed I enjoyed my Year of Trump. Over and over I was asked about how great it had surely been for me. Folks saw the *Vanity Fair* cover and increased name recognition and assumed it was all rainbows and unicorns. In their defense, I did not say much publicly about what it had actually been like. But some thoughtful reporters (and my friends and family) knew enough to recognize that this had been far from a glorious time.

One acquaintance Doug and I saw at an event in May said it perfectly, "I'm sure this has been a hard year for you both; what a tough space to occupy." That's exactly it—a tough space to occupy, straddling the world of being the storyteller and being the story. Like Cecilia in the Woody Allen movie *The Purple Rose of Cairo*, who somehow jumped into the movie screen and was stunned to find herself a part of the plot, as opposed to a mere observer of it.

In the end, the notion that I had it in for Trump was never more than a fiction—one that he created and the media perpetuated, but a fiction nonetheless. Some in the media held me up as a Trump foil, and Trump painted me as a nemesis, but I never wanted that, nor participated in it.

Some described me as "fearless" throughout these events. But I wasn't. I was fearful at times—for my safety and that of my family. For what the attacks might mean to my career, my relationship with my viewers, and some of my professional relationships. And yet I knew I had a job to do. And doing it felt empowering. In showing up at Trump Tower that day and later interviewing him for my special, I was taking control of my life, refusing to accept the status quo. Fear did come, but so did courage. If you can muster courage in the face of fear, you become more confident. You become tougher.

That doesn't mean being emotionless. Clearly I cry sometimes. I am human. But I also know how to play hurt. I have worries, and insecurities, just like anyone else. And yet I push through all of that in my quest to settle for more.

And "more" can come in surprising packages. As challenging as this year has been, it's also allowed me to do all the things so beautifully laid out in those John Denver lyrics my dad loved so much: to laugh, cry, and sing. Laughs in some of the darkest moments, thanks to my mom's sense of humor ingrained in me from birth . . . occasional tears when my own humanity would not be denied . . . and bouts of fear, courage, and eventually growth that have helped to make my life sing.

"How have you been dealing with it?" people kept asking as the Trump drama rolled on, month after month. "Well," I told them, "I've got a great husband, beautiful children, and supportive family members, friends, and co-workers. And I've had a lifetime of training."

Difficulty comes to everyone, and in far greater measure than I have experienced. My situation was temporary—a stressor, a distraction, but nothing compared to real suffering. The challenge of my Year of Trump was more about the folly of human interaction. And on that score, I did gain some perspective. Everyone gets knocked down in life. If we put ourselves out there at all, we deal with rejection, being hated, being bullied. It's universal. You learn to handle it, incident by incident. You toughen up and learn how to navigate the system.

Could twenty-two-year-old me have handled the indignities of the Trump fiasco—dealt with a leading presidential candidate talking about her bleeding, calling her a bimbo, a lightweight, a liar, crazy, sick, called for a boycott against her, and employed an attorney who encouraged 40,000 people to "gut" her—the way forty-five-year-old me did? Probably not. Some of my resilience was baked in by my parents, but most has come from practice—in my law job, my TV job, my life as an American woman.

Adversity is an opportunity, and one that has allowed me to flourish. It has made me stronger, my skin a little thicker. And as with any turmoil in your life, none of it is for nothing if you survive it and take stock. Imagine if I'd had no conflict prior to this. If I'd had no practice in how to shore myself up. If I'd only existed in my "safe space" with my "trigger warnings," I'd have had no means of coping.

This is why the Cupcake Nation mentality—"Everyone's a winner!"—is so dangerous. When we try to protect the young from any vaguely uncomfortable ideas or encounters, we do them a grave disservice. Being tested by different viewpoints in my life, being sometimes offended or occasionally hurt, or even targeted, is a big part of what prepared me for the challenges I've faced in my career—especially this past year. I had done the grueling sit-ups and my core was strong. I could withstand some gut punches.

Experience gives you a folder in which to put a new upset: Ah, yes, I'm being called a bimbo by the likely Republican nominee. I will file that with my bouts with workplace sexism. I'm being bullied, and people are calling me names? It's a magnified version of seventh grade. My safety is in danger because I did my job? I've been here too. It's like functioning when you're sick. You'd rather feel your best, but coughing and sneezing will not stop you from showing up. You do what makes you *you*, like being with your family and taking care of yourself and meeting your responsibilities, and you do it relentlessly until the crisis has passed. I've done this before, I survived, and so I know I can survive this too.

One day when I was working as a young associate for Bickel & Brewer in Chicago I took a walk outside with my boss, Bill Brewer. We had a talk about dealing with stress, and he told me something I draw on to this day in times of trouble: "Remember who you are." It sounds amorphous, but when something stressful happens to me, I often remind myself: "Remember who you are."

In other words: What defines you? Is it this latest stressor, or is it who you are as a person? Your relationships with your spouse, mother, father, daughter, son, sister, brother, friend? Your principles? Will those things be around even if this situation ends badly? Will you still be you? Who is that? Are *you* on the line? If not, then it can't be that bad. "Remember who you are" is the rip cord that releases me from almost any dark situation, because it reminds me that what I really value is almost never at stake.

When things were at their worst in my legal career, when I was toiling away at the office, calling my own voice mail (twice), and hoping to break a bone on the Kennedy Expressway so I could rest for a while, I was a stranger to myself. I had lost my joy, the essence of who I was. That was how I knew, beyond a shadow of a doubt, that I needed a change. That things could not continue as they were. Likewise, as stressful and maddening and relentless as the situation with Trump became, it was only in that moment of powerless resignation that this odd reality finally affected my sense of self. That was when I knew, once and for all, I had to act.

There is no historical precedent for Trump, or for how this election played out. But there is plenty of precedent in my own life for going through difficulty and coming out the other side a little stronger. And unlike the other rough eras to date—being bullied, losing my father, getting divorced—I am coming out of this one with a beautiful, healthy family, work I love, and colleagues and friends I adore. Most of all, I'm coming out of it having remembered who I am, as a person . . . woman . . . mother . . . wife . . . daughter . . . sister . . . friend . . . and professional.

Within hours of Trump's becoming the presumptive Republican nominee in May 2016, Hillary Clinton and groups supporting her released several attack ads showing moments in the Trump campaign in which he had behaved outrageously, especially toward women. Quotes about or pictures of me appeared in many of them.[1]

Watching these ads, I was struck again by how surreal this year had been, how much less fun it is to be the news than to cover it. And it occurred to me that this was exactly what my debate question foretold: his words about women being used against him in the general election. It had been, in other words, an important and prescient question. I knew a year earlier that this exact montage was coming; I just never imagined that I would end up in it.

24

Paying it Forward

B y July 2016, things had calmed down a bit in my life. Trump had stopped the nonsense. He and Hillary Clinton had secured their parties' respective nominations. And I was getting ready for the Republican and Democratic National Conventions. And then another national news story began to unfold in my life: Roger Ailes was sued for sexual harassment. The lawsuit was filed by Gretchen Carlson, an anchor whom Fox had just fired. Most of us had never seen such a complaint before, because our Fox contracts require us to arbitrate disputes in a private forum, so public lawsuits against the boss were unheard of. The majority of my colleagues dismissed the allegations as those of a disgruntled employee. But I had a different reaction.

The story sounded very familiar to me, because it had happened to me years earlier.

It started in the summer of 2005, when I was called up to New York—shortly after Brit Hume had told me I'd "captured the attention of Mr. Ailes." I had been with the company for just under a year—I was still a neophyte in the DC Bureau, working the 5:00 a.m. shift and plenty of weekends. By this point, I had figured out that Roger was not a politically correct guy—he would often make off-color jokes or comments about people, politics—pretty much any subject. (This was not a secret in the industry—Roger was praised publicly by many writers who found his provocative style amusing). At times his humor could be over the top, but it didn't bother me much—I'd worked in rough-and-tumble office settings before and had never been one to word-police my colleagues. However, Roger began pushing the limits well beyond humor; beyond anything I'd experienced, introducing explicit sexual innuendo into our conversations. At first it was just a comment here or there. But over the next six months, the remarks would get more frequent, and more direct, and then he made physical advances toward me.

As with others I have since learned about, there was a pattern to his behavior. I would be called into Roger's office, he would shut the door, and over the next hour or two, he would engage in a kind of cat-and-mouse game with me—veering between obviously inappropriate sexually charged comments (e.g., about the "very sexy bras" I must have and how he'd like to see me in them) and legitimate professional advice. This is part of what made it so complicated—it wasn't all a come-on—he also gave helpful work-related counsel, such as his suggestion about showing the audience my real self. But there would always be a stinger—and they got more explicit and disturbing over time. I kept a record of Roger's behavior, and have since shared the facts with those who investigated the case against him. I see no point in making all of the details public, but suffice it to say, he made sexual comments to me, offers of professional advancement in exchange for sexual favors, and, eventually, physical attempts to be with me—every single one of which I rejected.

I tried to laugh off the inappropriate comments, or pretend not to understand them, or to redirect the conversation to something work related, but I was deeply concerned. It was an upsetting, impossible dynamic. Here was this man, my boss, on the cover of industry magazines as "The Most Powerful Man in News." A man whose good opinion I desperately wanted, who could make or break my budding television career. I was beyond happy to be working there—I had finally achieved my dream. The last thing I wanted was this kind of monkey wrench thrown into our relationship. I wanted him to like me—professionally—and for him to help develop my career based only on my work performance. But he was trying to change the stakes for my advancement, and when that realization became inescapable, I felt a surge of panic.

Early on, I was still hoping it would end without confrontation. After all, I was in DC and only got up to New York every month or so. *Perhaps he'll lose interest*, I thought. *Perhaps he'll get the hint.* I was also bewildered that he would take such risks with someone he barely knew. *I am an attorney. How could he be so reckless?* Surely, I figured, he would eventually knock it off.

But in January 2006, Roger called me up to New York and we had a shocking exchange. I was nervous about going into his office, concerned he might start in again. Sure enough, he did. And then he crossed a new line—trying to grab me repeatedly and kiss me on the lips. I dodged the first two attempts, pushed him away, and immediately went to leave. His office was large and it took me a beat to get to the door, which was closed. As I walked away from him, he followed me and asked me an ominous question: "When is your contract up?" And then, for the third time, he tried to kiss me. I dodged him again and walked out—upset, rattled, and angry.

There was no more trying to deny his intentions. I knew I had a very real problem on my hands. Earlier, Roger had made sure I knew the stakes, telling me: "I don't like to fight, but when I do, I fight to kill." The message could not have been clearer: *If you tell anyone, I will destroy you.* He easily could have. He was merciless to his enemies, and Roger called all the shots at Fox. He had set up the management such that everyone was completely devoted to him. Loyalty was prized above everything—it was a prerequisite of working for him. It was well known that those who crossed him would soon be at the receiving end of planted hit pieces in the press. Look at what happened to Paula Zahn—he publicly humiliated her, he sued her, he tried to end her career—just for wanting to go to CNN. And she was established; she had power. But Roger had more, and was not afraid to use it. He was well liked by most in the building and well connected to everyone in the industry. And me? I wasn't connected at all. And I loved my job. And didn't want to lose it.

I left Roger's office that day and went directly to La Guardia Airport to catch the shuttle home. I hadn't even walked in before I called Willis Goldsmith, then the partner in charge of Jones Day's employment law practice, who agreed to represent me. I paced back and forth outside the terminal as he walked me through my options, most of which I already knew, and none of which was ideal. I realized Roger had crossed a line, but I had handled it without doing anything. I didn't want to sue. I didn't want to blow this up. Like most sexual harassment targets, I just wanted it to stop. I felt better having a lawyer in case Roger retaliated against me for rejecting him, but I knew the reality of the situation: if I caused a stink, my career would likely be over. Sure, they might investigate, but I felt certain there was no way they would get rid of him, and I would be left on the wrong side of the one man who had power at Fox. I'd get labeled a troublemaker, someone who is overly sensitive—all the things we too often hear about women who don't tolerate harassment. I didn't want any of that. I just wanted to do my job.

At the time, I wondered if I was the first or only target of Roger's advances. He was so brazen about it, I had the distinct feeling he'd done it before. I wrestled with the idea of keeping quiet. On the one hand, what if I said nothing and he did this to someone else? On the other hand, this was not the first time a male superior had come on to me, and I had no proof that Roger was a serial harasser. I tried to raise the issue with a female anchor who had been there longer than I had, to see if it had ever happened to her. She said she and Roger had always had a strictly professional relationship. I shared some of the details with my officemate Major Garrett, who was stunned and had never heard of Roger behaving that way.

And then, after much soul-searching, I decided I needed to bring the matter to a supervisor, which I did. That person—whom I have no wish to ensnare in a press melee by naming here—vouched for Roger's character, suggested he was likely just smitten, and recommended that I try to avoid him (which I hadn't realized was actually an option). To this day, I don't know whether this person pressed the matter further up the line at Fox, though no one ever contacted me. I figured I had managed to avoid compromising myself, and if I could steer clear of Roger for a while and get him to leave me alone, we could pretend the whole thing never happened. And I could get back to doing what I really wanted to do: reporting the news.

And so for the next several months, I did my best to avoid him. I offered excuses for why I couldn't swing by his office while in New York. I dodged his phone calls and then returned his messages after hours, when I knew he wouldn't be there. Major would see my phone repeatedly light up with the boss's name—me, a second-year reporter—and we'd share a look of aston-

ishment. I threw myself into work in the DC Bureau
(and there was plenty of it—this was around the time
of the Duke lacrosse case) and tried to be so good that
Roger couldn't ignore me—professionally—even if he
felt spurned personally. By the following summer, the
stalker had entered my life, and on that matter Roger
was appropriate and supportive. I also met and fell in
love with Doug, a fact I was sure to mention to anyone
who asked—including Roger.

By the fall of 2006, the Fox management team held
that off-site meeting, and Roger's top executives proposed pairing me with Hemmer for *America's Newsroom*. Lo and behold, Roger offered me the job. I
moved to New York in January 2007, and Roger never
sexually harassed me again. For the next nine years, we
had a professional relationship in which he was, for the
most part, a supportive boss, who mentored and looked
out for me. He gave me the chance to prove myself. He
promoted me during my maternity leaves. He and his
wife, Beth, had me and Doug to their home for dinner
parties. I got to know his son. And I filed his earlier
behavior away as a passing infatuation by a man who I
assumed had been having some marital difficulty.

As time went by, I always wondered if there were
other women who'd had similar experiences with
Roger. Years later, I met one. A friend confessed that

Roger had come on to her during her job interview, not long before my own exchange with him. She did not submit to his advances and, as in my case, he did not retaliate—she got the job. She had moved past the incident, and certainly did not want it revealed or turned into a legal matter. But I resolved then and there that if I heard of him doing this to another woman, I would again come forward.

In 2012, I learned that a reporter for *New York* magazine was writing a book about Roger. This reporter was no fan of Fox News, and certainly not of Roger's, and Roger became very focused on the project. He seemed to live in constant fear of it. He was so agitated about the book, I began to wonder whether he had something to hide—whether the harassment my friend and I had experienced was perhaps more pervasive. I discussed the issue with Brian Lewis, then the head of Fox PR and an executive vice president at Fox. I knew I was not at liberty to discuss my friend's incident, so I was careful in my choice of words. I confided to him that I believed Roger might have been inappropriate with women at Fox. Brian had never heard of such a thing. When the book came out, it hit Roger on every subject imaginable, but included only one notable reference to an inappropriate incident with a woman—from thirty years earlier. Even a reporter devoted to exposing

Roger offered no hint that Roger was a serial harasser. I felt reassured that he wasn't what I'd feared, that my superior's defense of him years earlier was sound.

In the years that followed, Roger hit his mid-seventies, fell into ill health, began using a walker for a time, and was in and out of the office for medical treatments. When I saw him, our conversations revolved mostly around my show or our families. My life was busy, and I never gave much additional thought to the matter. However, in the back of my mind, I still wondered whether another woman might someday come forward. Then came Gretchen's lawsuit.

When I first saw her complaint, despite my having been targeted by Roger, I felt ambivalent. I knew enough about Gretchen's tenure at Fox to know that executives other than Roger had long had issues with her performance, fairly or not. I wasn't discounting the possibility that she may have been harassed, but I wasn't entirely sure what to believe. Fox News' parent company, 21st Century Fox, quickly weighed in, announcing its "full confidence" in Roger—which came as no surprise. It also said, however, that it would conduct a review of the allegations. The scope of that review, and who would be performing it, was not addressed.

Almost immediately, three other women came forward to the *Daily Beast*—which identified them only as former Fox News employees. The details of their stories rang disturbingly true to me—I felt sick upon reading them. The questions pulsed through my mind: *Is this who he is? Did he truly never stop?* And: *How many others are there?*

Roger denied the allegations, and immediately began getting his ducks in a row—commencing an intense campaign inside Fox News to get the talent to speak out publicly on his behalf. I was approached several times, and several times I refused. There was no way I was going to lie to protect him. When I refused, he engineered hit pieces about me online, which cited "Fox News insiders," to suggest that I was being "selfish" for not defending him or looking to improve "my brand" by having a "feminist moment." It wasn't true, and it didn't work.

I understood my colleagues' wanting to defend Roger, since loyalty was an absolute job requirement. So was saying nice things about Roger (indeed, failing to compliment him enthusiastically in any press interview would always result in a rebuke). Many, including me, had experienced years of kindness from him—Roger was very good at cultivating the fealty he demanded. Most genuinely did not believe he was capable of that kind of behavior, although they did not know the experiences others had been subjected to behind closed doors.

The biggest downside to the PR campaign was the pressure it put on the victims—to whom the message was loud and clear: *We're with Roger. If you speak out, no one will believe you.* They were already afraid of Roger, and now they were worried about the major talent too. Would they be booked on this person's show again? Would they publicly be branded liars or ingrates by some of the best-known names in news? And what about Roger? What stories would he engineer about us? How would he try to discredit us? How would he punish us, without putting his fingerprints on it? When the allegations hit, *no one* thought Roger would get fired—including me. Crossing him was a major risk. Especially because Roger's emissaries were telling us we need not participate in the investigation, and made it clear we were facing "a loyalty test."

I was aware that my silence would speak volumes. But there was no way I was going to lie—especially when I might be called as a witness in the lawsuit against him or questioned in an internal review. I also wanted women who may have experienced similar behavior from him not to feel alone, or feel pressure from someone like me. Some would later tell me they felt relieved I did not speak out in his defense; it gave them permission to make the same choice.

This was an intense time: information was breaking daily—my phone was ringing nonstop, with colleagues trying to get my take, provide information, or pressure me into publicly backing the boss. I was still doing my show nightly, preparing for the conventions, finishing this book (or so I thought), and taking care of my children. The developments came rapid-fire, and I felt desperate for a quiet moment to gather my thoughts and decide what my next steps would be.

I spoke to my friend at Fox who'd also been harassed. She was as resolved as I that she would not lie. She and I agreed to quietly get the word out to other women who hadn't spoken out that we were prepared to go on the record with the investigators, so they would not fear standing alone. This took a lot of guts from my friend, who has little power at Fox. If she confided in the wrong person, her "disloyalty" would surely have gotten back to Roger. She was a fearless soldier in what would become an underground army of women—those resolved to be honest about his behavior. Still, resolving to tell the truth and actually doing it were two different things. The stakes were very high; our jobs were potentially in danger, and Roger was digging in for a fight.

And then, something critical happened: a source informed me that Roger was working to limit the review to just a small circle of staffers—those who had worked directly with Gretchen. He wanted the net cast very narrowly, to exclude virtually all of the Fox News talent. I knew what that would likely mean.

It was then that I realized I had a choice to make. I could sit back, let the process play out—limited though it might be—and keep my mouth shut. Or, I could ensure that the owners of Fox News Channel—Rupert Murdoch and his sons—understood they might actually have a predator running their company, and that a full-throated review was necessary.

It may sound like a no-brainer now, with 20-20 hindsight, but in the moment, I felt more anxious than I'd imagined I would. Telling the truth to an investigator who might come to me was one thing; ensuring the investigators got to me (and to other Fox talent) was another. The passive role felt more obligatory; an active one raised the stakes considerably. As of that early date in the process, I had my suspicions, but I didn't actually *know* what the truth was. The allegations online at that point were anonymous and undated. I knew of my story and that of my friend, but these were events from a decade earlier. Was I really prepared to get him in trouble for something we had long since gotten past?

To undermine this man who had done so much for my career, and who had my back in some ugly situations? I didn't want to hurt him. But could I stay silent? What if there were other victims? What if—God forbid—he was *still* doing it to someone? The choice became clear: honor my ethical code, or abide by my loyalty to Roger. There was no way to do both.

I had a long talk about it with Doug, who supported my coming forward but made clear he was with me whatever my decision. And then I spoke with Dana Perino, who had just finished an advance copy of this book.

"What did that cameraman Bond Lee say to you in Chicago?" she asked.

"Pay it forward," I told her.

"Pay it forward," she repeated back to me.

I put down the phone, and sat there for a long time. I glanced over at the draft manuscript: *Settle for More.*

The next morning, as I sat on my porch swing on the Jersey shore, I looked at some pictures of my children. There was one of my favorites of Yardley. In it, she is on top of a jungle gym, wearing a big smile, a white dress with red polka dots, and sneakers. Her long hair is falling forward, her blond summer highlights shining in the sun. A month earlier, she had fallen off the monkey bars and gotten stitches in her head. But she had conquered her fear and gotten back up there. My child, who will take this world by storm. My girl, who I pray will not have to make the same choices I did. My daughter, who deserved to have her mother stand up and say, *This man will not do this to another woman at Fox News. Ever.*

I picked up the phone and called Lachlan Murdoch. "You need to get your general counsel on the phone," I told him, "I have something to tell you." And he did. And then I told them the truth about what had happened to me all those years ago. It was hard—I was not looking to ruin Roger, but it was obvious this information would be damaging to him. In the end, however, I concluded that if Roger were taken down by an honest review of his conduct, it would be his responsibility, not mine. If mine were an isolated incident, he likely had nothing to fear. If it were part of an ongoing pattern, he would have only himself to blame for his undoing. Twenty years after I had refused to copy another case at Bickel & Brewer, I had again run headfirst into the realization that I had just one path forward.

Within days of that call, to its credit, 21st Century announced that it had hired the well-respected law firm of Paul Weiss to investigate Roger's conduct. As soon as Paul Weiss commenced its work, I was asked to and did appear at their law offices, where I told my story to the lawyers—the harassment during that six-month period at Fox, and the nine years of support and mentorship that followed. I wanted them to have the full measure of the man—the good along with the bad. Soon after, Roger was informed that I had gone on the record against him, something I had accepted would happen. By that point, I had become aware of many other victims—the underground soldiers were finding each other—including some women who were *still* being harassed by him in deeply unsettling ways. I figured if sharing my name with Roger would help the others stay anonymous, so be it.

The next thing I knew, someone leaked my name to the press as one of Roger's accusers. It was stunning and alarming to see such a private matter splashed all over the Internet. I had no wish to make my situation a public matter. Simultaneously, Roger tried to discredit me, getting the *Drudge Report* to print the lie that my complaint was all about a "hug [I] didn't like." Some of my colleagues, who loved Roger, felt angry, believing that story, believing I (and only I) had chosen to hurt him over what he claimed was nothing. I stayed silent, trusting that the truth would soon come out, and knowing that even if it didn't, I had followed my conscience. The upside of being "outed" was that more women reached out to me—current and former employees with nearly identical texts and messages: **Megyn, it happened to me too**.

Getting on the wrong side of Roger was nerve-racking—I was well aware of his vengeful streak. But the truth is, I was lucky—by this point in my career, Roger could not destroy me. That was not necessarily true for the other women who went on the record, all of whom were incredibly brave. Most were current Fox News employees, still dependent on him for their paychecks, many with families to support. Some were very young and very scared, with little ability to fight a smear campaign, or to move to a new shop—which is especially tricky in TV news. They, too, had been pressured to protect Roger. And yet somehow, they found the courage to risk it all. They want their anonymity, and I will respect their wishes, but as a result, they will never get the credit they deserve. All I can say is, I am incredibly proud of each and every one of them.

On July 21, 2016, as I sat in Cleveland, preparing for the Republican National Convention, I learned that Roger Ailes had been effectively fired—twenty years after he co-founded Fox News. Just like that, this man—who, to me, had been such a confounding mix of supportive, generous, infuriating, and cruel—was gone. Rupert Murdoch took over as acting chairman with his sons, Lachlan and James, at his side. And the Fox News Channel, in a way, began anew.

My colleagues at the convention were stunned and upset by the news. I was surrounded by turmoil, and some resentment. I was also surrounded by security guards, who escorted me in and out of the convention hall quickly and without stopping each night. The evening of the Ailes announcement, a woman and her daughter happened to catch my eye. The security tried to press past them, but I wanted to stop. The mother told me her daughter was a big fan. I put my arm around the young teen for a picture, only to realize she was crying, overwhelmed. I turned and held her for a long time—tears spilling from her eyes and, then, welling up in my own. I don't think I realized how much I needed that reminder that, while there may be an obvious cost to doing what you think is right, there are also real—though perhaps less visible—benefits.

My relationships with a few colleagues changed after these events. But for the most part, once people found out what Roger had been doing to the women of the company—which, as has now been publicly reported, was far more serious, sustained, pervasive, and disturbing than I could have imagined—many reached out to me. I was touched but not surprised. My friends at Fox are decent and kind. Most didn't mean to join some pressure campaign—they just misjudged a confusing situation. I received many messages—from friends and colleagues, including, once again, my beloved audio tech, Dion, who wrote me before anyone else did. I felt especially close to the victims, with whom I had an unusual bond. We had all been through it. We had all felt powerless to stop it. And eventually, despite enormous pressure, we had all told the truth.

I wish I could tell you I now have the solution that would prevent this from happening at another company. But I don't have it all figured out. One thing I would like to see is every corporation with a compliance director who does not depend on the CEO for his or her paycheck, who could receive reports about the boss like these. An ombudsman of sorts. But would that make the victims actually call? I honestly don't know. I want to believe the answer is yes.

I think the culture is changing a bit—it's already different from how it had been a decade ago, when Roger was harassing me. Back then, the papers were full of reports like that of the American Apparel CEO who had severely sexually harassed his female staff and, after paying off a few lawsuits, was allowed to run the company for another *ten* years. In 2016, when Roger's behavior was brought to their attention, the Murdochs acted quickly and honorably. Despite Roger's attempts to prewire it, the Paul Weiss review was not a white-wash. They were genuinely searching for the truth. When they found it, they knew Roger had to go. Sure, he was promised a separation payment, but he was cut loose and, more important, cut off from the women of Fox News. (Roger's harassment of women wasn't a deal breaker for everyone—it was widely reported that Trump used him as a campaign adviser.)

Many reporting on the Roger situation seemed to revel in the fall of a conservative giant. Some also seemed to forget about the humanity of his victims, resorting to victim blaming or shaming. Perhaps it was the Fox News connection, but questions surfaced a little too frequently, asking why these women didn't just quit. Why it took them so long to come forward. And why, for that matter, they chose to look so al-luring on the air. This was infuriating to many of us. Aren't we well past the days of *her skirt-was-so-short-she-invited-her-own-harassment* drivel? Most of the women in TV news are attractive, wear form-fitting dresses, and have their hair and makeup professionally done. Some wear no sleeves, dresses above the knee, and false eyelashes. That doesn't make them partners in their own harassment, as some suggested; it makes them broadcasters who want to look great when ap-pearing in front of millions of people.

For what it's worth, when I was being harassed, I was still wearing my Jones Day outfits—navy, black, and gray business suits with long sleeves and pants. And when I got bolder in my wardrobe choices? Roger never bothered me.

As for the attempts to blame the victims for not speaking out sooner, it is *management's* job, not that of the employees, to ensure that a company has ethical leaders who comply with the law, and to make certain that women feel safe to report any incident. That did not happen at Fox, and I suspect Fox is not alone. Roger maintained complete control at FNC—over the talent, the management, *everyone*. Not only did these women fear for their jobs, they feared being attacked by his PR and legal teams. They feared his many loyalists throughout the company who had risen to positions of authority but were protective only of him. This was a man who reportedly used private investigators and others internally to go after suspected enemies. He kept us all under careful watch—with security cameras and security locks requiring a Fox ID on every floor, guards patrolling the halls, and provisions in our contracts agreeing that our office communications may be monitored (this is standard practice at many shops). The point is: reporting about the boss—anonymously or otherwise—had daunting challenges at Fox. His victims, who I would later learn were typically vulnerable in some way—new to the company, going through a divorce, or having suffered a death in the family—were in an untenable situation. The entire structure was set up to isolate and silence them. Even those of us who did take the risk of reporting his behavior up the line didn't manage to effect any change. The bottom line is: the more we criticize harassment victims for their understandable reluctance to go on the record, the more women we'll shame into silence forever.

The thoughts I am left with are these: having meaningful controls in place to encourage reporting is critical—controls that account for employees' legitimate fear of coming after a powerful superior, especially a CEO. Having managers in place who understand their own responsibilities upon receiving such a report is equally important. (Sexual harassment training may help—it gives businesses some cover if they get sued—but it is far from a cure-all; we had it many times at Fox; clearly it wasn't enough.) As for the employees, there is strength in numbers. Women who have been harassed need to communicate with their colleagues, in particular, their fellow women. Men, too, can be harassed, and the same advice applies to them. One of the scariest things is thinking you are the only one, and fearing the task of taking on a king. If one's budget allows, retaining counsel may also help. Without Willis Goldsmith, I would have felt far less protected.

Finally, anyone being harassed needs to remember that no is an available answer. Roger tried to have me, and I didn't let him. I got out of his office with my self-respect intact, even if I felt demeaned. Most women I know have had to do this dance with a male superior at one point—trying to reject inappropriate behavior while also trying to avoid explicitly calling him out. But when push comes to shove, no is always there for you. It is not foolproof—as, sadly, any sexual assault or rape survivor can attest—but when dealing with a boss whose goal is not to forcibly overtake you but instead to see how far he can push you, it may offer an escape hatch. You may be flying the beautiful F-16, sleek and shiny and a powerhouse in the air, but when fire hits the cockpit, there's always the eject button to remove you from immediate danger. Get out of that room, get somewhere safe, and get help, in the form that works best for you.

I worked my tail off for the next ten years. I established myself as a serious person. I built my own power. And when the allegations about Roger hit, I used it. Perhaps there is some poetic justice in that. Times are changing for women in this country. We're putting up with less. Standing up for ourselves more. And making strides some never thought possible.

One week after Roger Ailes resigned, I watched as former Secretary of State Hillary Clinton became the first woman in US history to accept a major party's presidential nomination. In an arena in Philadelphia, her daughter, Chelsea, introduced her, the two women embracing onstage.

Mrs. Clinton then let go of her daughter, turned to the cheering crowd, and began.

25

Settling for More Today

Recently, I took the kids to visit my mom in Albany. During our stay, she taught them to gamble, trash-talk, and curse, and told them a horrifying story about a little child who goes swimming in the ocean and is eaten by a shark. She also suggested they start calling her "Beautiful Grand-ma-*maa*" in a British accent—though she said "Beautiful Nana" would suffice in a pinch. They're mulling it over.

While sitting at the dining room table, working on this book, I watched over my laptop as my mom accused Yates of cheating at Monopoly and then told him, "Yates. Is. Great!" Cue Yates's big smile. She went on, "But not as great as his Nana!" Cue bigger smiles—his and mine. Oh, Beautiful Grand-ma-*maa*.

Sitting there, watching them play, I smiled, thinking of how the Kelly family marches on. Nana, at age one hundred, finally agreed she might need some help taking care of things, so she moved in with my mom and Peter. "They'ah treatin' me like Lady Ho-sh Shit," Nana tells me. Being Lady Horseshit is apparently a good thing.

Patrick's daughter Susan got married. Peter walked her down the aisle in a beautiful outdoor ceremony. As she said her vows, the clouds above parted for a beat and the sun shone down upon her. Liza later said, "I knew my brother would find a way to say hello."

It's the end of what, by any measure, has been an extraordinary year. I've had many new experiences— some bad, some good. A few new party invitations came my way—including the *Vanity Fair* Oscar party and the Met Gala. Before the Oscar party, Doug and I went to a "night before" party in the Hollywood Hills. The home belongs to actress Helen Mirren but was being rented by Absolut Vodka. The decorations were exquisite. There were tiny red lanterns, white lights, white and red flowers, and votive candles everywhere. (There were also synchronized swimmers wearing 1950s-style bathing suits, because, hey, why not?)

They had flown in an award-winning bartender from London. I asked the host what one orders from such a bartender, and he said, "I recommend you just go over there and tell him what kind of a day you've had." Off I went. The tall, blond British barkeep, who was throwing glasses in the air like a juggler, stopped to ask what he could get me.

"Well," I said, "I've had a shit year. I'm exhausted. But I'm here in LA with my husband, and it feels like my first night off in a decade. What do you have for that?" (For the record: Absolut Elyx, citrus, and Earl Grey tea.)

It was a kick meeting people whose faces I had seen on the big screen or whose music I listened to, people whose work I admired. Meeting Taylor Swift was especially fun. She called me a powerful woman. I said the same to her. Then I realized I'm old enough to be her mother. Another Absolut Elyx, please!

Given that when not at the anchor desk I'm usually in jeans and a T-shirt, I enjoyed dressing up. I chose my Met Gala dress just a couple of days before the party. Busy with work, I was forced by my assistant to make a call on the offerings she had arranged to have waiting in my office. Mom offered to lend me a dress she'd just bought for herself at Fashion Bug, where I also used to shop in Delmar. It's black with sequins on it, "and of course," she said, "I look stunning in it."

Instead, I picked a black sheath with a metallic back by Badgley Mishka. The day of the Gala, I went to their salon. The designer, Rob, told me to try it on, and said Badgley and Mishka would be out to take a look. *Is that a joke?* I wondered. I had no idea if they were actual people, never mind alive and in this salon at that moment. (They are indeed real people.)

An interesting thing happened to me on the party circuit. Taking in these A-list, star-studded events, I realized something—they're not life-changing. They're fancy parties with lots of famous people, period. And no matter how famous they are, they're still just people. And I'm still me, the girl from Albany who wonders, whenever someone recognizes me on the street, *Why are they looking at me? Do I have something stuck in my teeth?*

These parties are like Saks Fifth Avenue at Christmastime—a visual delight, full of glitter and twinkling lights. The displays are mind blowing in their no-expenses-spared extravagance. But returning home to a comfy room with a fire burning, watching a favorite old movie, or playing Pie Face with my kids is pretty damn good too. (This is an actual game involving a face-full of whipped cream. My brother Pete ought to be getting royalties.) Often I feel like a fish out of water in all that fabulousness. It's not that I don't like being there, it's just that it doesn't quite jibe with who I know I really am—the tomboy on the tire swing.

Thankfully I have plenty of help staying humble. Not long ago I was in a restaurant with my friend Susan Lucci. We went to the ladies' room together. A woman in the bathroom could not believe she was laying eyes upon Susan.

"Oh my God! Susan Lucci!" this woman exclaimed. "*I love you!* I have never missed an episode of *All My Children*! *I love Erica Kane!* Oh, I cannot *believe* this!"

Susan was her normal kind self, smiling and thanking her fan.

Then the woman lost her smile, gave me the side-eye, and said, flatly, "I know who *you* are, too."

My Albany Law School Theory of Life—just when you think you're some sort of hot shot, life has a way of reminding you, *Yeah, not so much.*

I would not describe this past year as easy. But I have no regrets about it, either. I did my job, and controversy followed. At Fox News I honored my ethics, and paid it forward to the women coming up behind me, despite the risks of doing so. These events—very public and painful—tested me, and I survived. In fact, I was strengthened. They brought me and Doug even closer together, and reminded me of what's important in life. Unlike when I was younger and tried to go it alone, I leaned on those around me—often. Now those relationships are closer, too.

I was reminded that what M'Lady Amy said was true: there may be some cads in the world, but good men really are out there in abundance—I have them on my team, and I also happen to have three of them right in my apartment. When I look at my husband, I think, as my old friend Maureen used to say, *That's a real man.* Not just because he is smart and strong. It's because he's decent and good. Doug is a loving, involved father who respects me and our children and the life we are building together. That is the kind of partner I want to have, the kind of partner I want Yardley to meet someday, the kind of man I know our two sons will become.

Recently Doug and I had a particularly great day with the kids, one of those days with so much laughter and adventure, the kind that makes you feel like you want to stop time and just live that day over and over.

"It's too bad Thatcher isn't old enough to remember this day," Doug said to me after we put the kids to bed.

"It's all ingredients into the cake," I said.

Our little boy might not remember the details of what we did—how pretty the weather was, how sweetly his big brother and sister played with him, how his mom and dad held him—but all that warmth and love is going somewhere. Those experiences are making him the child and the man he will be.

The same is true of any human being. You can use the difficult times to shore yourself up, to prove to yourself you can handle anything, or you can lament your bad luck and cry in your soup about life being unfair. One is productive, and the other, most certainly, is not.

Tough times can be stressful, but they also have a way of centering us, of shining a light through the darkness. I learned this after the death of my father, which gave me a consciousness of my own mortality, and that has led to better choices. Knowing how little time we have has helped force me to pull myself out of sadness, debt, emotional armor, and a job and marriage I knew were not good enough. I've found a career that excites me, a husband I deeply love and respect, true friendships, and three beautiful children whose joy, love, and zest for life have brought those same things and so much more into my own. It's given me the gift of ambition—not for money, or power, or fame but for *more*: more human connection, more goodness, more time. The hard times remind you it *is* possible to change your life. To do better. To be better. To settle for more.

But settle for more is not a onetime thing. It's not like you redesign your life and then sit back and say, "Nailed it! Done." It's a framework for looking at life long-term and finding opportunities to make things better. And what "more" means at age twenty-five is different from what it means at forty-five; when you're starting out in your career versus when you're established; when you're single and unmarried versus when you're married with children.

Likewise, as I sat back and watched my mom and my kids play games in my mother's dining room, it occurred to me that settling for more at forty-five would be different than at seventy-five, my mom's age. Whatever age I am, I thought to myself, I will always settle for more of this—more games with my children, more laughs, more *fun*. That's what I need, it's what fuels me—and lately I haven't had enough of it, so that's something I'll be working on in the months to come. And I know I will find the balance.

Today I look at the future and see unlimited opportunity—for more meaningful time with my family, more work I find fulfilling, and, always . . . more John Denver.

I'll be a dandy and I'll be a rover.
You'll know who I am by the songs that I sing.
I'll feast at your table, I'll sleep in your clover.
Who cares what the morrow shall bring?

Acknowledgments

I generally find it challenging to convey the depth of my gratitude without hugging or singsongy tonal inflections. But I'll give it the old college try.

Thank you to my love and partner Doug, who personifies "more." He was the first person to read this manuscript and the one who helped me find the courage to write it in the first place. If every reader hates this, and every viewer leaves me, I'll still have Doug, so screw 'em.

To my children, Yates, Yardley, and Thatcher—amid the klieg lights, cameras, and craziness in my life, it's when I have you around me that I know why I'm here. Thank you for showing me. And remember what I told you: good little boys and girls never leave their mommies. Ever. Even for college . . . or marriage. Don't believe what others tell you.

Mom, Dad, Sue, and Pete—love and belated thanks for making fun of my feet, my pale skin, my bad haircuts, and all the rest, since I otherwise might have developed a big head along the way. I owe so much to you, like the ability to laugh at everyone. I mean every*thing*. Not every*one*. That would be wrong. I get that. I swear.

Dad, a million tomorrows have all passed away and I haven't forgotten the joy.

Peter Kirwan, thank you for loving us, and for always knowing when I need a hug, usually before I know it myself. You are magnificent.

To Nana, my eternal gratitude for the boatyard, the monster stories, the free rein, the swearing, and the look on your face whenever we laid eyes on each other. Soon you'll be with Pop Pop, dancing to "When Irish Eyes Are Smiling"—and they will be, right here, through joy of tears.

Liza, for the many laugh-so-hard-your-stomach-hurts moments (many via text during this past year), I will never be able to properly pay homage. As R. H. Sin put it, "Some women fear the fire, some women simply become it."

Jackie, Diane—here's to you being in the "rose" or "bud" category every year. And thanks for this guy Dougger, who clearly was taught by the women in his life how to level with the women in his life . . . and I have reaped all the benefits. Well, they're mostly benefits. Sometimes not. Occasionally. It really depends on the situation.

Ken and Will—I'm so lucky that the warm welcome you gave me never seemed to wear out. Your goodness, and that of your father, helped me believe early on in the magic of the Brunts; a decade in, I know it was real.

Huge props to my editor, Matt Harper, of Harper Collins, whose refusal to offer any false praise was actually very irritating but right in line with my own values and did, in the end, make this a much better book. (I think he's related to my mother.) To Brian Murray, Lisa Sharkey, Tina Andreadis, and all of the good folks at Harper, thank you for your unwavering support.

To Ada Calhoun, I will be forever grateful. Your ability to help me see my own life in the arc of a story was clarifying and even therapeutic. M'Lady Amy would be proud.

Speaking of M'Lady, my thanks to Amy—the woman without whom everything would be so different.

To my pal Dr. Phil, who through the airwaves one night found me, unhappy, on a sofa in Chicago: Oprah says the people she's helped are her legacy. That's also true for you, and I am beyond grateful to count myself as one of them.

To all of my friends at *The Kelly File* who kept the show afloat during one hell of a year, thanks for being in the foxhole with me. I am extremely proud to work with you, you cynical mo-fos.

Tom, Abby, and Emily, thank you for taking every risk with me, and for shoring me up whenever I've wavered. You don't get anywhere near enough credit for your strength. Tommy, I can't think of a man better suited to take the baton and run.

Janice Dean and Dana Perino, two of the most beautiful women I know—ever heard the term "magnificent badass"? Doug once found it on a greeting card. I think it belongs to you.

To Chris and Vincenza, for all the nine-year-old-boy humor and haircuts and lip gloss, and for never letting me "roam alone"—*mille grazie*. You turn the sow's ear into a silk purse better than anyone, but it's your love and friendship that get me through the roughest days.

To Debra, who encouraged me to "rise"—thank you for the fire hose when everything was aflame. Who the hell would have thought some hedge fund guru could bring calm and serenity into a person's life?

To Rebecca and Andrea, who remind me what true friendship is all about, and who accepted me before I had actually figured it out.

True gratitude to Willis Goldsmith, who has always

had my back, and always believed I could do it all, whatever "it" was. (And who graciously chose not to make a big deal out of that deer-fur-in-the-rental-car-grill that time I was late for trial. The important thing is, no one was hurt. Well, no one who is a human.)

To the selfless, generous, divine Meredith—thank you, thank you—why are there no words better than "thank you"? I'm so grateful we found each other over the Eagles and Sting and Stevie Nicks, and I hope in some way, I've made you proud.

Cait Hoyt, Matt DelPiano, Alan Berger, Kevin Huvane, and my incredible team at CAA, much respect to you for seeing the landscape ahead, and for steering me toward what is true and good. Cait, you are a force of nature. Matt, thank you for your class, and for laughing at my stupid jokes. (I realize I'm basically paying you for this but somehow it still means something to me.)

To our viewers, my thanks and respect and ongoing commitment to keep earning your trust and loyalty. You humble and inspire me.

And last but not least, to Lachlan Murdoch, who had the courage to do what's right, and showed grace, humility, and kindness under pressure—you have my enduring admiration.

Notes

CHAPTER 10: LAWYER, BROADCASTER, JOURNALIST

1. Jarrett Murphy, "CBS Ousts 4 for Bush Guard Story," CBSNews.com, January 10, 2005, http://www.cbsnews.com/news/cbs-ousts-4-for-bush-guard-story-10-01-2005/.

CHAPTER 14: ALL THE DAYS OF MY LIFE

1. A. J. Jacobs, "I Think You're Fat," *Esquire*, July 24, 2007, http://www.esquire.com/news-politics/a26792/honesty0707/.

2. "Hillary Clinton Outraged in the Congo," You-Tube video, August 10, 2009, https://www.you-tube.com/watch?v=xiaI2EZ9ubw.

3. "Charles Gibson Describes Reporting on 9/11 Attacks, Extended Interview," YouTube video, September 11, 2013, https://www.youtube.com/watch?v=xA4LMYvitqg.

4. Linda Saslow, "Vows: Megyn Kelly and Douglas Brunt," *New York Times*, March 16, 2008.

CHAPTER 15: THE BEST LINE

1. Maane Khatchatourian, "Gwyneth Paltrow Says Industry Discouraged Women from Being 'Ambitious,'" *Variety*, October 9, 2015.

2. Maureen O'Connor, "Megyn Kelly Destroys Guy Who Called Her Maternity Leave 'a Racket,'" *Gawker*, August 8, 2011, http://gawker.com/5828842/megyn-kelly-destroys-guy-who-called-her-maternity-leave-a-racket.

3. "A Quarter of New Moms Return to Work 2 Weeks after Childbirth," *Chicago Tribune*, August 20, 2015.

4. "Lactate Intolerance," *The Daily Show with Jon Stewart*, August 11, 2011, http://www.cc.com/

video-clips/08acdo/the-daily-show-with-jon-stewart-lactate-intolerance.

5. "Anchor Management," *The Daily Show with Jon Stewart*, March 3, 2010, http://www.cc.com/video-clips/0rtdn2/the-daily-show-with-jon-stewart-anchor-management.

6. For example, see Tom Brokaw, "Time 100: Jon Stewart," *Time*, April 18, 2005.

CHAPTER 16: NOW EVERYONE'S HERE

1. David Carr, "For One Night at Fox, News Tops Agenda," *New York Times*, November 11, 2012.

2. *Lou Dobbs Tonight*, May 29, 2013.

3. *The Kelly File*, May 31, 2013.

4. Christopher Santarelli, "'I Had an Abortion' Shirt Sales Stir Controversy at University of North Carolina Wilmington," *Blaze*, April 19, 2012, http://www.theblaze.com/stories/2012/04/19/i-had-an-abortion-shirt-sales-stir-controversy-at-university-of-north-carolina-wilmington/.

CHAPTER 17: READY FOR PRIME TIME

1. "*Kelly File* Exclusive: William Ayers Pressed on Controversial Past," Fox News, June 29, 2014,

http://www.foxnews.com/us/2014/06/29/kelly-file-exclusive-william-ayers-pressed-on-contro-versial-past.html.

2. David Masciotra, "'Megyn Kelly's Eyes Are Very Cold': Bill Ayers on His Fox News Appearance, Education 'Reform,' and the Problem with the Ivy League," *Salon*, September 18, 2014, http://www.salon.com/2014/09/18/megyn_kellys_eyes_are_very_cold_bill_ayers_on_his_fox_news_appearance_education_reform_and_the_problem_with_the_ivy_league/.

3. Ward Churchill, "'Some People Push Back': On the Justice of Roosting Chickens," from an excerpt published www.kersplebedeb.com.

CHAPTER 19: ELECTION SEASON

1. Ryan Buxton, "Wayne Barrett: Donald Trump Tried to Bribe Me with an Apartment," *Huffington Post*, October 2, 2015, http://www.huffingtonpost.com/entry/wayne-barrett-donald-trump-bribe_us_560eaabae4b0dd85030bb2d5.

2. Mark Bowden, "Donald Trump Really Doesn't Want Me to Tell You This, But . . ." *Vanity Fair*, December 10, 2015.

3. *The Kelly File*, May 20, 2015.

4. The Bloomberg poll question, on April 6–8, 2015, was about which candidates the surveyed Republican or Independent would consider supporting for the 2016 Republican nomination. For Trump, only 9 percent said "Seriously Consider," and 62 percent said "Never Consider."

5. Nicholas Confessore and Karen Yourish, "Measuring Donald Trump's Mammoth Advantage in Free Media," *New York Times*, March 15, 2016.

6. Paul Bond, "'It May Not Be Good for America, but It's Damn Good for CBS,'" *Hollywood Reporter*, February 29, 2016, http://www.hollywoodreporter.com/news/leslie-moonves-donald-trump-may-871464.

7. Tim Mak, "Ex-Wife: Donald Trump Made Me Feel 'Violated' during Sex," *Daily Beast*, July 27, 2015, http://www.thedailybeast.com/articles/2015/07/27/ex-wife-donald-trump-made-feel-violated-during-sex.html.

CHAPTER 20: THE FIRST DEBATE

1. *Celebrity Apprentice*, season 6, episode 1, March 3, 2013.

2. Interview with Thomas Roberts, MSNBC, August 7, 2015.

3. Lauren Carroll and Clayton Youngman, "Fact-Checking Claims about Donald Trump's Four Bankruptcies," Politifact.com, September 21, 2015, http://www.politifact.com/truth-o-meter/statements/2015/sep/21/carly-fiorina/trumps-four-bankruptcies/.

4. Harry Hurt III, "Donald Trump Gets Small," *Esquire*, May 1991.

5. Julie Baumgold, "Fighting Back: Trump Scramble Off the Canvas," *New York*, November 9, 1992, 43.

6. Zeke J. Miller, "Trump Blasts 'Nasty,' 'Unfair' Debate Questions," *Time*, August 7, 2016, http://time.com/3988424/republican-debate-donald-trump-complaint/; David Weigel, "Donald Trump: 'Megyn [Kelly] Behaved Very Badly,'" *Washington Post*, August 7, 2015.

7. Brett LoGiurato, "Donald Trump Is Having a Meltdown after Megyn Kelly and Fox News Cut Him to Pieces during the Debate," *Business Insider*, August 7, 2015.

8. Frank Bruni, "A Foxy, Rowdy Republican Debate," *New York Times*, August 6, 2015.

CHAPTER 21: FALLOUT

1. Mark Hensch, "2016 Contenders Criticize Trump for Megyn Kelly Remarks," *The Hill*, August

8, 2015, http://thehill.com/blogs/ballot-box/
gop-primaries/250651-2016-contenders-criticize-
trump-for-megyn-kelly-remarks.

2. Neetzan Zimmerman, "Trump: Megyn Kelly
Had Blood Coming Out of Her 'Wherever,'" *The
Hill*, August 7, 2015, http://thehill.com/blogs/
blog-briefing-room/250641-trump-megyn-kelly-
had-blood-coming-out-of-her-wherever.

3. Paul Solotaroff, "Trump Seriously: On the Trail
with the GOP's Tough Guy," *Rolling Stone*, September 9, 2015.

4. Sara Jerde, "Fiorina: Women Know What Trump
Meant about My Face," TalkingPointsMemo.
com, September 16, 2015, http://talkingpoints-
memo.com/livewire/carly-fiorina-donald-trump-
responds.

5. Harrison Jacobs, "Donald Trump Is Going Off on
Megyn Kelly Again," *Business Insider*, September
22, 2015.

6. David W. Dunlap, "1886: Without Fear or
Favor," *New York Times*, August 14, 2015.

7. Megyn Kelly, "How to Deal with the
Haters," *Time*, February 9, 2016, http://
motto.time.com/4203136/megyn-kelly-deal-
with-haters/.

CHAPTER 22: RELENTLESS

1. Kyle Becker, "All 117 Donald Trump Tweets about Megyn Kelly," IJR.com, March 5, 2016, http://ijr.com/2016/03/564685-here-are-all-x-tweets-donald-trump-has-ever-sent-out-about-megyn-kelly/.

2. Bob Cusack, "Trump: I Didn't Try to 'Woo' Megyn Kelly," *The Hill*, January 6, 2016, http://thehill.com/homenews/campaign/264894-trump-i-didnt-try-to-woo-megyn-kelly.

3. Here's the full statement: "As many of our viewers know, FOX News is hosting a sanctioned debate in Des Moines, Iowa, on Thursday night, three days before the first votes of the 2016 election are cast in the Iowa Caucus. Donald Trump is refusing to debate seven of his fellow presidential candidates on stage that night, which is near unprecedented. We're not sure how Iowans are going to feel about him walking away from them at the last minute, but it should be clear to the American public by now that this is rooted in one thing—Megyn Kelly, whom he has viciously attacked since August and has now spent four days demanding be removed from the debate stage. Capitulating to politicians' ultimatums about a

debate moderator violates all journalistic standards, as do threats, including the one leveled by Trump's campaign manager Corey Lewandowski toward Megyn Kelly. In a call on Saturday with a FOX News executive, Lewandowski stated that Megyn had a 'rough couple of days after that last debate' and he 'would hate to have her go through that again.' Lewandowski was warned not to level any more threats, but he continued to do so. We can't give in to terrorizations toward any of our employees. Trump is still welcome at Thursday night's debate and will be treated fairly, just as he has been during his 132 appearances on FOX News & FOX Business, but he can't dictate the moderators or the questions."

4. Erik Wemple, "The Sexism in Donald Trump's Latest Swipe at Fox News's Megyn Kelly," *Washington Post*, January 26, 2016.

5. Cooper Allen and Paul Singer, "Six Takeaways from the Iowa Republican Debate," *USA Today*, January 29, 2016, 5.

6. "The Internet Freaks Out over Megyn Kelly's New Haircut," *Extra*, January 29, 2016, http://extratv.com/2016/01/29/the-internet-freaks-out-over-megyn-kellys-new-haircut/.

7. T. Becket Adams, "Trump Attacks Megyn Kelly

Again after Winning Florida," *Washington Examiner*, March 15, 2016.

8. Maureen Dowd, "Will Trump Be Dumped?" *New York Times*, March 19, 2016.

CHAPTER 23: THE TRUMP TOWER ACCORDS

1. Lynn Vavreck, "Insults and Ads: How Gender Hurts Trump but Doesn't Lift Clinton," *New York Times*, April 30, 2016; Cortney O'Brien, "Hillary PAC Highlights How Trump 'Respects' Women in New Ad," Townhall, May 10, 2016, http://townhall.com/tipsheet/cortneyobrien/2016/05/10/trumps-controversial-comments-about-women-again-in-spotlight-as-hillary-pac-releases-new-ad-n2160908; Amie Parnes, "Clinton Launches Blitzkrieg on Trump," *The Hill*, May 12, 2016, http://thehill.com/homenews/campaign/279619-clinton-launches-blitzkrieg-on-trump.

About the Author

MEGYN KELLY currently serves as anchor of the Fox News Channel's *The Kelly File*, the top-rated news show on cable. Throughout her tenure with the Fox News Channel, Kelly has covered breaking news, moderated presidential debates, and interviewed some of the best-known figures of our time. In 2014, *Time* magazine recognized Kelly as one of the 100 Most Influential People in the World. Before joining Fox News, Kelly served as a general-assignment reporter for WJLA-TV (ABC 7) in Washington, DC, where she covered national and local stories of interest. Prior to her career in television news, Kelly practiced law for nine years, the majority of which she spent as a litigator at the law firm of Jones Day in Chicago, New York, and Washington, DC. She lives in New York with her husband and three children.

THE NEW LUXURY IN READING

We hope you enjoyed reading
our new, comfortable print size and found it
an experience you would like to repeat.

Well – you're in luck!

HarperLuxe offers the finest in fiction and
nonfiction books in this same larger print size and
paperback format. Light and easy to read, HarperLuxe
paperbacks are for book lovers who want to see
what they are reading without the strain.

For a full listing of titles and
new releases to come, please visit our website:

www.HarperLuxe.com